SPORT, CULTURE AND THE MEDIA

)03

5

ISSUES in CULTURAL and MEDIA STUDIES

Series editor: Stuart Allan

Published titles

SPORT, CULTURE AND THE MEDIA
The Unruly Trinity

David Rowe

OPEN UNIVERSITY PRESS
Buckingham · Philadelphia

Open University Press
Celtic Court
22 Ballmoor
Buckingham
MK18 1XW

email: enquiries@openup.co.uk
world wide web: http://www.openup.co.uk

and
325 Chestnut Street
Philadelphia, PA 19106, USA

First Published 1999

A catalogue record of this book is available from the British Library

ISBN 0 335 20202 0 (pbk)   0 335 20203 9 (hbk)

Library of Congress Cataloging-in-Publication Data
A catalogue record for this book is available from the Library of Congress

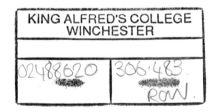
Typeset by Type Study, Scarborough
Printed in Great Britain by Biddles Limited, Guildford and Kings Lynn

To the Rowes and Henders:
great prizes in the lottery of families

CONTENTS

SERIES EDITOR'S FOREWORD

Despite its obvious significance for any exploration of popular culture, sport has not received the attention it deserves within cultural and media studies. This neglect may be attributable, in part, to the difficulties associated with achieving a sufficient degree of critical distance to investigate something which is such a familiar part of everyday life for so many people.

David Rowe's *Sport, Culture and the Media: The Unruly Trinity* has at its centre precisely this aim of de-familiarizing an array of our most taken-for-granted assumptions about media representations of sport. In order to discern how sport has become intimately interwoven throughout the varied realities of everyday experience (even for those people who do not consider themselves to be sports fans), he makes a number of important analytical connections across otherwise disparate areas of enquiry. At stake is the need to examine the structural, institutional and organizational frameworks shaping how media discourses of sport are produced, disseminated and, in the final instance, negotiated by the audience. Projected against this conceptual backdrop, in turn, is a cogent critique of the forms, conventions and practices associated with different sports texts, especially those in the press, radio, television, film and still photography. Such an approach works to bring to the fore a host of intriguing, and frequently unexpected, insights. Indeed, as Rowe proceeds to demonstrate, 'in engaging with sport and media, the personal and the political, the serious and the fun-loving, the po-faced and the ironic, can be combined in the most surprising and productive ways'.

The Issues in Cultural and Media Studies series aims to facilitate a diverse range of critical investigations into pressing questions considered to be central to current thinking and research. In light of the remarkable speed at which the conceptual agendas of cultural and media studies are changing, the authors are committed to contributing to what is an ongoing process of re-evaluation and critique. Each of the books is intended to provide a lively, innovative and comprehensive introduction to a specific topical issue from a fresh perspective. The reader is offered a thorough grounding in the most salient debates indicative of the book's subject, as well as important insights into how new modes of enquiry may be established for future explorations. Taken as a whole, then, the series is designed to cover the core components of cultural and media studies courses in an imaginatively distinctive and engaging manner.

Stuart Allan

ACKNOWLEDGEMENTS

Why would anyone not a dedicated masochist write an academic book? A relish for self-inflicted punishment must be the best qualification for the task. What really sustains the author (apart from ego and stimulants) is that, one day, the work (in both senses) will no longer be theirs. The book, conceived and executed in solitude, is finally a social product – it is written for people and, without those precious people, the book could never be written.

With the usual nervousness about advertent and inadvertent omissions, I thank on this occasion those who come to mind as indispensable: my family in the UK, especially the ones who haven't been acknowledged before – Joanna, Oliver, Alex and Tony – and my family in Australia who always get a mention: the inimitable Daniel and Madeleine. The longstanding and more recent friends and colleagues I honourably mention this time around are Therese and Grace Davis, Sue Dean, Mick Dwyer, Geoff and Dimity Lawrence, Helen Macallan, Kevin Markwell, Jim McKay, Toby Miller, Chuck Morris, Jules Pavlou-Kirri, Deborah Stevenson, Alan Tomlinson, Garry Whannel and Dave Whitson.

I thank my other immediate academic colleagues for being exemplary workmates, and publicly acknowledge my debt to the lifesaving, ever-engaging administrative double act, Shelagh Lummis and Kerry Beaumont (deft architect of the index). Richard Lever also provided some very handy research assistance at strategically significant moments. The Research Management Committee of the University of Newcastle provided generous funding for the study of sports journalists. Finally, Stuart Allan was as congenial a series editor as Justin Vaughan and Gaynor Clements were encouraging publisher and editorial assistant (respectively). I hope that this book bears some reasonable resemblance to the object they had in mind.

David Rowe

PREFACE: IMMERSED IN MEDIA SPORT

Introduction: a day in the life of the media sports consumer

All over the world, spanning many time zones, people of otherwise very different cultures, languages, religions and political ideologies are having a similar daily experience. Various aspects of the 'typical' day I am about to describe are representative of life in the more affluent reaches of late capitalist societies, but they are by no means unknown in even the poorest and least economically developed (by western standards) nations.

This daily round goes something like this: you wake up to the sound of the alarm clock radio, and as the news of the day is reported and anticipated considerable prominence is given to seemingly bizarre cultural practices. They involve individuals and groups getting together and agreeing to engage in physical activities bound by rules (or even laws) in which people may be allowed to strike various parts of others' bodies with various parts of their own. Or they may be forbidden from having any kind of bodily contact at all. Often, they will be required to propel objects of various shapes and sizes using various implements or body parts towards designated targets of diverse kinds, while others do their best to stop them. Some people are paid huge sums of money for partaking in these activities, while others do it for fun or by compulsion at school. The ones who get paid do so because many more people want to watch them in operation in the same time and space or by means of electronic transmission. Those spectators also want to watch, read and listen to other people who get paid for talking and writing about what those who are exerting themselves are doing or what others have said or written about it. What is shown, said and written provides many opportunities in many contexts (like playgrounds, pubs, bus queues and traffic jams) for people to discuss what has happened and what has been communicated about what has happened in a spiralling and self-amplifying discourse.

To an inter-planetary visitor all this movement by a few people and interest in it by many more would seem like some kind of viral contagion, a collective insanity (or at least irrationality) perhaps brought back in the dust attached to moon rocks. For earthlings, however, it is an omnipresent part of their lives whether they like it or not. It is so pervasive that, like water or electricity, it is really acknowledged only when its supply is interrupted by natural disasters or industrial disputation. We on earth call it **sport**. As we have seen, however, this phenomenon is only partially about its actual practice. In fact, what occurs on fields, courts, courses and other prescribed venues is at the bottom of an inverted pyramid of sports watching, selling, marketing, sponsorship, presentation and discourse. Sport is a contemporary medium for performing many tasks and carrying multiple messages and, as such, is increasingly indistinguishable from the *sports media*. This constellation of institutions and practices that supplies the means by which messages involving sport are communicated is not restricted to the print and electronic forms as they are conventionally conceived. 'Data' about sport are all around, with seemingly every animate and inanimate object capable of functioning as a *medium of sports culture*.

This point becomes clear as we resume the routine daily tasks commenced above and observe the extent to which sport has insinuated itself into the warp and weft of everyday life. At the breakfast table there is plenty to read. Not only does the morning paper carry many pages of sports results and analysis (usually conveniently placed on the back page or in a 'pull out' supplement), but the cereal boxes may be covered with bright endorsements by prominent sportspeople. Befuddled breakfast conversation can stay on safe ground if it covers only the results of the previous night's games or the latest engagement between a 'sexy' female pop singer and a 'hunky' footballer. As the breakfast dishes are stacked for washing, regular sports news updates are given by the radio or by breakfast television. The visit to the bathroom may well involve contact with the range of soaps, deodorants and colognes promoted by runners, tennis players, boxers and the like. Perhaps patches of tattooed skin proclaiming undying love for Manchester United or the Chicago Bulls are in need of cleansing. Next comes the big decision about what to wear, often meaning a difficult choice over which company's sports logo will emblazon T-shirts, shoes, hats, socks and jackets. The Nike 'swoosh', perhaps, or the Reebok flag insignia or, then again, maybe the three stripes of Adidas?

Once out over the threshold, public space is suffused with signs of sport –

much to the chagrin of dedicated sports haters and to the mild irritation of the merely indifferent. Billboards, hoardings, the sides of buses, and numerous other available surfaces carry advertisements featuring celebrity sportspeople endorsing fast food chains, new car models, leisurewear brands, health insurance and sundry other goods and services. Many fellow travellers and pedestrians have also turned themselves into walking brand promotions, displaying corporate sports logos and colours. Flashing electronic signs and newspaper stands on street corners carry news about footballers transferring between teams for multimillion sums of money, coaches and managers sacked, and forthcoming sports fixtures on television. Shop windows and street stalls display all manner of sports paraphernalia for sale, from collector's cards to supporter's scarves, and, if a local team is about to take part in a significant sports contest, messages of support decorate the streetscape, 'go the Blues, Reds, Cowboys, Bruisers etc.' urgings in 'respectable' shop windows are visible alongside the illicit fan signatures, endorsements, insults and threats characteristic of sports graffiti.

Leaving public territory for the institutional world does not mean entering a 'sports free zone'. In workplaces and educational establishments, conversational space in available breaks is likely to be filled with talk of sport and about sports talk as athlete-endorsed hamburgers and isotonic drinks are consumed, and personal boundaries and identities are marked with photographs and banners on desks and walls declaring sporting affiliations. The sports cyberworld will be illicitly contacted when employers and teachers think that computers and their Internet access are being put to more 'serious' use. The predictive and analytical skills of workmates are likely to be applied to 'sweeps' at the time of famous horse races, sports result 'tipping' competitions, in sports betting on the 'net', and in pursuit of the perennial dream of a rich retirement after winning the 'pools' by accurately predicting the results of a number of sports contests. On the journey home, **media** headlines may be sighted about the latest sports scandal (Rowe 1997a) – a famous sportsman and film star on trial for the murder of his wife, a swimmer caught with performance-enhancing drugs in her bloodstream, a basketball player announcing that he's HIV-positive, allegations of corruption of referees and match-fixing connected to international sports betting rings. Back again at the domestic hearth, there will be myriad opportunities to receive information about sport in the electronic and print media, or via home computers (whose 'educational' uses may also involve software sports games), and there is likely to be 'live' sports coverage or edited highlights on the multi-channels of free-to-air or 'pay' television. As the alarm clock radio is being checked for the morning and the sleep timer switched on to guide the listener into sleep, quite possibly the last sounds of the day to be registered by the conscious and unconscious self, as at the moment of waking, will be of sport.

This is a picture of a sports impregnated world which does not rely on actual engagement in physical activity. People do so, of course, and in large numbers – but to nothing like the extent that they watch, talk and read about it (McKay 1990; Brown and Rowe 1998). It is increasingly hard to remember a time when sport and the media were not deeply entwined in a relationship of such systematic intensity that it has been characterized as a 'complex', with any apparent primacy given to sport or media varying between Jhally's (1989) conception of the 'sports/media complex' and Maguire's (1993) notion of the 'media/sport production complex'. The adjusted formulation used in this book is that of the '**media sports cultural complex**', which signifies both the primacy of symbols in contemporary sport and the two-way relationship between the sports media and the great cultural formation of which it is part. As I have noted above, the sights, sounds and 'feel' of sport are everywhere – shrilly piping out of televisions and radios, absorbing acres of newsprint, and decorating bodies whose major physical exertion has commonly entailed walking between different leisurewear stores in suburban shopping malls. Media sports **texts**, of course, do not appear *ex nihilo* – that is, they are not beamed in from outer space, already formed and with unknown origins. An industrial infrastructure of daunting proportions manufactures them for us, peopled by specialists who are unequivocally in the sports discourse business. As a consequence, whether certified 'sports nuts' or the vaguely interested, largely indifferent to or actively dismissive of sport, we are all required to confront and negotiate the power and presence of the sports media.

Sport, Culture and the Media: structure and outline

In seeking to comprehend the phenomena and accomplish the task set out above, *Sport, Culture and the Media: The Unruly Trinity* is divided into two parts which reflect the different emphasis on sports production and reception. Part I, 'Making media sport', focuses on the organizational structures and professional ideologies that shape the production of media sports texts. It opens with an introduction to the field, 'Understanding sport and media: a socio-historical approach' (Chapter 2), which provides a brief historical and sociological overview of the developing relationship between sport and media as a prerequisite for the production of media sports texts, showing how the institutions became mutually dependent in an increasingly extensive exchange of exposure and rights fees for content and audience capture. The heightened prominence of sport in print reportage (including specialist sports, business and general journalism), magazines, still photography, radio, film, video and television is outlined. Themes of media power, the reproduction of ideologies of dominance, and the position of the sports media in contemporary culture are highlighted as crucial to the ensuing analysis. The links between the conditions under which media sports texts are made and the meanings and ideologies that they generate are proposed as the key twin foci of a cogent and instructive understanding of the relationships between sport, culture and the media.

This is not to suggest that production and reception of texts are distinct processes which have no bearing on each other. The reverse is the case, because what is produced in the media always operates with notions of how a text might be received, just as how it is received (positively, negatively or not at all) depends first on whether the text has been produced for consumption in the first place, and then on the conditions which are only partially under the control of the text producer (such as whether it is being 'displayed' to a man or woman, sports fan or sports hater, and so on). By provisionally separating media sports text production and reception along these lines, it is possible to grasp the complex way in which media sports texts are made and unmade in a continuous process involving the representation of a cultural form by media organizations, its transformation through these acts of representation, and then its further transformation (including challenges to the media's representation of sport) by other interested parties (such as sports administrators, performers and fans). In so doing, it is possible to challenge two common, flawed and opposing arguments (both partially defensible) – either that the media are so powerful that they are progressively exterminating sport 'as we know it' (with sports fans reduced to the playthings of media moguls) or that sport is so powerful that the media are forced (in a pleasingly mixed metaphor) to fawn over it like hungry dogs (with sports fans ever more indulged and pampered by sports television, radio and the press).

Chapter 3, 'Working in media sport: the discipline of sports journalism', examines the professional status of sports journalism as a sector of journalism in general. Based on an international study of sports journalists in the print and electronic media, it demonstrates how the makers of media sports texts have difficulty in securing high professional standing, not least because they are expected to observe the strictures of journalistic objectivity while also developing close ties both to their subjects (athletes and other sports workers) and to their audiences (predominantly sports fans). The resulting tension is shown to have a significant impact on the formation of stories and to produce sharp divisions between different sub-disciplines within sports journalism. The cultural significance of what otherwise might be seen as merely an internal power struggle within a media profession is, it is argued, symptomatic of a more general societal ambivalence concerning the importance and 'seriousness' of popular culture and a 'squeamishness' about its commercial dimensions. Hence, 'Money, myth and the big match: the **political economy** of the sports media' (Chapter 4) concludes the first part of the book by assessing the relative power of major sports and sports organizations and of media corporations and proprietors.

The development of new economic 'synergies' and media technologies are examined in this chapter along with sharply contrasting local and 'amateurist' sports media. Economic forces are shown to be central to the manufacture of the form and content of media sports texts without establishing absolute powers of determination over them. These considerations inevitably involve questions of cultural politics and there follows an examination of familiar debates about politics in and of sport from a largely unfamiliar perspective – the rights associated with the concept of cultural citizenship. The sports media are shown to be caught between a 'neutralist' entertainment stance, their traditional 'Fourth Estate' role, and the Olympian ideology of sport as supra-political. The media sports scandal is briefly discussed as a massively conspicuous media event that cannot be contained by the 'sport-and-politics don't mix' edict which, to a substantial degree, problematizes the notion of a separate sphere of sports journalism. This discussion prompts a reconsideration of the political responsibilities of the sports media which, as in the case of other media genres, are shown often to be compromised by economic imperatives. This semiotic and ideological instability and 'contestability' are then addressed in Part II, 'Unmaking the media sports text'.

In this second part of the book, the activities of reading, decoding and deconstructing sports images and information are shown to be connected to but not entirely governed by the industrial forces that have 'supplied' them. A series of readings of 'typical' media sports texts of various kinds is conducted in which each text is shown to be deeply inscribed with ideologies of power, so demanding an overall critique of the concept of an entirely open text amenable to an infinite range of meanings. At the same time, media sports texts are shown to be available for multiple readings according to time, context and readership, and can be seen to be subject to general representational shifts as responses to organizational and wider social changes. In Chapter 5, 'Taking us through it: the "art" of sports commentating and writing', there is an analysis of several types of spoken and printed media sports texts (such as 'live' commentary, routine sports reports and sports gossip), noting how each constructs particular versions of the sporting and surrounding worlds. The language of sport – sometimes called 'sportuguese' (John Hargreaves 1986) – is also appraised, and the role of sports metaphors in non-sporting discourses as bearers of populist meaning, thereby tracing the two-way flow of sports texts and social ideologies.

Words, although a vital component of media sports culture, are by no means its only medium. In 'Framed and mounted: sport through the photographic eye' (Chapter 6), the still, visual media sports text is appraised, concentrating on the aesthetic **codes** that govern the composition of sports photographs. Particular attention is given to the representation of gendered and racialized athletes' bodies in orthodox sports news photographs and publicity stills. Visual metaphors, especially in advertising, are shown to work alongside print captions in the accomplishment of various sporting associations and connotations. In concluding Part II, 'Screening the action: the moving sports image' (Chapter 7) interrogates media sports texts in sound and vision – the television broadcast, filmic treatment of sport and sport-related themes. The ways in which sport as myth makes itself readily accessible for the discharge of a variety of narrative and ethical functions are appraised, alongside the efficacy of such symbolic deployments of sport in the light of their substantial dependence on specific and pre-existing audience histories.

This discussion returns us to the territory traversed in this Preface – the relationships between sport, culture and the media that are always everywhere in process, influencing and being influenced by each other in a perpetual dance of assertion and counter-assertion. There are both traditional and novel aspects of this process, but also little doubt that, at the much-hyped dawn of a new millennium, it is subject to profound and rapid change. A short Afterword looks to the future of media sport which, in technological capability if not yet in widespread cultural practice, has arrived. 'Sport into the ether(net): new technologies, new consumers' (Chapter 8) closes the book with a consideration of the trajectory of media sport, both in terms of the texts being generated ('reality' media sport), the relationship between the institutions of sport and media, and the exchanges between sport 'producers' and 'consumers'. The capacity of new media technologies to subvert current prevailing textual relations and practices in sport is assessed in the light of what is already known of the history of media sports development. Once again, the linkage between the conditions under which media sports texts are made and the meanings and ideologies that they generate is shown to be in need of constant review.

Conclusion: looking towards sport and media

A trained capacity to decode media sports texts and to detect the forms of ideological deployment of sport in the media is, irrespective of cultural taste, a crucial skill. It is no exaggeration to assert that such a key critical competency is an important aspect of a fully realized cultural citizenship (Murdock 1992; Stevenson 1995) in the era of the omnipresent sports image. It is important, then, to understand the dynamics of the relationship between sport and the media. We need to be able to analyse their mutual roles as social institutions (including assessing the traditional sports fan lament that 'TV has taken over sport'), and to develop a knowledge of the institutional processes, practices and motivations that bring media sports texts of various kinds to their willing and unwilling audiences. It is also incumbent on us to be able to criticize their (separate and mutual) interaction with other social institutions, groups and individuals, not least by interrogating the ideologies of repression and exclusion embedded within such seemingly innocent and exhaustingly available elements of popular culture.

In examining the production and content of mainstream media sport texts we also encounter the points of dissonance and resistance, the places where different meanings and practices of and for sport are made and played out. The requirement is not to treat the sport–media nexus as a closed system of commercial exploitation, massified communication and unreflexive image consumption, but to acquire the critical means to establish an authoritative grasp of the structural, institutional and organizational framework governing their production, dissemination and reception. This is not as grim a task as it sounds, because to gain critical knowledge and acumen in this or any other corner of the popular world involves the pleasure of trading heedless absorption or numb indifference for knowing reflection or informed appreciation (in its broadest sense). In engaging with sport and media, the personal and the political, the serious and the fun-loving, the po-faced and the ironic, can be combined in the most surprising and productive ways.

Part I
MAKING MEDIA SPORT

2

UNDERSTANDING SPORT AND MEDIA: A SOCIO-HISTORICAL APPROACH

The world of sports in the age of mass media has been transformed from nineteenth century amateur recreational participation to late twentieth century spectator-centered technology and business.

(Michael Real 1998: 14)

Introduction: when two worlds collide

Before launching into an extended analysis of how media sports texts are made and interpreted, it is necessary to have an historical and sociological understanding of the relationship between the institutions of sport and media. There is, after all, no necessary reason why they should be connected in any but the most perfunctory of manners. The practice of sport, in the first instance, is physical play: it is an embodied experience, demanding move- ment, the corporeal manipulation of time and space, and often the hard clash of bodies against other bodies or against immobile hard surfaces. In fact, it is this bodily aspect of sport that prevents game contests like chess and Scrabble from being fully recognized as sports. Most conventional defi- nitions of sport stress that, whatever else happens when we are in the pres- ence of sport, whole bodies or their selected parts are in motion (or, in the case of sports like shooting and archery, exhaustively trained to minimize it). A conservative but, in terms of the analytical sports literature, representative approach like that of J. Bowyer Bell separates sport and other playful activity in a straightforward way:

> Certainly, all sports are games but equally certainly not all games are sports. War games or diplomatic games are matters of analogy, not sports events. Sports are play in a closed universe, seemingly isolated from society's other activities. More to the point, some play is a game,

not a sport. Essentially a sport is a *repeatable, regulated, physical contest producing a clear winner.*

(Bell 1987: 2, original emphasis)

Such prescriptions of what ought to be called a sport are often contested, but at both official and unofficial levels dispute is not so much over whether a game contest has to be physical in order to count as sport, as over the physical status of the activity that claims to be a sport. Thus, Bell (1987: 3) rules out chess as a sport because 'structurally, the physical element is irrelevant' and dice because 'winning depends, if honesty rules, on lady luck not an adept toss', but admits darts to the sporting pantheon despite its lack of 'intellectual challenge or a vastly demanding physical strain'. The strong sense of physically based hierarchy in according the title of sport is made clear in the reluctant admission that 'For the purist, there is the problem of video games. Alack, it appears that, however crude the game, the winner, physically adept, is playing a sport' (Bell 1987: 3). The sports spectator, therefore, is witnessing a physical activity predicated on precise calculation of the winners and losers, or, in the 'unfortunate' (certainly for sports marketers) absence of a clear result, stated and measurable criteria for declaring a draw or tie.

The 'practice' of media – in terms of both production and reception – is much less physically dependent. Film and television directors, camera operators, music producers, writers and so on may require plenty of physical stamina and, in some cases, an extraordinary 'eye' or 'ear', but, the questionably accountable area of awards aside, tend to be assessed on aesthetic rather than physical, quantitatively measurable criteria (such as the influence of writers rather than their ability in a head-to-head contest to put assessable words on the page). As text reception activities, viewing and reading, are, of course, sensory and sensual activities, and can elicit physiological responses (by provoking fear, sexual arousal and so on), but they are hardly in the same league (forgive the pun) as completing a marathon or knocking an opponent to the canvas. While the value and status of different media texts is hotly disputed – Milton versus Mills and Boon, or Verdi versus The Verve, etc. – the outcome is rarely as self-evident as Brazil 3, Germany 0 or an individual world record in swimming.

Similarly, sport and media, as organizational complexes, have different reasons for being, personnel, skill requirements, relations with government and non-government agencies, and so on. In short, 'getting physical' in sport and 'making symbols' in media might be expected to remain different cultural pursuits with few compelling reasons to engage each other on a regular basis. Yet, over the past century, the boundaries between these two institutions have blurred sometimes to the point of near invisibility, and they have become so mutually indispensable that, as asserted in the Preface, one is literally unthinkable without the other (literally, because it is almost impossible now to 'imagine' sport without the mind's eye conjuring up replay, slow motion and multi-perspectival images, accompanied by the inner voice of phantom sports commentators). How did this intermeshing of sport and media occur? In search of an answer, we must look to the great changes that have refashioned the structure and rhythm of the lives of most of the world's inhabitants – the rise of **capitalism** and industrialism in general and the advent of mass consumption and the **commodification** of leisure time in particular. In order to develop this argument, I shall first sketch in very briefly the twin histories of the institutions whose convergence provides the rationale for this book.

The rise of sport

Most scholarly histories of sport (such as Guttmann 1978) trace the origins of structured physical play in different societies and epochs, but argue that what we have come to recognize as sport, like the nation-state or adolescence, is of much more recent and specific origin. There are many 'folk' games still played today in human groups organized around tribes, small to medium-sized settlements, and even extending to the 'urban villages' of the metropolis. The ancient Olympic Games are routinely judged to be the birthplace of sport, but it would be historically fallacious to conceive of the development of sport into its modern manifestation as arising out of a steady evolutionary process, the origins of which can be traced directly to the ancient Greeks. This is not only because the original, 'ancient' Games were discontinued for at least sixteen centuries (according to Hill 1992: 6, terminating in either AD 261 or 393) until revived in 1896 by the French aristocrat Baron Pierre de Coubertin (although there had been attempted revivals in both Greece and England in the intervening period). It is also because sport as a recognizable social and cultural institution is not universal but emerged in a particular location (Britain) at a particular time (early industrialization). There is a danger, of course, in proposing such a foundational argument, of 'cleaning up' the messy origins of contemporary sport and of failing to acknowledge its qualitative and directional changes. Without wishing to 'essentialize' the diverse and chaotic world of sport, it is none the less important to appreciate that the constituent elements of what is now globally identifiable as sport became manifest in response to a unique combination of historical factors which, once established, took on a logic and life of its own (an argument not unlike, perhaps, Max Weber's (1930: 182) thesis that an historically contingent meeting of Calvinism and Protestantism created the 'spirit of capitalism' which, once it had taken firm hold, then 'escaped from the cage'). What were these formative forces and conditions out of which sport was created in Britain, and especially that part of it that 'is forever England'? An Anglo imprint so strong that the German writer Agnes Bain Stiven stated that 'England was the cradle and the loving "mother" of sport', while an aristocratic compatriot remarked that in Germany the English word '"Sport" is as untranslatable as "gentleman"' (Prince Puechlser-Muskau, quoted in Elias 1986a: 127).

First, there is the longstanding practice of physical or 'rough' play and of periodic competition. Elias and Dunning (1986a) describe the 'folk football' events when the inhabitants (especially the young men) of small settlements engaged in playful activities like the attempted conveyance of inflated pigs' bladders from one village to the other, and a corresponding obstruction of this passage – both tasks to be achieved by any means possible! Not only did such events take many hours (even days), but also they sometimes resulted in serious injury. The more organized game contests such as boxing, wrestling, football, horseracing and cock fighting took place principally on market, feast, harvest and holy days well into the nineteenth century (Clarke and Critcher 1985: 53). They often incurred the wrath or moral concern of dominant political and religious forces who abhorred the wasteful and dissolute behaviour – drunkenness, wagering, violence and sexual promiscuity – that often accompanied these 'proto-sports' tournaments. Ruling elite anxiety concerning the leisure pursuits of the general populace is a feature of all social history. Elias and Dunning (1986b: 176), for example, describe an order by 'King Edward III in 1365 to the Sherriffs of the City of London' that 'able bodied men' who were at 'leisure' on feast days should engage only in militarily useful 'sports' using bows, arrows and other approved weapons. Those who engaged in 'vain games of no value' like stone throwing, handball and football did so 'under pain of imprisonment'. Not all authorities have taken quite such a 'hair shirt' stance, but they have recognized the highly political nature of permitting, prescribing and proscribing popular pastimes. Weber (1930: 167), for example, notes that it was even necessary for Kings James I and Charles I to make the *Book of Sports* (sport used here in the most general sense of pleasurable diversions) into law in order to permit 'certain popular amusements on Sunday outside of Church hours', legislation that was inspired by a struggle for power with the Puritans, for whom:

> Sport was accepted if it served a rational purpose, that of recreation necessary for physical efficiency. But as means for the spontaneous

expression of undisciplined impulses, it was under suspicion; and in so far as it became purely a means of enjoyment, or awakened pride, raw instincts or the irrational gambling instinct, it was of course to be strictly condemned.

(Weber 1930: 167)

There is little doubting what would have been the Puritans' disapproval of almost everything that characterizes the culture of sport today – the ecstasy of the moment of victory, the chauvinistic pride when a fan's team wins, the 'rawest' of human feeling from high states of euphoria to violent impulses (Kerr 1994), and the ever-expanding possibilities to gamble not only on the outcome of a sports contest (or, in the case of the 'pools', many simultaneous sports contests), but also on a seemingly infinite range of mini-outcomes (such as predictions of scores, scorers, timing of significant game developments, and so on). Sport can be seen to be an important symptom and a partial cause of a move away from a social order founded on the repression of physical play and its pleasurable *accoutrements* to one which not only accepts such pursuits, but also promotes and 'makes capital' from them. The constituents of the contemporary 'carnivalesque' (Bakhtin 1968) may have changed, but – as Hughson (1998) notes in his analysis of soccer hooliganism – sport is still a significant site of struggle between the controllers of social space and the controlled.

From the late eighteenth century onwards, the sea change in social organization caused by the spread of factory labour, the growing concentration of the new industrial proletariat in the cities, the circulation of popular democratic and revolutionary ideas, and the mobilization of radical political movements – in short, the capitalist, industrial, urban and political revolutions that unfolded across the nineteenth century (Nisbet 1967) – made control and surveillance of 'popular amusements' more difficult. This increased degree of 'licence' provoked an intensified 'moral panic' (Cohen 1980) about popular leisure among the established landed class and the emerging capitalist class alike. Pressure built up, therefore, for greater control over working-class activities outside work as part of a more general subjection to industrial capitalism's time and work-discipline (E.P. Thompson 1967). Workers were expected to turn up for work on time and in a fit state for arduous and often dangerous shifts in mines, mills and factories – any residual tolerance of seasonal, intermittent and ill-disciplined agricultural labour was being swept away by the industrial capitalist demand for efficiency and reliability. Such calls for commitment to work and restrained leisure led, for example, to the banning in 1860 of the ancient football game in Ashbourne, Derbyshire, leading to a Court Circular carrying an

'Obituary: Death of the Right Honourable Game Football' (Anon. 1992: 5). At the same time, there was a movement to promote healthy physical activity and to discharge 'unhealthy' urges among the citizenry.

It was this line of moral thought that led, somewhat bizarrely, to the staging from 1850 of the 'Olympian Games' in the small English town of Much Wenlock, Shropshire. The Games' founder, Dr William Penny Brookes (who developed a close association with Baron de Coubertin) was strongly in favour of school physical education (especially in state, non-fee-paying institutions) and believed that farm labourers (whose work under more intensive farming methods was becoming as rigidly prescribed as that of their industrial counterparts) should be given compulsory physical training. In extolling the virtues of outdoor exercise, he observed that 'true manliness shows itself not merely in skill and field sports, but in the exercise of those moral virtues which it is one of the objects of religion to inculcate' (quoted in Hill 1992: 10). Hence, through compulsory physical education and sport in state schools, and the imposition of more rigid rules governing sports like boxing, cricket and football outside it, elite and religious groups believed that they could maintain discipline within the working class.

The fear that the 'idle' leisure of the 'common man' would lead to physical degeneracy, a weakened kingdom unable to defend itself (or to attack others), and a debauched nation sapped of moral fibre spread in the nineteenth century to the young men of the 'officer' class. For example, Thomas Arnold, the headmaster of Rugby (public, which is to say private, fee-paying) School, famously promoted sport as a means of promoting discipline, cooperation, leadership and 'purity'. As Clarke and Critcher note:

> The encouragement of organised sport was simultaneously a means of controlling the characteristically anarchic behaviour of public school-boys and of redirecting the public school ethos towards a model of what would subsequently be defined as 'muscular Christianity'. Thus both the traditional clientele of the aristocracy and the new market of the sons of the bourgeoisie could be retained for the public schools, refurbishing an image tarnished by low morality and dubious academic accomplishment.
>
> (Clarke and Critcher 1985: 62)

Baron Pierre de Coubertin was much taken with this 'healthy body, healthy mind' aspect of sport, and by the noble idea that, while excelling at sport would make the citizenry more able to wage war effectively (France, after all, had suffered an ignominious recent defeat in the Franco-Prussian War), meeting other physically and morally fit young people from all over the world in international sporting competition every four years would enhance international understanding and make actual military combat less likely. The legacy of this notion of a '*pax Olympia*' was highly visible during the Winter Olympics in Nagano, Japan, in February 1998, when President of the International Olympic Committee (IOC), Juan Antonio Samaranch (strongly backed by Michael Knight, the New South Wales minister responsible for the 2000 Summer Olympics in Sydney, Australia), called on all countries to observe an 'Olympic truce', just as US-led forces massed for a possible military strike against Iraq. The strong moral impulse (much degraded, as we shall later discuss) behind the modern Olympic Games (first staged in Athens in 1896, not too far from the Gods' home on Olympus) was, then, less a legacy of the ancient Greeks than the product of a model of competition influenced by the English and adapted by the French.

Profitable play

If there was a strong morally and physically improving element fostering the development of organized sport in nineteenth-century Britain, there was a less edifying, baser force at work also – capital and profit. Importantly, the commercialization of sport and the commodification of athletes (transformed from casual 'players' into sportsworkers selling their athletic labour power as 'products' bought and sold on the sport market) opened up a deep schism within the institutional **ideology** of sport itself. For lovers of sport like de Coubertin and Arnold, being an *amateur* (derived directly from the French word for lover) was to adhere to higher values of selfless devotion to the sport, fellow team members and competitors. Indeed, the ethos of sport they were promoting explicitly opposed the 'unworthy' practice of 'playing for pay' or of constructing entire sports (like prize fighting) around gambling and money making. Attitudes to the business and work possibilities of sport were clearly marked by social class at both ends of the hierarchy. For those who had inherited wealth (especially through land ownership), there was no material need to earn money from sport, but for the emergent entrepreneurial capitalist class who accumulated wealth by making and selling goods and services, and for the members of the working class who had no means of support other than their own labour power, professionalized sport held many attractions. Thus, while 'upper crust' sports like rugby split into two codes in England in 1895 (and Australia in 1907) over the issue of player payment and compensation for loss of work through travel or injury, and the International Olympic Committee to this day eschews the paying of prize money to athletes (since 1981 questions of eligibility to compete and remuneration have been left to the individual international federations – Hill

1992: 240), the penetration of the logic of capital accumulation into sport has been such that, as Cashmore (1990) has noted, the term 'amateur' has increasingly become a term of abuse in sporting culture.

'Pure' amateurism in sport, if it ever existed, quickly died, and in the case of rugby union (the amateur side of the split), a long period of 'shamateurism' ended in 1995 with such suddenness that it now threatens to swamp in commercial terms its long-time 'professional' antagonist – rugby league – while multimillionaire tennis players like Andre Agassi and Pete Sampras are now permitted to take part in Olympic competition. Estimating the current global value of the 'sportsbiz' is no mean task, given the range of economic activities which it can claim to embrace, but in 1988 Neil Wilson (1988: 8) noted that 'Official figures in Britain estimate that more than [US]$4 billion is spent on sport each year, more than on motor vehicles. In Britain, sport-related activity employs 376,000 people, more than the chemical industry, or agriculture or the combined electricity and gas industries.' A decade later, a report by the Confederation of Australian Sports valued sport's economic activity in that country (with a population less than one-third of Britain's) at AUS$8 billion, with the sports sector directly employing '95,000 people in 1995–96 – more than the rail, grain, electricity and clothing industries' (Boreham and Pegler 1998: 3). In the same year as this report was released in Australia, the eight-year TV rights to the National Football League in the United States alone were sold for US$17.6 billion (Attwood 1998: 39 – see Chapter 4). It can easily be seen, then, that the sports industry (without factoring in its contribution to ancillary industries like clothing, food, beverages and transport) is growing and in global proportions.

How can such large sums of money be generated in and through sport? In examining the flow of capital, the initial source lies in the willingness of some people to pay for the privilege of sport spectating. This ability and desire to be entertained by those who specialize in and excel at particular activities – a phenomenon periodically present in pre-industrial societies in the shape of travelling groups of troubadours and actors – grew as part of a more general development of the division of labour in capitalist and industrial societies, as the new complexity and profusion of mass produced goods and available services demanded a much wider range of occupations, skills and tasks (Durkheim 1960; Marx 1967). Furthermore, the now rigid and carefully calculated segments of work time in factory (and later office) labour created its own alternative – leisure time – that demanded an equivalent level of planning and organization in order to be utilized to the full (Brown and Rowe 1998). This 'rationalization' (M. Weber 1968) of the rhythms of work and leisure in the eighteenth and nineteenth centuries was accompanied, as we have seen, by the growing standardization of the rules of various sports and strong pressure from the authorities to stamp out the most dangerous and destructive pursuits – in the name both of propriety and also of labour force efficiency (a gin-sodden or injured worker is also an unproductive one). This process (which he links to a more general 'civilizing process') is described by Elias (1986b) as the 'sportization of pastimes', whereby:

> The framework of rules, including those providing for 'fairness', became more precise, more explicit and more differentiated. Supervision of the observance of the rules became more efficient; hence penalties for offences against the rules became less escapable. In the form of 'sports', in other words, game-contests involving muscular exertion attained a level of orderliness and of self-discipline on the part of participants not attained before. In the form of 'sports', moreover, game-contests came to embody a rule-set that ensures a balance between the possible attainment of a high-combat tension and a reasonable protection against physical injury.
>
> (Elias 1986b: 151)

This 'figurational' perspective judges the development of organized sport to be evidence of a general shift away from the unrestrained bodily expressions that left the participants in some physical jeopardy (ranging from pub brawls to 'knock down', bare knuckle fighting) to a more disciplined activity in which a clear division existed between spectators and performers. In the case of fist fighting, for example, it evolved under the 1867 'Queensbury Rules' and subsequent restrictions into a boxing contest in a ring of prescribed size over a specified number of rounds of limited duration between only two fighters, both wearing padded gloves, permitted only to strike particular parts of the body ('no hitting below the belt!'), and so on. As the discretionary income of the industrial proletariat increased, especially by organizing through trade unions to wrest a little more of the capital surplus from the bourgeoisie, the possibility arose of reclaiming and expanding that capital surplus by 'packaging' and selling spectator access to those sports which could attain the requisite, pleasurable 'high-combat tension'. Nineteenth-century entrepreneurs (in the case of the first cricket tours these were often, not too surprisingly, publicans – to the extent that Cashman (1994: 71) describes them as 'the first cricket administrators, [who] viewed cricket as an extension of public-house entertainment') created the conditions for a sports business in much the same way as other leisure pursuits became paying concerns. They relied on supplying services which were attractive to consumers – and made to seem even more so by lively advertising and promotion – but which could be accessed only at a cost, which was set at a level that reflected the 'scarcity' of what was to be watched and the superiority of the view of proceedings. In this way, sport became another component of the burgeoning entertainment industry which, as Goldlust (1987) notes, has over the past two centuries supplanted so much uncommodified, self-reliant leisure:

> The successful growth of spectator sport was premised on a set of well established entrepreneurial principles that applied throughout the 'entertainment' industry. As determined by the organisers, a price, or a range of prices was fixed, the payment of which entitled any member of the public to be admitted to a venue in which the performance or event would take place. The venue, be it a circus, vaudeville house, concert hall, theatre, cinema or stadium, was physically constructed in a manner that limited the potential audience to a finite number of paying customers who, from variably privileged vantage points – depending on the price they were prepared to pay – could experience that performance or event. Through the construction of some form of physical barrier or boundary, those unwilling to pay the cost of admission or unable to gain entry to the venue, because all the legally sanctioned audience space was already committed, were excluded.
>
> (Goldlust 1987: 73–4)

The ease with which sports contests could be enclosed and 'screened' for paying customers varied with the nature of the sport; it was much harder, for example, in large, open-air football, cricket and baseball grounds than for roofed boxing or wrestling buildings and tents. It was also more profitable to set up permanent venues in the large, population-dense urban centres than to rely on travelling sports exhibitions, where transport and sustenance costs were high and venue security and comfort standards low. The 'classical' mass production capitalist principle of producing as much of the same commodity as cheaply as possible took hold in spectator sport from the late nineteenth century onwards. By the second decade of the twentieth century, 'Spectator sport was [now] attracting massive crowds' (Clarke and Critcher 1985: 74), especially of working-class men. On this basis, a whole economy of sport developed as:

- sporting clubs and associations were formed by subscribing members
- competitions were established with attractive prize money
- imposing venues with large crowd capacities were built
- a labour market (often feudalistic until player revolts) grew up to handle the transfer and valuation of professional and semi-professional 'sportsworkers'

- state funds were donated to the development of sport
- sportswear and fan merchandise were manufactured and sold
- and (of particular significance for this book), newspapers, magazines, newsreels, films, radio (and, later, television) programmes became devoted to sport.

The initial development of the commercial side of sport paralleled that of other forms of entertainment, with more and more information about sports events and the people involved in them (especially the new sports celebrities) provided by a panoply of publications from newspaper sports columns to specialist sports newspapers and magazines. But prime dependency on paying spectators physically transporting themselves to particular events limited its potential for expansion. A vast, untapped audience existed which could, by means of developing audiovisual technology, be relieved of the necessity to travel to sports events – instead, the games would come to the audience (Rowe 1996). Yet how could this large, dispersed 'crowd' which was never likely to meet each other nor approach a sports stadium be turned into a 'market' capable of turning a profit? The answer, of course, is that listeners and viewers – especially the latter, on account of television's power to simulate 'real time', sensory experience – would not pay directly to see sport (except by bearing the cost of electronic equipment, electricity and, in some countries, a licence). Instead, another party (advertised businesses) would arrange and pay for them to watch sport and selected messages through a third party (television). While this 'free-to-air' television transmission of sport is now supplemented and even threatened by a re-institution of direct payment for service though subscription and pay-per-view TV, it is still overwhelmingly dominant on the most important sports media occasions (like the Olympics) when the sheer size of the audience generates enormous advertising, sponsorship and TV rights revenue. The vast popularity of sport, then, became an economic resource in its own right which can be readily harnessed by external economic interests. For this reason, the economy of sport in the twentieth century has developed in such a way that it is no longer reliant on a direct, monetary exchange between spectator and 'exhibitor'. Yet sport not only is of economic significance, but also has political and cultural dimensions.

Political football

National governments, on behalf of the nation-state, have invested heavily in sport and sports television (through national, public broadcasters) because of the highly effective way in which sport can contribute to nation building. In countries divided by class, gender, ethnic, regional and other means of identification, there are few opportunities for the citizens of a nation to develop a strong sense of 'collective consciousness', of being 'one people'. One significant exception is war, for which sport is often claimed to be a substitute, so that 'in the course of the twentieth century, the competitive bodily exertions of people in the highly regulated form that we call "sport" have come to serve as symbolic representations of a non-violent, non-military form of competition between states' (Elias 1986c: 23). The idea of sport as a 'symbolic representation' of war has sometimes been taken further, to the extent that it is seen as a functional substitute for it, discharging military aggression between countries in a relatively harmless way. This 'war minus the shooting' proposition is most famously associated with George Orwell, but he saw sport as anything but a benign diversion, instead judging international competitions to be malign manifestations of militaristic nationalism:

> I am always amazed when I hear people saying that sport creates goodwill between the nations, and that if only the common peoples of the world could meet one another at football or cricket, they would have no inclination to meet on the battlefield. Even if one didn't know from concrete examples (the 1936 Olympic Games [the so-called Nazi Olympics], for instance) that international sporting contests lead to orgies of hatred, one could deduce it from general principles.
>
> (Orwell 1992: 37–8)

The English, according to Orwell, were leading 'young countries' like India and Burma (at least in 1945 when his article was published) astray by exporting their 'obsession' and arousing 'even fiercer passions'. In the ensuing half century, there have been many more examples of what Orwell would have regarded as 'nations who work themselves into furies over these absurd contests, and seriously believe – at any rate for short periods – that running, jumping and kicking a ball are tests of national virtue' (Orwell 1992: 38). Sometimes the consequences of such heightened emotion can be fatal, as in the 1994 'revenge' murder of Colombian footballer Andres Escobar, who was summarily executed outside a bar by an enraged fan after Escobar had scored the own goal that precipitated his team's exit from the World Cup finals. Probably the most famous direct linkage of sport and military combat is the so-called 'soccer war' in 1969 between El Salvador and Honduras, where border tensions were 'touched off' by riots following a soccer World Cup qualifying match between the countries. Not only has the entwining of national and sports culture tightened in many countries and spread to others, but also the possibilities of exposing all the globe's citizens to such 'symbolic representations' of national progress and international competition have grown with the institutions of sport and media.

Just as it was in Britain that the social institution and cultural form of sport first emerged, it was the British state, through its public broadcaster the British Broadcasting Corporation (BBC), that pioneered the use of great sporting occasions as festivals of nationhood, so that 'broadcasting would produce a new form of national event: in extending major occasions of state and of sport throughout the land it would make a royal wedding a nation's wedding', and demonstrating 'the centrality of the BBC's sport coverage of notions of Britishness and national identity' (Whannel 1992: 20, 21). Other countries quickly appreciated this symbolically unifying power of national and, especially, of international sport, so that great sporting moments like the Super Bowl in the USA, the Melbourne Cup in Australia, the FA Cup Final in the UK, Hockey Night in Canada (Kidd 1982; Gruneau and Whitson 1993), and global media mega sports events, like the Olympics and the soccer World Cup, have become orgies of both nationalism and commodification ('commodified nationalism', perhaps).

Apart from the state political usages of sport – most notoriously, as Orwell noted above, Adolf Hitler's attempt to use the 1936 Berlin Olympic Games as a vehicle for the assertion of Aryan supremacy – the overall cultural significance of sport cannot be underestimated. For example, most of the historical accounts of sport drawn on above reproduce the inequality of its gender order, with women athletes and spectators rendered more or less invisible or marginal (Jennifer Hargreaves 1993a; 1994). Yet there is a powerful 'herstory' in sport: a series of tales of women who have fought for the right to play sport, be paid properly for it, supported by sponsors like their male counterparts, wear what they choose while competing, secure appropriate media coverage, and so on (Blue 1987; Guttmann 1991). If culture is the 'stuff' of everyday life – the frame through which we experience, interpret, mould and represent everything that surrounds us – then sport occupies, as noted in the Preface, an uncommonly prominent position within it. The economy of sport is, then, more than the exchange of money for tickets, of wages for performance on the field of play. There is also a **cultural economy** of sport, where information, images, ideas and rhetorics are exchanged, where symbolic value is added, where metaphorical (and sometimes literal, in the case of exchange-listed sports clubs) stocks rise and fall. This cultural (and material) economy of sport has developed through 'cottage industry' and early industrial and capital accumulative phases to a full blown, sophisticated complex. Once elements of sport had become rationalized and industrialized, they necessarily entered into relations with other economic entities which acted as conduits, carrying sports culture far beyond its places of origin. As noted above, the institution (which, more accurately, is a constellation of diverse but related structures and practices) that has become crucial to the destiny of modern sport is the media.

It is the media that not only have created the capacity for sport to reach its staggering global audience but also 'service' that audience, that reproduce and transform sports culture through an endless and pervasive process of showing, 'sounding', discussing, depicting – in short, of representing sport in myriad ways. Before we can proceed to an analysis of the sports media, we must first understand, through cultivating a socio-historical sensibility, not only why contemporary sport needs the media so desperately, but also why the media have an equal and urgent need for sport.

The rise of the mass media

As in the case of the physical play and game contests that mutated into sport, **communication** using a variety of aural and visual media is an ancient practice, from cave paintings and 'sagas' told around campfires through religious icons and hand-written books, to satellite broadcasts and computer graphics. A key element of the rise of capitalism and industrialism was the transformation of small scale and technologically rudimentary media into an institutional complex of enormous social, cultural, political and economic importance. These 'mass media comprise the institutions and techniques by which specialized social groups disseminate symbolic content to large heterogeneous and geographically-dispersed audiences' (Bennett *et al.* 1977: 9, adapted from Janowitz 1968). The standard accounts of the development of mass communication (such as Bittner 1983; McQuail 1987) chronicle the 'take off' points, such as the invention in 1450 of the Gutenberg press which gave birth to print, and, later, the arrival of radio transmitters and, then, the cathode ray tube that brought us television. To see these technological developments out of social context is, however, also to view the development of media as an inevitable, evolutionary process. But the history of media, like that of sport, is a much more complicated tale of struggle, in this case between powerful groups (first the church, then the state) to control the circulation of 'dangerous' texts (like officially unapproved versions of the Bible) and other, often less powerful groups and individuals (political movements, trade unions, unaffiliated people asserting their rights of liberty) who wanted access to them and to the means to circulate their own texts. Not only did the rise of representative democracy, citizenship and the nation-state demand a free and efficient media as a political imperative, but so also did the new capitalist class require the capacity to display its goods nation-ally and, later, internationally in obedience to an economic one. McQuail traces our contemporary notions of the 'ideal' newspaper to:

> The 'high bourgeois' phase of press history, from about 1850 to the turn of the century, [which] was the product of several events and cir-cumstances: the triumph of liberalism and the ending, except in more benighted quarters of Europe, of direct censorship or fiscal constraint; the establishment of a relatively progressive capitalist class and several emergent professions, thus forging a business-professional establish-ment; many social and technological changes favouring the operation of a national or regional press of high information quality.
>
> (McQuail 1987: 12)

The establishment of the values and practices of 'good' journalism (fearless independence from government and other powerful groups, a commitment to rooting out corruption, an authoritative voice on which the public can rely, and so on) was followed by a more overtly commercial concern with adver-tising. The 'quality' newspapers could exercise political influence by reaching a relatively small but powerful readership, as Hartley (1996: 14) notes in his comment on the 1835 painting by B.R. Haydon, *Waiting for The Times*, in which one gentleman impatiently covets the broadsheet in the hands of another, anxious not to remain 'absent from the imagined community of VIP readership'. As Curran (1981a: 25) notes, attempts by the British ruling class to deny this level of power and influence through the media to others by imposing stamp duties and harshly enforcing laws of libel and sedition, para-doxically also helped a nineteenth-century radical press (like *The Poor Man's Guardian* and the *Northern Star*) to flourish by slowing 'the development of a mass market for newspapers, and consequently the development of expen-sive print technology to service it, while the duty on advertisements limited the growth of advertising expenditure on the popular press'. Campaigns against 'the taxes on knowledge' were as much driven by capital accumu-lation as by appeals for freedom of thought and expression – the removal of many political impediments to newspaper production allowed the economic power of 'new money' entrepreneurs (especially press barons like Lord Northcliffe and, a little later, Lords Beaverbrook and Rothermere) to assert itself. Thus, cheaper, widely distributed papers, made attractive to advertisers by toning down political rhetoric and to readers by sensational copy, edged out the radical, 'disreputable' press (Curran 1981b) and created and then ser-viced a different market to that of 'highbrow' newspapers.

The new technological capabilities of the media meant that the content of the popular 'penny dreadful' scandal sheets that were sold on the streets could be readily disseminated in a manner that reflected the economic power generated simply by the exposure of large numbers of people to imprecations to buy products and services. The emerging 'yellow press' (associated in the USA with Joseph Pulitzer and William Randolph Hearst) was not much admired by the guardians of nineteenth-century media morality, but, just as occurs in the contemporary world, the immediate riposte was that demonstrable public demand for 'bad' journalism had to be satisfied, and that no group of privileged individuals had the right to dictate what the 'masses' wanted to read and see. Disputes over media morality and ethics, and especially their political and economic power, are no less apparent long after the daily newspaper first made its mark. Indeed, as Schultz (1994) argues, they may have been exacerbated in the current 'information age':

> As the engines of global economic growth switch from industrial to information production, the rhetoric which, for two centuries, has legitimised the media as more than just another business needs to be re-examined. More than any other industry the media have been characterised by 'deeply ethical' debates about role and responsibility – profit was never the sole criteria [*sic*] on which the media were judged. But as the profits generated by the media continue to grow the tensions between serving the public and making money are also likely to escalate.
>
> (Schultz 1994: 61)

This idea that the media are 'not just another business' sits particularly uncomfortably with developments in the late twentieth century that have seen the media's principal currency – information and images – become also the prime unit of exchange, and the role of the media far exceed that of the idealized 'vocation' of nineteenth-century 'quality' journalism. The intensification of debates about media power and responsibility is, however, a product of expansion of the whole media sector, rather than, as media moralists often suggest, linked to a specific development like the invention of television, the circulation of glossy magazines or the marketing of paperback books.

News and entertainment

The mass media, as we have seen, had from the outset two major, sometimes conflicting functions. The first involved the 'serious' notion of news gathering and processing as part of the Fourth Estate which acted (at least ostensibly) as a watchdog on the powerful and as an important influence in the key process of nation building by communicating the nation to itself (Schlesinger 1991). It was no longer necessary to listen to a town crier to hear the news of the day or to rely on rumour and gossip to be informed about what was happening outside the individual's or small group's immediate experience. The great journals of record and opinion leaders such as *The Times* of London or the *New York Times* and, later, the public broadcasters like the BBC and those in the former British colonies or dominions on which they were modelled, like the Australian and Canadian Broadcasting Corporations (ABC and CBC respectively), were and are key media organizations in the formation of an informed 'public sphere' (Habermas 1989). The extent to which the mass media successfully fulfil this important function of challenging the powerful and promoting informed citizenship has always been hotly disputed, not least because to own or control a major media organization (or an 'empire' consisting of many different organizations operating in a single medium or, even more powerfully, across different media) is a significant form of power in its own right (Golding and Murdock 1991). However unflattering the 'verdict' might be on the capitalist press or on state broadcasters in regard to their sincerity and effectiveness in serving the people at large and protecting the weak from the abuse of power by ruling elites, there is no doubt that major media organizations are highly sensitive to allegations that they ruthlessly exploit their command of the channels of mass communication to their commercial and political advantage. As Windschuttle (1984) argues, the conventional defence of commercial media organizations (and, we might add, even of some increasingly entrepreneurial public media) against criticisms of dereliction of public duty is to construct the idea of the 'public interest' within a type of 'free market model' which, in the case of newspapers, positions them as:

> simply in the business of satisfying the demand for news. So the principal criterion of selection is public interest. The concept of 'public interest' is usually interpreted in two ways: what the public is interested in; and what is in the public's interest. This produces a dual approach to the business of editing. It means the news media have to both 'give the public what it wants', which is often taken to be 'human interest' or largely trivial material, and to fulfil its 'duty' to record the important events of the day.
>
> (Windschuttle 1984: 262)

Because the public interest can never be absolutely understood but can easily be invoked, and because terms like 'trivial' or 'human interest' can be endlessly debated, newspaper proprietors and editors (and their equivalents in television and radio) can claim that they are only biased against what is boring and off-putting for their publics. If they do not cover news stories about their commercial or political opponents, or represent them un-favourably if they do, it can be claimed by media organizations that it is in response to an audience-pleasing imperative. Here the rather abstract concept of the public interest can be easily translated into measurements (ratings, circulation, sales) of what the public can be shown to be interested in.

This second function of the mass media, then, has rather less lofty am-bitions and a somewhat reduced emphasis on ethical accountability; it is to entertain the populace using the new media technologies (which allow texts to be rapidly reproduced and disseminated) to communicate cheaply with large numbers of people. In this way, it is no longer necessary to go to a con-cert to hear music, to watch a play in performance to experience drama, and so on. Furthermore, the popularity of this media content can be used to advertise the myriad goods whose mass production demand an equivalent level of mass consumption (Dyer 1982). As Brierley puts it with disarming directness:

> Advertising arose out of the industrial revolution. Overproduction of mass market goods through new manufacturing techniques and low consumption meant that consumer goods companies needed to stimu-late demand. New channels of distribution such as transportation and mass retailing opened up the possibility of reaching new markets.
>
> (Brierley 1998: 39)

In order to be effective, advertising had to connect with the powerful social myths already in circulation (Leiss *et al.* 1990) and also situated in a highly visible media site where it was available to facilitate the trade in goods and services. Popular media texts could, then, be used as a lure to bring unknow-ing and perhaps reluctant consumers into the orbit of commodity culture. In 'capturing audiences for advertisers' – as Smythe (1977) has influentially argued – for the purpose of mass consumer persuasion, the mass media could now be subsidized by those same advertisers to provide cheap (as in the case of newspapers whose cover price is only a fraction of their produc-tion cost) or free (as in much 'free-to-air' television) media content that would provide the opportunity for an unprecedentedly massive 'window display' for goods and services.

As the mass media developed into large-scale, formal, bureaucratic organizations in the business of producing news, culture and entertainment in a manner which imitated the continuous process production methods of factories, they also displayed an insatiable hunger for content – the vast spaces of print and air time had to be filled in fulfilling their dual informa-tional and entertainment functions. It is impossible to imagine newspapers

or radio news bulletins being cancelled on the grounds that nothing sufficiently newsworthy happened in the world today, or no new records or
films being released this week because of a temporary talent shortage, or
blank pages in magazines and empty TV screens on account of a failure to
come up with anything sufficiently diverting. This is not only because news
is always being made and culture produced that is of interest to somebody
somewhere, but also 'dead air', blank screens, empty pages and goods-free
shops cannot be tolerated by the media and cultural industries. The economics of the commercial media are premised on the continued availability of
'new' material (however familiar in form and predictable in content) which
will constantly stimulate popular attention. In this way, the mass media can
be seen as an institutional space which must be filled on a daily space in
order to function, rather than in more conventional terms as a supplier of
cultural goods on the basis of established and measurable demand.

The publicly funded media, furthermore, are charged as we have seen with
the additional responsibility of fostering national culture, a sense of belong-
ing to the nation which brings its various citizens together across the barriers of locality, class, age, race, ethnicity, gender, and so on. The public media
are no less required to provide continuous content than the commercial
media, although their revenue does not derive directly from selling goods
and exposing audiences. Nevertheless, for public media to fail to produce
copious quantities of information and entertainment would imply the
unthinkable – that the nation is not being dutifully served or, worse, that
during breaks in transmission it does not exist! All media – public or private,
large or small – have to deal with the question of a public. While it is mis-
leading to reduce media relations simply to one group of people (the audience) accepting or rejecting the product of another (journalists, film-makers,
pop musicians, television directors, and so on), there is no doubt that, ultimately, audiences are crucial to the success of media enterprises.

The media, especially in corporate and public form, are expected to be
accountable to their audiences – they are literally at their service. Despite
widespread belief in the ease of audience manipulation by unscrupulous
advertisers, television executives and press barons, it is striking that media
professionals see their publics often as fickle, mysterious and essentially
unknowable. In a crowded marketplace where most cultural products that
are sold will lose money, or where success is dependent on stopping the listener from 'touching that dial' or the viewer from switching the remote control, it is necessary to minimize the risk of failure in an uncertain 'task
environment' (Hirsch 1971). Managing that task environment is a delicate
activity: it is necessary to 'second guess' what audiences want; to act on
previous successes by giving them more of the same while judging when they

have become bored or satiated with a particular format; to offer the requisite level of novelty without alienating the audience with something too far 'out of left field'. Making media texts is, then, both a creative and a conservative activity, requiring a judicious appreciation of the swings between cycles of standardization, when a successful formula (like TV 'infotainment' shows or teenage 'splatter' movies or costume dramas) is found and reproduced, and cycles of diversification (like the sudden 'breakout' of punk music, ironically 'postmodern' violent films or 'weird' TV serials) when novel approaches and material are desired (Peterson and Berger 1975). What subject could possibly satisfy all these competing and disparate demands? The answer – for so many editors and programmers the dream solution to the perennial problem of contacting and holding media audiences – is sport.

Having it both ways: sport meets media

Sport provides the mass media with many precious qualities. In terms of audiences it is able regularly to deliver large (sometimes enormous), often extremely loyal cohorts of readers, listeners and viewers. The linkage between sport and media did not await the arrival of the age of television. As Michael Harris (1998: 19), for example, demonstrates, 'cricket was drawn into the content of the London newspapers' well before 1750 as part of the 'widening circle of commercialization within what might begin to be described as the leisure industries' and the 'emergent urban activity which became closely associated with the elite groups in English society'. Newspapers, therefore, were key promotional tools as entrepreneurs began to 'construct a business around public recreation' (M. Harris 1998: 24). The core audience of sports fans (and the derivation from 'fanatic' is frequently appropriate) is a reliable 'commodity' which can be profitably sold to advertisers, and on occasions a much larger and less committed audience can be drawn in to take part in the great national and international spectacles which generate their own momentum of interest through their sheer size and 'cross-media' visibility. Just as television has, like fashion, its new seasons, sport has its equivalent of serials and blockbusters. The established sports can 'bubble away' in their rolling time slots (in some cases becoming global, year-round offerings courtesy of satellite television), while the media machine periodically gears up for national and international mega media sports events which, in a self-fulfilling fashion, become compulsive viewing and reading matter (because they are nearly impossible to escape). Consider, for example, the scarcity of personal space impervious to images and information concerning the summer Olympics during the competition period in any society with a reasonably well developed media infrastructure. Sport not only produces audiences faithful to the media which are displaying it, but also is productive of other forms of loyalty, such as to products (as the sponsors of sports competitions and the companies which heavily invest in sports related advertising, like Benson and Hedges, Coca-Cola and McDonald's, can attest) and also to city, state, county, region or nation (an emotion much prized by governments and much exploited by commerce). In countries like Australia, where sensitivity to media and cultural imperialism exists as a result of its earlier colonial status and current openness to media products from the dominant English language centres of production, sport also supports the idea of local loyalty by counting towards legislated quotas of local audio-visual media content (Cunningham and Miller 1994).

For all this valuable emphasis on predictability and loyalty – to the extent that many sports in the media take on the appearance of sought-after brand names with a high recognition factor (Lash and Urry 1994) – sport also possesses the highly desirable quality of novelty and unpredictability. Media **discourse** before, during and after sports events is variously about prediction, judging what has been predicted against what is actually unfolding, and then reflecting on and seeking to find explanations for what has transpired (Eco 1986). In other words, while, for example, 'live' sport on television may have the stylized and easily anticipated quality of the soap opera **genre** (see Chapter 7), it is always capable of a surprise outcome which refuses to follow slavishly a script that has been apparently prepared for it (Harriss 1990). This 'uncertainty principle' of sport – and hence media sport – explains why result fixing, like a boxer 'taking a dive' or a soccer goalkeeper deliberately letting in a goal, is so scandalous. In sport's famous clichés 'it's never over until the fat lady sings' (in this case a scenario borrowed from opera) or 'the game is never over until the final whistle' (a tautology masquerading as wisdom). This 'emergent' quality of sport in the media helps meet the perpetual audience need for something new and different alongside what is familiar and known. It also provides the media with the cornerstones of news gathering and delivery – constant updates, reported results, highlights, behind-the-scenes information, and so on. Sport, then, stands at the confluence of the two principal functions of the mass media – news and entertainment – and is carefully structured into the 'softer' spaces of news bulletins and newspaper sections. It simultaneously supplies the material to be reported on and a substantial amount of the infrastructure of reporting. As content, sport can absorb a lot of media space and time. A test cricket match, for example, is a single sports event which can occupy a television schedule from morning to early evening, followed by some packaged late night highlights and frequent news reports, for five days. Variations on the same sports story can appear on the front, features and 'op ed' pages of newspapers, as well as in the regular sports sections, supplements or 'tear-outs'.

It is little wonder that the relationship between sport and the media (especially in television) is commonly described as the happiest of marriages, with both institutions becoming mutually dependent in an increasingly extensive and expensive exchange of exposure and rights fees for sport in return for compelling content and audience capture for the media (Rowe 1996). Like all enduring relationships, however, there are many points of tension, power plays, negotiations, compromises, disagreements and secrets. Many of these visible, partly obscured and hidden elements of the sport–media nexus will be analysed in the following chapters as we attempt to understand how media sports texts are manufactured, 'unwrapped' and consumed. This might be an all very interesting but not terribly enlightening exercise in the description of cultural production if making media sport was just a technical matter, a value-neutral process whereby sports information and action is disseminated and a little (or even a lot) of money is made on the side. But this is not the case; power over media sports production brings with it other forms of power – economic, social, cultural and ideological – which often seem elusive or the existence of which is denied altogether by those who believe that 'it's just business' or 'it's only a game'. The final task in this summary socio-historical analysis of sport and media is to propose that the (conscious or unconscious) exercise of power is not an unfortunate by-product of the media sport production process, but is, in fact, central to it.

Conclusion: sport, media and cultural power

The heightened prominence of sport in print reportage (including specialist sports, business and general journalism), magazines, still photography, radio, film, video and television is incontestable. What we are to make of this observation is much less easily established. A number of propositions can be offered to explain the spectacular growth of the sports media. Blandly, it can be suggested that it is produced by the efficient operation of the market in cultural goods, services and information, a benign example of how popular taste is accommodated by the cultural industries. Alternatively and more sinisterly, wall-to-wall media sport can be seen as the extension of the 'bread and circuses' policies of dominant groups, perpetually distracting the population with trivia while getting on with the business of ruling a grossly unequal world to their own advantage by making sure that oppositional values are discredited and neglected. These well known polarized perspectives, described over a quarter of a century ago by Cohen and Young (1973) as the commercial *laissez-faire* and mass manipulative models, have between them a range of different positions which gravitate, in emphasis rather than in their totality, towards one or other end of the analytical spectrum. Even less conclusive is the approach which stresses the inconsistent, contingent, negotiated or emergent relations between media, sport, culture and society. Instead of the master **narratives** of consumer freedom versus mass oppression, there is a more modest and qualified attention paid to the historical and institutional conditions which produce outcomes that can only be pronounced upon after close and unprejudiced inspections of particular instances of media sport on a case-by-case basis. From such a perspective it is not possible to speak of the state of the sports media in general, but only of the diverse complex of sites and processes out of which are produced many different, historically conditioned circumstances.

Here, then, commercial and media forces can be said to have wrested control of a sport from 'the people', but over here 'the people' have successfully resisted the blandishments of sports media commerce, or have accepted the need for economic rationalization, or have formed alliances with more 'sympathetic' commercial enterprises or governments to repel the clumsy incursions of 'buccaneering' businesspeople, and so on. The cost of such an open, flexible and indeterminate approach is, however, the loss of explanatory power arising from a concern with the uniqueness of each instance of media sport rather than with the common features out of which patterns and trends can be discerned. For this reason, the analysis of the sports media must move in different directions, carefully weighing the macro and micro, general and specific influences which, in combination, work to fashion everyday life out of the social resources at hand. Thus, as Foucault (1980) observes, there are different forms and effects of power which are in play at different levels throughout the social world. Power is not necessarily a negative concept: it ranges in character from the exercise of the grossest and subtlest forms of oppression to the capacity to effect dramatic or cumulatively progressive change. Power also operates in environments – like the domain of the sports media – often dismissed as trivial and harmless. The 'trick' is to recognize the many forms, directions, sites and effects of power without optimistically inflating the success of resistive strategies or playing down the capacity of established power structures to assert themselves with an almost effortless and invisible force.

In this book I am interested in three main manifestations of power. The first is at the institutional level – the manner in which the institutions of media and sport have come together, the ways in which one may be said to have dominated (or even consumed) the other, the extent to which their interaction has had a mutually modifying effect. The second is at the symbolic level – how the institutionally provided and moulded media sports texts can be interpreted and used, sometimes accepted and revered, on other occasions rejected and ridiculed. The third is at the relational level – the wider social and cultural ramifications of the development of a giant, partially globalized media sports cultural complex – that is, the extent to which this great 'engine' of **signs** and **myths** itself symbolizes and helps create our current 'being in the world'. By gaining a better knowledge and understanding of how media sports texts are produced and what they might mean, it is possible to learn more about societies in which 'grounded' and 'mediated' experience intermesh in ever more insidious and seemingly seamless ways.

This chapter has covered a good deal of ground in attempting to establish a socio-historical framework for the study of sport, culture and the media. Many corners have been cut in the process, because to do a thorough job would have taken up the whole of this book – and probably several more volumes. I have tried to demonstrate something of how sport and the media developed as social institutions and then intersected and interpenetrated as the rapid growth in industrialized leisure and large scale consumption, coupled with the requirements of modern nation building, created the circumstances for a long lasting and increasingly intense union. Such developments, I have argued, need to be interrogated rather than merely documented, because the enormous investment of capital, human labour, political rhetoric, social effort and cultural space that has produced contemporary media sport has created the conditions for the playing out of many forms of power to:

- 'discipline' 1 billion people across the world in 1988 to watch the single event of the opening ceremony of the Seoul Olympics (then the 'largest television audience in history' (Rogers 1993: xiii) until inevitably exceeded by the opening of the 1996 Atlanta Olympics, with its 'estimated viewing audience of 3.5 billion around the world' (Gordon and Sibson 1998: 209) and, no doubt, again to be topped at Sydney 2000)
- determine the destiny of large companies and their employees
- influence the policies of government
- constitute much of the verbal and visual imagery in circulation
- occupy the ground of so much social discourse.

Clearly, all that the media sports cultural complex has at its disposal is a power not to be easily dismissed.

Where is the point of entry for probing the media sport behemoth? It is as well to remember (in order not to 'fetishize' them) that media sports texts, as the product of human activity, have to be manufactured by human subjects according to accepted and imposed procedures and values. The personnel traditionally charged with supplying and/or interpreting these texts are quite commonly regarded as the 'least cuddly' of their profession, 'notorious for going sour with drink and age' (McGuane 1992: xv). They are known by the professional title 'sports journalist'.

Further reading

Briggs, A. and Cobley, P. (eds) (1998) *The Media: An Introduction*. Harlow: Longman.

Curran, J. and Seaton, J. (1997) *Power Without Responsibility: The Press and Broadcasting in Britain*, 5th edn. New York: Routledge.

Elias, N. and Dunning, E. (1986) *Quest for Excitement: Sport and Leisure in the Civilising Process*. Oxford: Basil Blackwell.

Goldlust, J. (1987) *Playing for Keeps: Sport, the Media and Society*. Melbourne: Longman Cheshire.

Guttmann, A. (1978) *From Ritual to Record: The Nature of Modern Sports*. New York: Columbia University Press.

3

WORKING IN MEDIA SPORT: THE DISCIPLINE OF SPORTS JOURNALISM

> I have done every job in provincial journalism, everything but Saturday afternoon sport, because even vultures will throw up on something!
>
> (Terry Pratchett 1990: 13)

Introduction: flesh, blood and sports journalists

There is something deeply paradoxical about the professional status of sports journalism, especially in the medium of print. In discharging their usual responsibilities of description and commentary, reporters' accounts of sports events are eagerly consulted by sports fans, while in their broader journalistic role of covering sport in its many manifestations, sports journalists are among the most visible of all contemporary writers. The ruminations of the elite class of 'celebrity' sports journalists are sought after by the major newspapers, their lucrative contracts the envy of colleagues in other 'disciplines' of journalism. Yet sports journalists do not have a standing in their profession which corresponds to the size of their readerships or of their pay packets, with the old saying (now reaching the status of cliché) that sport is the 'toy department of the news media' still readily to hand as a dismissal of the worth of what sports journalists do. This reluctance to take sports journalism seriously produces the paradoxical outcome that sports newspaper writers are much read but little admired.

How can we explain, putting aside the wider question of the surprising lack of occupational prestige of journalists as a group – according to Curran (1998: 90) 'former standards of accuracy are declining, at least in the eyes of the public' – the rather low esteem in which sports journalists are held within their chosen profession? Or, even if journalists in general retain high or even growing repute, why does the American writer James Traub (1991: 35) note that after a short stint as a sports writer, 'The experience taught me that the trend of increasing prestige for the press, observable in such coverage sectors as business and politics, has not been universal'? In looking for an answer to these questions, it is necessary to understand the more general ambivalence concerning the value of popular culture and of attempts to take it seriously. Sports journalists, furthermore, are caught in a particularly difficult bind because of the different, sometimes contradictory professional demands made on them; they are expected, often at the same time, to be objective reporters, critical investigators, apologists for sports and teams, representatives of fans, and, not unusually, to have performed in sport at elite levels. Their readers, listeners and viewers are more than a little uncertain about the value of their work. As Hornby (1992: 136) pronounces in his obsessive fan's paean to soccer, *Fever Pitch* (the film of which is discussed in Chapter 7), 'Sports journalists and armchair Corinthians are the Amazon Indians who know more than we do – but in another way they know much, much less.' Such questioning of authoritative knowledge recurs repeatedly in lounge and bar-room discussions of sports journalism: What do they know anyway? Can they really feel it? Are they too close to it? Often lying behind such doubts is a lingering resentment, from non-sports colleagues and sports fans alike, that sports journalism is something of a 'lurk' – a case of 'nice work if you can get it'.

These conflicts over the identity and conduct of sports journalists go beyond a little jockeying for position in the professional pecking order: they have far-reaching ramifications for the process of making media sports genres and texts. By inspecting the 'coalface' of media sports production, it is possible to 'de-naturalize' media sports texts and so to understand that they are particular creations and constructions arising from the complex, contradictory forces that make culture. At the same time, we begin to see something of the cultural politics of sports journalism, especially the way in which sports texts mediate understandings of social issues within sport and between sport and the society in which it is embedded. The seemingly 'automatic', neutral procedures of media sports text production are thereby revealed as wedded to the negotiation and promotion of power relations in their various forms.

In this chapter I shall explore the practice and status of sports journalism (with the major emphasis on print) in teasing out key aspects of the making of sports texts. In so doing, I shall draw on a research study (with some interview extracts presented here also found in Rowe and Stevenson 1995) I conducted in the mid-1990s, which involved over 40 interviews (not all conducted by me) with working sports journalists (mostly print, but also television and radio) from three different English-speaking countries (Australia, UK and New Zealand). A key element of the study was the sports journalists' self-assessment of their own and their colleagues' work activities in different sports media (all identifying names of individuals, organizations and places, it should be noted, have been removed in presenting these interview data). It is important to understand (although not be limited to) what sport journalists think about what they do because, despite appearances to the contrary on occasions, they do not robotically churn out pre-programmed content. However urgent the deadlines, limited the vocabulary and familiar the organizational routine of sports journalism, it should never be forgotten, as Schudson points out:

> Journalists write the words that turn up in the papers or on the screen as stories. Not government officials, not cultural forces, not 'reality' magically transforming itself into alphabetic signs, but flesh-and-blood journalists literally compose the stories we call news.
>
> (Schudson 1991: 141)

Despite the development of computer programs like the 'Zybrainic Sportswriter', which can automatically compose sports data fed to it by non-journalists, so allowing '*The Monroe City News* in Missouri [to] become the world's first newspaper to use a computer instead of journalists to write its sports reports' (Sydney Morning Herald 1993: 79), there is a human body and brain behind the sports news.

My concentration on print sports journalists reflects the continuing predominance of the written form as the vehicle for what we call journalism (rather than commentary or presentation) and the numerical strength of print journalists as compared with the rather smaller departments of the electronic media. Henningham (1995: 14), in a national survey of Australian sports journalists conducted in 1992, notes that 'Sport is the biggest single speciality in mainstream news media', accounting for almost 11 per cent of all Australian journalists, 80 per cent of whom worked for newspapers (as opposed to exactly two-thirds of non-sports journalists). As the study did not 'count [the] many more journalists who work for specialist sports publications or non-news sports programs on television and radio' (Henningham 1995: 14), it can be seen that the number of 'accredited' and 'non-accredited' sports journalists is very substantial. While there may be some peculiarities of the Australian context (to be discussed below), related studies in countries like the USA (such as Garrison and Salwen 1989; Salwen and Garrison 1998) indicate that sports journalism is, indeed, the largest sub-discipline in the profession and that print is at its heart. This is not to ignore the movement of sports journalists from print to radio or television, and the increasing tendency for them to range across media so that, in a single day, a sports journalist might write stories, provide radio reports and commentary, and take part in TV studio discussions. It is notable, however, that print credentials carry the most weight, reflecting the continuing power of newspapers to set the agenda for the electronic media. Although we see the 'imprint' of sports text production practices on the back (and, not infrequently, the front and middle) of every newspaper, we are somewhat less likely to observe and reflect on the factors that brought them to the page. A good starting point, then, is to consider what it might feel like to be a practising sports journalist.

Sports journalists: 'shabby reputations' and professional problems

To be a sports journalist is to engage in an occupational specialization that combines the general responsibilities of the profession with the particular demands imposed by the object to which those professional practices and ethics are directed. In principle, then, sports journalists are no different from those with any other assigned 'round' or 'beat'. Court reporters relate the events of important trials; law reporters address difficult legal issues; police reporters go to crime scenes and get unattributable briefings from the constabulary; business reporters watch the share market and pick up on the rumours (often planted) of corporate plays; and sports reporters get the best seats at the biggest games, inform others of what happened, and are meant to use this privileged vantage point to expose the hidden workings of the sports machine. This 'democracy' of journalistic disciplines does not, however, exist in pure form. A hierarchy of esteem (if not always one of salaries or profile) exists which places the 'serious' disciplines (like the politics round) at the top end and the 'lighter' ones (like the entertainment page) at the bottom. Sports journalists, whose subject suffers from the twin disadvantages of popular appeal and a focus on the body rather than the mind, tend to gravitate towards the lower echelons. As Salwen and Garrison (1998) discovered in their survey of over 200 members of the US Associated Press Sports Editors:

> Issues related to professionalism, which included ethics, were major concerns to both sports journalism and journalism in general, according to the respondents. Sports journalists who elaborated on these concerns as they relate to sports journalism believed that their shabby reputations cultivated over the years haunt them in this age of professional prestige and accountability. In this regard, we can see how the historical roots of sports journalism affect the field today.
>
> (Salwen and Garrison 1998: 98)

Two levels of response to the researchers' questions can be seen to be at work here. When asked to consider journalism in general, 30 per cent of Salwen and Garrison's respondents ranked 'professionalism' second only to the 'reader related' category (31 per cent) of the nine most important problem areas (Salwen and Garrison 1998: 93). These sports journalists appear to be reflecting on the overall decline of journalism's occupational prestige – a fate that it shares with other professions like medicine and law (Macdonald 1995). When addressing sports journalism in particular, respondents ranked 'professionalism' first in the list of problem areas, although only 21 per cent of them did so (Salwen and Garrison 1998: 93). The probable explanation of this survey outcome is that the sports journalists saw their own discipline as so beleaguered that they spread the range of important problems rather more widely, with seven of the nine most important problem categories selected by 8 per cent or above of the total, compared with only four out of nine for journalism in general. Thus, if the profession of journalism is felt to be currently 'in trouble' by many journalists, then the discipline of sports journalism is believed never to have been out of it. Salwen and Garrison note that this 'historical baggage' weighs down sports journalism and allows sporting figures like the late A. Bartlett Giamatti, once president of Major League Baseball's National League, to state:

> My impression is that editors generally ignore the sports section. They ignore it in the sense, and it is an important one, that the same set of editorial standards for accuracy, competence, distinguishing fact from opinion, rewriting, and editing are simply not applied consistently or rigorously to sports sections as they are applied to all other sections of the paper.
>
> (Giamatti, quoted in Salwen and Garrison 1998: 89)

In finding sports journalists guilty of sins of truth denial, dubious ethics and misplaced apostrophes, there is a suggestion – not uncommonly held within and without the sports discipline – that sports journalists are a breed apart. Indeed, this term was used by a provincial British sports journalist in describing the special demands of the job:

> I think the [sports] news is different, you are a different breed . . . it's a very specialist area, sports fans don't suffer fools, you need to know what you're talking about. You can't just put anybody on sport, you've got to be certain he's a fanatic . . . you have to live and breathe it to an extent, you have a vast knowledge, especially like myself, a special editor of a particular sport . . . because rugby in Barchester is the be-all-end-all, really . . . If you're giving statistical information you've got to

be on the ball, you've got to get it right, because you can guarantee if you don't get it right somebody will pick it up. It only has to happen a couple of times and you get known as the person who gets it wrong, who can't get it right. So you have to live and breathe it, you have to be armed always with facts.

(Alan)

In sharp contrast to Giamatti's notion of an indifferent tolerance of inaccuracy, this sports journalist is acutely aware of the demanding nature of the readership, to the extent that the journalist is expected to display, on pain of getting 'known as the person who gets it wrong', the same fanatical attention to sporting statistics and facts as the fans themselves. It is by meeting such demands that sports journalists sometimes seem to become detached from the wider profession and attached to the world of sports fandom (we could call this 'anorak' journalism).

As Henningham (1995: 13) points out, the almost uniquely isolated position of sport in media organizations helps foster such feelings of professional difference, with the 'ghetto structure of sports departments in newspapers and broadcast media organisations' turning them into something of an occupational one-way street. Young sports journalists, once they have entered the sports department, tend to remain there rather than moving on to other, more prestigious 'rounds'. With sports departments being their 'own little empires, with a sports editor, sub-editors and reporters, all of whom handle nothing but sport' (Henningham 1995: 13), sports journalists operate in a rather enclosed world, achieving upward mobility by moving towards the position of sports editor by 'leapfrogging' between media organizations or gaining internal promotion. But they remain largely confined to the sports arena – according to Henningham (1995: 13) 'sports editors never become editors of newspapers' – trapped in the journalistic equivalent of the 'Land of Boobies' in the child's story *Pinocchio*, where boys never had to study but spent their time 'in play and amusement from morning till night' (Collodi 1911: 196). This is not such an unkind analogy in the light of Henningham's (1995: 14) finding that sports journalists are happier in their work than non-sports journalists, with only 17 per cent 'dissatisfied' with their jobs, and half the level (13 per cent) of 'very high' job stress levels than other journalists.

In my study of sports journalists, a young, university-educated journalist on a provincial newspaper, who subsequently transferred to different journalistic specialisms such as music, stated that he found 'sport a bit of a dead end', with less recognition than 'police or council or general reporting' (Christopher). A much more experienced career British-born newspaper sports journalist working in New Zealand (interviewed, it should be noted in the interests of ethnographic colour, some 32,000 feet above Afghanistan and Turkey), reflected on the joys of travelling the world reporting on major sports events while also recognizing that 'we certainly are looked upon as rank old hacks by some other branches of journalism' (Rodney). This jour- nalist noted that many promising young journalists were deterred from entering the sports specialism by this poor professional reputation. It is important to probe why it is widely believed – not uncommonly even by sports journalists themselves – that the sports pages are characterized by inaccuracy, incompetence, technical weakness and ethical failings. This is not a reputation confined to print, as one indigenous Australian journalist, who trained as a sports broadcaster before moving into other areas of radio, remarked of the cool reaction of his new non-sports colleagues to his career background: 'I mean there is that stigma attached to sport, that it's not really news as such' (William). What, then, are the prevailing standards by which all journalism is assessed, and which determine what counts as 'news as such'?

While there is considerable disagreement about the core criteria of good journalism – we need only contrast the highly subjective 'new journalism' (Wolfe and Johnson 1975) with the canon of objective reportage – it is useful to outline a conservative prescription for what journalistic values and prac- tices ought to be, and then to compare them with the failings – real or imag- ined – of sports journalists. In a diatribe against journalism educators who subscribe to a cultural studies approach, Windschuttle (1998) has outlined 'the three characteristics of journalism that most teaching in the field upholds':

> First, journalism is committed to reporting the truth about what occurs in the world . . . Second, the principal ethical obligations of journalists are to their readers, their listeners and their viewers . . . Third, journal- ists should be committed to good writing.
>
> (Windschuttle 1998: 11)

In another place I would take issue with Windschuttle's rather crude and mechanical journalistic manifesto, but it is probable that such prescriptions are frequently taken by journalists and non-journalists as the yardstick of 'good journalism'. It is immediately apparent that much contemporary (and no doubt previous) journalism of all kinds does not observe these strictures. 'Truth' can be manipulated by governments or proprietors or 'spin doctors' and sundry other media manipulators; the interests of readers may be sacri- ficed for those of advertisers or journalistic careerists; what appears on the page may be a ragbag of clichés and plagiarisms – see, for example, the trenchant criticisms of contemporary journalism by crusading public intellectuals like John Pilger (1998) and Noam Chomsky (1989; Herman and Chomsky 1988). Yet, as we have seen, if journalism in general is open to such charges, sports journalism, lowly placed on the 'totem pole', is doubly so. In part, these criticisms are made by connecting what sports journalists do with who they are. Garrison and Salwen (1994: 40–1) describe them as 'overwhelmingly white, male, college-educated and thirty-something'. For most journalistic disciplines, the bulk of this description would hold except for the 'overwhelming'. As Henningham (1995: 14), for example, notes of the sexual composition of the profession in Australia, there are almost nine male sports journalists for every one female, but among their non-sport counterparts, the ratios are still close to two-thirds male, one-third female. In teasing out what is common to journalism and specific to sports journalism, and reasonable critique from snobbish prejudice, we can make use of a technique developed by the FBI in tracking down serial killers and urban terrorists – profiling.

Profiler: the strange case of the sports journalist

Empirical studies of the sports journalism discipline (like those noted above) provide a handy snapshot from which to build up a more detailed picture of the social characteristics of sports journalists and attitudes (including their own) to their professional practice. The areas covered in Henningham's (1995) study (which is succinctly interpreted in principally quantitative terms by its author and so demands considerable elaboration and cross-comparison) that I shall concentrate on are social characteristics and related attitudes; work satisfaction; political orientation; and ideas on the media's role and ethics. The image of the sports journalist that emerges from the matches and mismatches of available data and attitude is of a journalistic speciality that benefits from the privileges of inherited social advantage while suffering from its association with the socially and culturally disadvantaged. This rather convoluted argument is necessitated by the contradictory and ambivalent attitudes that abound in constructing the image of the sports journalist.

Sports journalists (as briefly mentioned earlier) are not drawn from the ranks of the working class. This is a hardly surprising observation in an occupation requiring relatively advanced non-manual skills and, as Henningham (1995: 15) found, sports journalists are every bit as middle class in origin as other journalists. However, the research subjects in Henningham's Australian survey, unlike those in Garrison and Salwen's (1994)

US-based study, had on average lower levels of educational attainment than non-sports journalists (but somewhat higher than the general population). Although this picture is variable, a perceived pattern of sports journalists moving into the specialism without a university education, coupled with the vexed issue (Rowe and Stevenson 1995) of the recruitment of un-trained, unaccredited personnel on the basis of their achievements (liter-ally) in the field of sport (the celebrity athlete turned sports writer), contributes to the negative image of much sports journalism even from within the discipline. As one sports journalist for an Australian broadsheet newspaper put it:

> Well I think in this country you've been able to get away with some pretty lazy writing being a sports journalist. I mean some of the career paths into sports journalism have been ex-players who decide they want to do something with their sport when they finish playing. They might have been a great player who played a hundred times for Australia but whether they can string two words together is another matter, but they have been allowed to do that because of who they were. Or even, racing is a good example, a lot of people who got into racing journalism were strappers or kids who, you know, there was more of an opportunity if you were involved in a sport to become a sports writer. That is not to say that all people who have come out of an active sporting career can't write, it did mean in that sense that the standard of the writing was not as high, and they were not trained as closely or as professionally as other journalists.
>
> (Martin)

The negative attitude of journalists (both sports and non-sports) who had trained 'in-house' in the orthodox way to those who had entered the pro-fession on the basis of their sporting expertise is common. Suspicions of involvement in 'ghosting' – the common practice in the entertainment print media of celebrities putting their names to texts that they have not written – hang over the heads of all sports journalists (certainly in early career) who are practising or former elite sports performers. As one Australian print journalist, a former international sportsman who has now published widely in the international sports press, exclaimed:

> I was highly offended in the first two articles I did [while still a player] that, you know, I got a great reaction and people said 'were they ghosted?' No, they fucking were not ghosted! And nothing I've done has ever been ghosted! I've done ghosting for friends and I don't mind doing it, but I think to have some resentment towards someone like me

when I look at joining the *Messenger* now, you know, you've got to start out, basically. I don't know, I stand to be corrected but I think you've got to have a degree before you can be a first-year cadet – although I think if you have a degree they might start you at third year or something like that, but it is a very arduous process and circuitous route to get to a decent grading in journalism. Now the short cut that I took to that, to circumvent all that, was to have a field of expertise where I would have some authority to write things . . . [It's] by no means only sport, people make their names in computers, and don't come that route because people want to read what they have to say. Now I consider myself very fortunate to have circumvented that, I never would have had the wherewithal to have done it the other way. I stumbled into journalism, found that I loved it, but I never would have done it the other way. I never would have stuck it for a four year cadetship, doing shipping rounds and nonsense like that. I was lucky and so far so good it's worked out well.

(Philip)

This experience of 'stumbling' into sports journalism from another occupational area – including elite sport – is a common and, in many cases, by no means an illegitimate one, but it does not do much, from a credentialist point of view, for the status of the specialism, especially when it is accompanied by the ethically dubious practice of ghosting. In 'paying their dues' on the shipping and garden fete rounds, many journalists expect to bank up professional experience that is recognized as a qualification for the job – including sports reporting. The movement into their ranks of those unqualified or underqualified in journalistic terms not only questions the value of such experience, but also raises the broad issue of the authority of the writer and critic who has not been what he or she is describing at the highest level – an Olympic athlete, opera singer, chef, and so on. This tension between competing forms of authority – sporting and literary – in a discipline of journalism that is already subject to considerable scepticism concerning its quality and worth leads, as is noted below, to an anxious pressing of claims to professional and even artistic legitimacy.

While this difficulty in restricting labour market entry – especially in cases where 'ingress' is on the basis of demonstrated physical rather than mental and literary prowess – may negatively affect sports journalism's prestige, it does not automatically depress its social class composition. As McKay (1991: 11) has noted, in terms of the general population, participants in sport 'have a relatively high level of income and education'. Henningham (1995) found, furthermore, that, while indistinguishable from other journalists in socio-economic class terms, sports journalists are more likely to be Anglo and male than their colleagues in the wider profession. A degree of caution is needed here – there are no doubt other equally WASP (White Anglo Saxon Protestant)-dominated journalistic specialisms (business and political reporting spring to mind), but these may be protected from criticism by their concern with 'serious' matters of state and economics. In other words, the social homogeneity that is barely questioned in some areas of journalism becomes, in the negative stereotype of the sports journalist, a sign of the 'hack'. A 'clubbish' image of sport journalism begins to emerge when it is seen to be resistant to entry by women (according to Van Zoonen (1998: 129), masculinity and a subjective attachment to sport and sportspeople is definitive of sports journalism) and/or those of non-Anglo background. In my (qualitative) study it was sometimes remarked that, for example, in Britain there were few Asian and Afro-Caribbean sports journalists 'coming through'. One British former editor and current sports columnist noted the irony of the largely mono racial/ethnic composition of sports journalism, 'Just as an increasing number of sportsmen have become black'. He went on to remark that:

> Barry Brain, the sports editor of *The Watchdog*, told me that he was very consciously bringing on Black sports writers because he did feel they had a perspective that was missing in the sports pages, but not very many are doing that. Again, I just don't know how many guys there are who are any good at it.
>
> (Darren)

The under-representation of non-Anglo people in the sports media could be the journalistic equivalent of 'stacking', the practice in sport of (often unconsciously) assigning black athletes to 'race appropriate' sports, team and coaching positions which rarely involve tactical decision making and leadership (Cashmore 1990). From this perspective, sports reporting and commentary largely involves white people in a 'non-manual' occupation authoritatively judging the sporting deeds of largely silent and objectified non-white people using their bodies to make a living. The outcome (if not the intention) is racist and ethnocentric in that the culture of sports journalism can be seen to be replicating a very old and damaging structure of inequality that reserves key 'gatekeeping' positions for dominant social groups even as subaltern people appear to be making progress in the area in question.

The view that diversifying the 'body' of sports journalists not only is a matter of social equity but also is likely to produce fresh insights and approaches was also expressed when he reflected on the dearth of good

female sports reporters in Britain and the pattern of those who had specialized in sport becoming discouraged and moving to other specialisms:

> Every sports editor starts off paying lip service that he wants women to
> read the sports page, and one effective way of getting more women to
> read the sports pages is getting more women to write on sport pages –
> there is a natural identity there. And then they get bored with it or there
> aren't enough women around and it fades away again. I think it's a
> great shame because I think, I read a piece that Sue Knott wrote in *The
> Sunday Times* a few weeks ago, an interview with Ray Kennedy, the
> footballer with MS [multiple sclerosis]. Now that was something very
> few men could have written – if any, I suspect – because it had a special
> sympathetic perspective, human perspective and did illuminate the situ-
> ation for people very well indeed. He talked to her in a way he might
> not have talked to a man, there's a kind of macho culture in which they
> hold back some of these really personal things. I'd like to see a lot more
> of that.
>
> (Darren)

While the recruitment of female sports reporters was partly advocated here
as a tactic to increase circulation and partly to supply a more traditionally
nurturant, non-combative feminine quality to the sports page, it nevertheless reveals the predictability of approach of much current sports journalism
and the limited experiential base of its practitioners.

Henningham (1995: 15) records in his study that sports journalists were
less likely than non-sports journalists to have 'experienced or had knowledge of newsroom prejudice' relating to race, ethnicity or sex. Of those few
sports journalists in his study who were female, women journalists were far
more likely than their male colleagues to agree that it is 'more difficult for
women to get ahead in journalism' (36 per cent compared to 85 per cent,
although their non-Anglo counterparts did not tend to attribute to ethnicity
an equivalent level of obstruction to upward occupational mobility).
Because they had not experienced prejudice and discrimination on the
grounds of race, ethnicity or sex themselves, or had not been sensitized to
the negative experience of others (not least because most of their immediate
colleagues had similar backgrounds), most of the sports journalists in this
study were not much troubled by social structural inequities.

This cosy picture of the sports desk as a WASP male enclave is reinforced
to a degree by Henningham's findings that sports journalists tended to stay
in the same job and, indeed, profession, for longer than their non-sports colleagues and (as mentioned above) were generally more satisfied with, and
less stressed by, their jobs than journalists in general. When questioned on

the relative importance of different characteristics of those jobs, sports journalists were significantly (in statistical terms) attracted to their job's pay,
security and fringe benefits, and significantly less concerned with the editorial policies of their organization (Henningham 1995: 16). The last
characteristic connects with the political orientation of journalists; as we
saw in Chapter 2, western news media workers have traditionally prided
themselves (though sometimes only with the aid of self-delusion) on their
fiercely guarded critical independence from governments and big business
enterprises (even when the latter are their own employers). Yet, the sports
journalists whose attitudes are recorded in studies like Henningham's are
more politically conservative than non-sports journalists (almost twice as
likely to vote on the Right), and more positive and optimistic about the current state of press freedom, concentration of ownership and control, and so
on. The 'splendid isolation' of the sports department has no doubt partially
insulated it from the 'improper interference' by proprietors and managers
that bothers journalists in other departments. Greater priority, as a result, is
given to news functions like 'get information to the public quickly' and 'concentrate on news of interest to the widest possible public' rather than 'provide analysis and interpretation of complex problems' or taking the role of
sceptical 'adversary' in dealing with public officials and businesses (Henningham 1995: 16). Here the traditional sports reporting and recording
function comes to the fore (see Chapter 5) at the expense of the analytical
and investigative tasks of the news media.

Crusaders and cheerleaders

The engaged, 'crusading' media role is less appealing to those sports journalists (the majority, it seems) schooled in the work of describing sports
events and passing on news about them, rather than interrogating and probing them. These findings are not inconsistent with those that find sports journalists more ethically principled than other journalists on issues like 'using
confidential business or government documents without authorization' or
'badgering unwilling informants to get a story'. Sports journalists may be
less tempted to 'cut corners' in the interests of the 'big scoop' not only
because much of their work involves interpreting what is already publicly
known and visible, but also because they are heavily dependent on cultivating good relationships with sportspeople, officials, sponsors and so on. The
penalties of being 'frozen out' by the 'usual suspects' (the providers of off-
the-record insider information) are serious for journalists on any round
(Chibnall 1977), but are likely to be worse than most in sport, especially

outside the capital cities or where the journalist has been overly reliant on sporting camaraderie and has not developed other analytical resources and 'quotable' sources. A provincial British print journalist whose main work task was to cover the local soccer team made clear the professional and ethical difficulties that may arise (what he called 'the big tightrope of doing the job') when there is a high level of dependency and concentration on a single sports operation:

Gareth: If you are working for a national paper, for example, or even a paper covering a number of teams, you don't have the daily contact and you float in and out as it were. You may upset people at a particular club but that doesn't really matter because you're not going back for a few more weeks. But in this instance you have hit the nail on the head, my job does entail speaking to the manager, the Baddington manager Brian Snout, and my job is to speak to him basically every working day. But, yeah, that's right there can be occasion, OK you ring up in the morning and the manager, whoever it may be over the years, is not very happy about what you wrote last night and then you kick off with having to defend what you've written before you move onto, you know, what's happening today type of thing. It is important, of course, that you do manage to bridge that gap because at the end of the day you depend on ringing the manager to get the information, so if you criticize them a bit too heavily and, the following morning he says, 'I'm not very happy with you', and puts the phone down, then the job is made that much more difficult.

D.R.: If there is a kind of embargo by the manager, and he refuses say to speak to you, would that make it virtually impossible to do your job?

Gareth: Um, no. In fact two or three years ago I did have a set to with Fred Wild, the previous manager. The team were doing badly and the paper generally, not totally what I'd written, but I'd been criticizing, and other writers on the paper as well on the sports desk were having their two pence worth . . . As a result of that he said we were trying to get him the sack and he had no intention of cooperating with us in future, so he refused to speak to us, to the paper in general. That meant that for a period we had to go along with, you know, we weren't banned from the club, there was no suggestion of that. It was just purely that I didn't have access to the manager to obtain the information on a daily basis, but I was still able to go along, report the matches in the normal way, and pick up information as best one can.

There are other contacts that a journalist has, naturally, he doesn't rely purely on the manager, although it is the manager that they normally deal with on a day-to-day basis, quote on a day-to-day basis. It doesn't mean that you don't get unidentified sources and, therefore, you can't quote people anymore, and you're having to say 'this is believed to be happening' and 'that may be happening'. In some ways it takes the pressure off a little bit right away, you no longer have the worry, as I mentioned earlier, of having to get back onto the manager the following morning and take flak for the criticism you might have given him overnight, because, you know, you've no longer got that worry of having to speak to him. Basically, you can sit back and let fly willy nilly. He's got to, the manager's got to suffer in a way, because you're going to feel even more free to criticize.

D.R.:   And, of course, he did in the end get the sack.

Gareth: That was about twelve months later.

This exchange reveals the complexity (familiar, of course, to journalists on many other rounds where the 'object' to be reported on and the associated sources are fixed and limited) of the relationship between sports journalist and principal source. It is a relationship of mutual dependency – the sports entity needs media coverage and the media worker needs a story – which can break down or get out of balance. In this instance, 'normal service' was resumed without compromising journalistic integrity (indeed, the journalist felt liberated by not having to deal with the source on a 'daily basis', so being licensed to 'let fly willy nilly'), but it is not difficult to imagine less ethical outcomes (arising out of, as Murphy (1976) discovered in his study of provincial journalism, the network structure of the local elite).

Broader areas of ethics on which sports journalists were not questioned in Henningham's study include the perils of becoming too much of a 'cheerleader' for sports teams (see Chapter 5) and a 'mate' of athletes rather than an independent journalist, and on the inevitable temptations (not unknown to travel and wine journalists, among other specialisms) of the 'perks' that go with the job (travelling with the team, entertainment, open access, free tickets, and so on). It is at this point, where the ethics of journalism rub against the enviable 'on the side' opportunities of the sports round, that critics of sports journalism (in some cases, no doubt unreasonably) see it as the compromised ally of the sport and entertainment business rather than as a legitimate arm of the news media.

In this section I have tried to flesh out the shadowy glimpse of the sports journalist schematically presented in Henningham's article. He concludes by judging contemporary sports journalism as something of a throwback – perhaps one that would be approved of, as discussed earlier, by Windschuttle (1998: 17) to 'an older model of journalism, more objective and "fact based", more in tune with the commercial imperatives of the media, less questioning of the ideological and sociological role of journalism'. Henningham is also concerned by the lack of 'angst' and the absence of a 'self-critical approach' by sports journalists whose profile, as developed out of the survey, is of a rather complacent group of white male professionals from comfortable backgrounds with enviably 'cushy' jobs. This picture does not altogether match that emerging from my qualitative study of sports journalists or that reported in Salwen and Garrison's quantitative and qualitative studies. Methodologically, these variable 'findings' may stem from the different types of data generated by 'pencil and paper' survey-style interviews and exploratory, semi-structured interviews.

It is likely that the more thoughtful and self-critical responses of the sports journalists in my study were artefacts of the selected research method, which involved interviews of at least twenty minutes' duration (often much longer) and a series of inquisitive and sometimes discomfiting questions. It is also possible that sports journalists are generally satisfied with their lot but feel less so when reminded by interviewers that they tend to be poorly regarded by their non-sports peers. Most of the interviewees in my study described both the pleasure and pain of their jobs as producers of media sports texts. For example, a female sports journalist on a broadsheet Australian newspaper (necessarily, as we have seen, unrepresentative of her occupational group) expressed both a sense of international variation in the prestige of sports journalists, a desire for greater recognition, and the joy of sports writing:

I think, perhaps, they're treated better in Britain than we are here, we're all dying to be treated the way they are in America, where they're generally seen as the top echelon of journalism in sport over there, and it would be lovely to be felt that way here. But people generally assume that have nothing to do with it, that it's much easier than other forms of journalism, and because it's sport, it's a physical activity, that there's nothing intellectual about it. It's not true, I did all the other things when I was a cadet, but the thing that gave me most stimulation was sports writing. You have the most freedom, you make many more decisions on your own about how it should be approached, and particularly now that sport is so professional, you have to know about finance and economics and courts, because it's always ending up in the courts these days, and you've got to be able to encompass all those areas. If you can't do that then you're not going to survive in professional sports. The way it is, you really have to be able to turn your hand to anything, and you've also got to be a good writer, because sport is a very descriptive type of writing, expressive, you've got to be able to make people feel that they were there. So, that's why I like it, it just gives you so much [more] breadth than the other sections.

(Nancy)

Like virtually every interviewee in the study, this sports journalist was keen to assert the degree of difficulty and required skill level of the specialism. Journalists, editors and other sports writers are often frustrated and resentful about their professional standing, and anxious to improve it. The shifting positions of sport in the general cultural hierarchy and in the narrower culture of journalism are the determinants of the standing of sports journalism. In Chapter 2 we noted how sport in its various forms, at different historical moments, is claimed by different social groups. Dominant groups (such as the nineteenth-century British aristocracy and the twentieth-century bourgeoisie) have often embraced sport and prescribed approved forms of it for subordinate groups in the interests of character building, discharging 'unhealthy' urges, physical fitness, and so on (Ingham and Loy 1993). We have also seen that great sporting events, especially when carried simultaneously to all parts of the country by the electronic media, have contributed vitally to the process of nation building (Whannel 1992). Yet the very popularity of many sports, the possibilities they offer of cultural democracy, have made them also questionable to social elites, especially when they have moved beyond the noble 'disinterested practice' of amateurism (Bourdieu 1978) into the less edifying world of mass entertainment.

Sport's reliance on the moving body has also been at odds with those who have developed a culture of refinement through aesthetics and contemplation, as Urry (1990: 45) has noted in the social-class inflected split between forms of tourism typified by the 'collective' and the 'romantic' gaze. Organized sport also moves in and out of fashion; for example, in the 1960s it was seen by many in the counterculture as a popularly digestible form of militarism, but in the following decade supporting a sports team became a way for middle-class male intellectuals to demonstrate that they really were 'men of the people' (Rowe 1995). In contemporary Britain, soccer's remarkable recent wave of popularity has washed over groups in very different positions in the social hierarchy of 'Cool Britannia' (Miller *et al.* forthcoming). Non-sports journalists have not been immune to this epidemic of sports fandom nor have they been blind to its possibilities for professional advancement, while proprietors, managers, programmers and editors have, in many cases somewhat belatedly, realized the commercial value of sport and have provided more capital and human resources for it.

What do these long term trends and recent changes mean for the profile of the sports journalist? As I mentioned above (and not unlike the position of tabloid journalists in general), sports journalists are reasonably socially advantaged professionals whose 'patch' is a form of popular pleasure with a lowly reputation in some quarters. If the development of their professional discipline has been stunted by a somewhat comfortable, socially homogeneous male culture of 'giving the facts' and 'mixing with the players', it is, because of its expanding audiences, commercial clout and cultural profile, also currently in a state of flux. In order to improve our understanding of the making of the media sports text, it is helpful to examine more deeply, as Schudson (1991) noted above, how in the specialism of sport the 'flesh-and-blood journalists [who] literally compose the stories we call news' negotiate the various and conflicting demands that are made on them.

Talking to the sports talkers

In the excerpts from interviews with sports journalists presented earlier in this chapter it was apparent that, in going about their everyday duties, they are subject both to the occupational problems that beset all types of journalists (such as their relationships with sources) and others that, while not altogether exclusive to sports journalists, are particularly common to and pressing for them (like their status with fans and professional peers). Because the stereotype of the hard-bitten sports journalist is such an established one, it is tempting to discount the differences between them. While it is unquestionable that sports journalists tend to be white, middle class and male – for example, Creedon (1994a: 100) notes that the US-based Association for Women in Sports Media found that 'only 3% of the nation's 10,000 print and broadcast sports journalists are women' – differences and tensions exist between practitioners with similar social 'profiles', while we can also anticipate that the breaches already made in the bastion of sports journalism by women and non-Anglo people will widen. Divisions may emanate from involvement in different genres in the same medium (such as between tabloid and broadsheet journalists) or in different sports media (such as print versus broadcast), and complicate even further an already complex process of media sports text production in which fans, fellow journalists, athletes, sports administrators and sponsors are also implicated.

If we consider, for example, the case of Caroline, a female sports editor on an Australian radio station using a contemporary pop music format, it is clear that she must negotiate rather different work-related issues than a male journalist on the sports desk of a major newspaper. First, there is the matter of gender affecting the conduct of her work, such as in the 'danger zone' of the male sports dressing room, the scene of various confrontations over rights of access by female sport journalists, most famously symbolized by the 'Lisa Olson "incident" ' (Kane and Disch 1993) in which the *Boston Herald* reporter was subjected to 'locker room' sexual harassment in 1990 by some players from the New England Patriots football team. Caroline displayed acute awareness of the pioneering role of women sports journalists like Lisa Olson, whose public campaign against her treatment led to fines imposed by the National Football League and guarantees of gender equity in the conduct of sports journalism:

> I know I have come in on the shoulders of other women who have had to take football teams to court for not letting them in the dressing rooms. I know that, I know that a few years ago I probably wouldn't have been let within coo-ee [Australian slang for close proximity!] of a football dressing room, but because other women have done that I have been fortunate, I have had a slightly easier ride . . . they make sure there is an area where the players and the media can be. The players if they want to be naked can be in another room, and then get dressed and come out and talk to all of us, male and female . . . and in the end instead of me having to trot over to them, they come trotting over to me because they know me.
>
> (Caroline)

While acknowledging the preponderance of men in sport's journalism, Caroline saw the discipline as no more 'cliquey' than other rounds (like the parliamentary) that she had worked on. In replying to a question about whether she socialized (in bars and similar venues) with people in the sports industry, the reason given for not doing so was not exclusion on grounds of gender but the limited, straight news requirements of the radio station:

> No, I have never done that, because I have never had the time, and also, too, because since sport is not the huge priority of the station as a whole, and our news services as a whole, I don't have to go delving, delving and get all these little scoops, and bits and pieces. It's not the way our format really works with a music station, with news on the

hour, and although I think it is a good news service and they do take it seriously here, it's not something where you need to have all this dirt digging and delving and finding out little whispers in corners over a beer. So, if I was strictly on a round and I had to do that, I would do it, but in this situation I don't have to.

(Caroline)

This female radio sports editor, who in response to the radio news room requirement, with its limited personnel and urgent deadlines, of being 'jacks and jills of all trades', became responsible for the area by default, because 'I discovered I was the only person in this news room who either (a) liked sport at all and (b) had any interest in it.' The station format required a clear division of labour between media, with the radio providing the kind of old fashioned 'fact based' reportage identified earlier by Henningham (1995), leaving the more investigative coverage to print and the more detailed game analysis to television:

Well, the parallel with print is very similar to what it does in news. With radio, with newspapers, it's almost the same as basic hard news, other news. I see radio as a means of getting information through fast, not deep information. At the newspaper end they can go digging and delving and they can talk about what happened minute by minute through the match [but] a lot of people out there like following their favourite team but they don't want to read the absolute nuts and bolts. They just want to know the score . . . With television again, I think television is like a different kettle of fish altogether because my view is the sort of people who are watching television aren't listening to us and vice versa, you can't really have two sound sources on at the same time, so we'll find our job is more very much just to give the brief stuff – who won, who was the highest scorer, and let the other media go with the big post-mortem stories.

(Caroline)

Another female radio journalist who was required to conduct in-depth interviews did not find gender unimportant in her work (as did Caroline) but, rather, was able to use traditional gender roles and identities in her favour:

I think it [being in a minority as a female sports journalist] is an absolute advantage because most of the people you have to speak to are men, and for whatever reason, I guess it comes back to playing mothers and fathers, men will tell women something that they won't tell other men. So if you're talking about getting an interview and getting somebody to say something different, it's a real advantage being a female because you can play the softer side, and make the person relax and they do start telling you more than they would tell somebody else if they had the curtains or the barriers up. And I think the same for women. Women obviously know how to talk to women, whereas I think some men don't. So I think it's an advantage, I really haven't struck any disadvantages yet.

(Teresa)

Such neutral or positive experiences of gender in sports journalism – which run counter to those which might be expected – are not, of course, universal. For example, one young female print journalist found it more difficult for a woman to get 'a rapport going' with the predominantly male sportspeople with whom she had to deal on a professional basis, stating that it was:

hard for a female reporter because there is a lot of sexist attitudes. I'm sure a lot of people would just say 'what would you know about sport?' . . . It would be harder for them than a guy, I'm sure.

(Diana)

Yet a more experienced female sports journalist in a published interview, the late Wanda Jamrozik, turned this gender exclusion to her advantage, arguing that the 'insider trading' (journalists acquiring privileged information about sportspeople that they did not publish because 'it would betray the trust of friends') in sport 'was much greater than in other areas that I'd worked as a journalist'. By being forced to be on the outer in male-dominated sport (although less so when assigned to cover female sport, an editorial practice which many female sports journalists feel to be a form of ghettoization and marginalization), Jamrozik experienced less 'foreclosing on the things you might write about' after 'selling your soul' like, for example, the mostly male journalists on the 'traveling media circus that follows the professional tennis around' (quoted in A. Smith 1997: 91).

While it is not possible from my qualitative study to make claims of statistical representativeness and validity, it was striking that most of the female sports reporters interviewed were, on average, younger and with higher levels of educational attainment than their male counterparts. Baird's (1994) study of Australian women sports journalists (which used both quantitative and qualitative methods) found this to be precisely the case. Comparing her data with Henningham's mostly male respondents reveals that her sample of women was twice as likely to be tertiary educated than sports journalists in general (although well behind US levels of education), with only 21 per cent over 30 years of age compared with 60 per cent of all Australian sports journalists as found in Henningham's (larger) study. In Britain and Australia, at least, there is an apparent gap in 'cultural capital' between new entrants to the discipline of sports journalism (including university educated women) and longer serving reporters (mostly men) who had received only a secondary education – and in some case had not even completed that. This division is often replicated in the journalists' location in tabloid and broadsheet newspapers.

Tabloids, broadsheets and fanzines

A copious amount of sports copy is often taken to be a 'sign of the tabloid', yet the intensive coverage of sport by the broadsheets replicates the familiar, wider classification of the press into 'worthy' and 'unworthy'. One veteran British tabloid sports journalist saw this split in explicitly hierarchical terms, and inverted it by strongly asserting the high levels of skill (such as those of economy and speed) required by the tabloid sports press and expressing great antipathy towards 'patronizing' colleagues on the broadsheets with their 'wonderful degrees' who fail to appreciate such professional accomplishments:

> What pisses me off about my so-called colleagues on the broadsheets is their patronizing manner when it comes to tabloid journalists. They give the impression they want to wash their mouths out when they refer to tabloid journalism. Well, I can assure nearly all of them that I can do their job, they can't do mine. They're not good enough. And I mean that sincerely, they're not good enough to work for *The Daily Front* newspaper, they'd be totally lost. To be able to write and inform their readers in five hundred words of exactly what's happened and why, they couldn't do it. They need two thousand words and bore the arse off people. You know, I mean I fall asleep on a Sunday reading some of them, you know they go on and on with their long words and they think they're clever. I mean this patronizing crap that they come out with . . . The good broadsheet journalists, the McIlvanneys of this world, they will never patronize their colleagues on the tabloids, they're too big for that, they're big men in every sense of the word. They know we have a difficult job and most of us do it extremely well . . . Most of them wouldn't last a month on a tabloid newspaper because they're not good enough. I have no hesitation. They've all got wonderful degrees, no doubt, all went to university, but they couldn't do our job, wouldn't know where to start. It would destroy them . . . We've all got a job to do and most of us do it extremely well, otherwise we wouldn't still be doing it.
>
> (Calvin)

The unflattering image of the tabloid sports reporter is, indeed, powerfully imprinted on the minds of many university-educated sports reporters and editors. As one sports editor on a British weekly magazine put it, 'I think sports journalists just tend to be real, particularly with the tabloids, the tabloid hack element. I find it's a stereotype that is actually largely, really true' (Alistair), while his counterpart on a broadsheet newspaper stated, 'there are very great differences between what, say, a tabloid soccer man does . . . and what one of the quality people [does], especially the people on the *Independent* or the *Guardian*, which are very much writer driven' (Philip). This assertion of the 'quality' writing function over and against that of 'hack' journalism is constantly made by those who wish to elevate media sports texts, especially of the print variety, almost to the status of art. Sports journalism is not the only specialism where aspiration and current standing are strangers. One British freelance sports journalist and academic placed the sports round at 'second bottom of the pile, second only to media journalists. Media journalists have got a real chip on their shoulder, they believe they are seen to be the lowest of the low – and very often they are' (Sidney). Once again, the status of journalists who cover popular culture is believed to be poor, the lowly cultural status of sport and television rubbing off onto the journalist responsible for reporting on them. The possibility of transcendence is offered by turning formulaic writing into artistic expression:

> there are people who have turned it into such an art, feature writing and the atmosphere, who recognize sport as being much more than just a knockabout between two competing sides of individuals but as part of the culture of the country and the society and the sociological aspects of sport . . . They elevate their own sport to something bigger and greater really, and they write, and because they can write well and capture the atmosphere and the social reflections in sport, then I think they actually become recognized as rather better than your average results recorder. I think that's particularly true again of the broadsheet press. It's less true of the tabloid press. I have to say on the tabloid side . . . on reflection it might be, given the number of pages devoted to sport in tabloids and given the way they're known to sell papers, that actually in the hierarchy, in the pecking order of tabloid newspapers, sports journalists might be better regarded.
>
> (Sidney)

Once again the broadsheet–tabloid split is invoked here as corresponding to the relative quality of sports journalism, although it is conceded that, in the more popular (or populist) newspapers, journalistic status may be determined by different values – commercial rather than aesthetic. Repeatedly in this study a rather heroic picture of certain sports journalists emerged, which showed them to be capable of reaching beyond sport into the more universal and profound sphere of individual motivation, the 'human condition', the state of society, and so on. Here sports reporting becomes first sports writing, and then writing which uses the subject of sport only as a literary pretext. So, by using sport as a vehicle for the exploration of wider subjects and themes rather than being 'consumed' by it, the 'art' of sports writing resists classification as just another product of the toy department of the news media. As in other forms of art, however, this quality tends to be attributed only to a few, unusually gifted individuals:

> I also think somebody like McIlvanney is not only the best writer on the sports pages, he's probably the best writer on the paper. He has demonstrated that writing sports pages does not have to be inferior to writing the general news or being a foreign correspondent. There are very few writers who live up to those high standards but there are some. Ian Wooldridge I would say is probably the best writer on the *Daily Mail*, certainly one of the best. There's even the *Sun*, for example, although it does some deplorable things in its sports pages, you know, over-personalizing, vendettas against the England manager, and so on. There is some very good boxing writing in the *Sun* – very vivid. So I try to develop the idea that sports writing doesn't have to be downmarket simply because it's about sport, and that many a sporting experience can be as much a seriously deep psychological study of a man and a player and motivation. McIlvanney is probably the best example of that, particularly in boxing, where he reaches a very profound level, I think, in understanding what it is that drives sportsmen on to do what they do and why some sportsmen are greater than others.
>
> (Darren)

This model of what has been acidly called the 'sports journalism is high literature of the Mailer-in-Esquire school' (Diamond 1994: 16) is especially prominent in the USA, with its stronger tradition of celebrity sports writers, for whom, 'Sportswriting, at its best, is an art form accomplished with a work ethic' (Richman 1991: 337), although perhaps threatened with 'death' at its own hands in producing, 'Sportswriting [which], at its worst, panders to the lowest tastes of readers, offering rumor instead of information, jokes instead of passion, opinion instead of insight' (Richman 1991: 337). For Darren, the approved of 'hardboiled' style of quality sportswriting is unusually extended to embrace some tabloid sports journalists but, as we have seen, sports journalism in general remains a highly stigmatized specialism.

The critiques quoted above of much current sports journalism and pro-motion of 'superior' writing are paralleled in the unfavourable comparison of the best textual material produced by the print media and the standard programming of the broadcast media, which are seen to be overly reliant on 'fact-based' reporting and live coverage. Rivalry between sports media personnel is readily apparent, often over who gets priority access to sports performers after a game (usually the broadcast media – Rowe and Stevenson 1995) and over the appropriate job specifications in the sports media. As a British sports columnist asserted:

> There is a distinct shortage of investigative reporting on TV and radio. I'm hopeful that Radio 5 will commission some serious investigations. As you know some of these debates in sports are pretty fundamental stuff about the commercialization of sport, drugs in sport, many things that touch on serious social problems, and I think the sporting press generally has been slow to see that. I think newspapers are getting better but there was very little sign until very recently that television was prepared to do that. In fact, the point I made to the BBC the other day was that the number of actually scripted programmes about sport is minimal. Now I accept that live sport is live television, it's wonderful television, but there is also scope behind the scenes for doing much more, both on personalities and on issues relating to sport, than they're doing at the moment.
>
> (Darren)

It is felt by many sports journalists that there needs to be a more critical and inquiring approach to sport, and, for the print journalists at least, this change of tack has been forced on them by the broadcast media's seizing of much of their traditional territory of describing sports events. Several print journalists argue that they need, in the age of live radio and television broadcasts, text services, and so on, to find a new role that enhanced the media services already provided by the broadcast media. But some believe that the lack of an established culture of sceptical inquiry and distance from sources makes this transition difficult:

> but the greatest problem, far and away with Australian sports journalism, and I don't limit it to Australian sports journalism, is there is always a tendency towards sycophancy and biographies being hagiographies, and that whole line of Johnnie Bloggs was the greatest there ever was – and it doesn't matter that he's won five grand finals in a row now and can high jump ten metres, you never saw such a modest bloke who loves his wife! Look at him here with his two kids . . . the

great problem with sports journalism is there is way too much sycophancy.

(Philip)

Philip notes, for example, that one leading sportsman (who cannot be
named on grounds of defamation!) is regularly presented favourably in the
press as a family man and 'nice guy', but that, 'If we had the world deadshit
Olympics and I was a selector, I would send him'. He also describes the
problem of being in the position (also commonly experienced by pop music
and other entertainment journalists) of being granted an exclusive interview
with a sporting superstar who is 'savvy about the media ways', and then feeling inhibited by this privilege:

> the great man has agreed to speak to me. It is really something – the
> only print article he gave when he was out here and we did get on very
> well. It would have been, if I had really wanted to have a go at him, it's
> bloody difficult, he's given me twenty minutes and he ain't given any-
> body else twenty minutes.

(Philip)

Such criticisms by sports journalists themselves that the print and broadcast
media are not doing enough critical, investigative work are usually made in
the name of their Fourth Estate function. It is argued that society – especially its vast cohort of sports fans – is being let down by lazy, compromised
and trivial sports journalism.

This reputation (justified or not) for sycophancy in sports journalism is
widespread among other types of journalist and sports fans alike, meaning
that contemporary sports journalism is caught in a critical pincer movement
both from inside and outside the profession. The growth (at least in British
soccer) of 'cottage industry' sports publications – 'fanzines' and now 'netzines' – is perhaps a symptom of a failure of sports journalists and other
writers to serve their audiences to their satisfaction. In such cases (as is discussed in Chapter 5) sports fans have seized the means of cultural production by publishing amateur print texts, creating their own sports web pages,
and so on. Sports journalists generally do not see fan involvement in making
media sports texts as a threat, with some of the more professional looking
publications like the British football fanzine *When Saturday Comes* being
established as a hobby by professional journalists (Shaw 1989), and some
contributing to them under a *nom de plume*. Most (in my study, at least)
have little interest in fanzines, as indicated by a tabloid sports journalist:

Calvin: Yeah, one newspaper, the *Independent*, publishes a fanzine
column, don't they? Maybe we could do that. I don't even

> bother to read it in the *Independent*. I don't know why, I just
> haven't got around to doing it.
>
> D.R.: So you've never been tempted to moonlight on a fanzine?
>
> Calvin: No [*laughing*], the only freelance stuff I do is a bit of broad-
> casting. But I'm basically lazy and I don't go looking for work.

This candid remark, made in jest, returns us (not accidentally) to the image
of the indolent and complacent occupant of the toy department, enjoying
life 'on a good wicket'. We have seen here the self-perceptions of sports
journalists, as relayers and producers of sports information and analysis,
oscillate between assurance and anxiety. Despite, then, its machine-like
appearance, the media sports cultural complex does not always run
smoothly and efficiently, pumping out sports stories with the ease of the
Zybrainic Sportswriter. Some of the cogs in this machine have doubts.

Conclusion: hacks and hipsters

This chapter has examined closely several of the structures, principles and
practices which shape, through sports journalism, the voluminous quantities
of media sports texts that are available to us every day. In particular, by comparing external and internal opinions of the profession of journalism and its
sports discipline, it was possible to see how culture is created out of a complex mix of diverse and multidirectional forces. For example, it might be
expected, given the major importance of sports journalism as an attractor of
audiences and as a supplier of content for print and broadcast media alike,
that the sports specialism would have a status commensurate with its
'pulling power'. In fact, we saw that, despite the common impression of
sports journalism as a comfortable and privileged enclave of white, middle-
class men travelling the world watching games at other people's expense,
many sports journalists felt professionally insecure and unappreciated. As in
other parts of this book, these circumstances recalled the work of the soci-
ologist Max Weber (1968), in this case his distinction between class and
status. Just as for Weber it was possible for groups and individuals to wield
considerable socio-economic power through class location but not be highly
regarded by others (that is, be rich but with relatively low status), it is also
often the case that the economic power of the sports department (in terms
of the large number and handsome remuneration of personnel; importance
for circulation, ratings, advertising revenue, and so on) is at variance with
its cultural power (low professional reputation and esteem). For this reason,

sports journalists often craved equal status with 'serious' journalists or even recognition of their writing as 'art'.

I observed that the economic power of sports journalism does seem, somewhat belatedly, to be raising its professional status, but that this improvement is at least as significantly due to sport being very much in vogue. Of course, the current fashionability of sport is in part related to its skilful promotion as a 'hip' cultural commodity – a phenomenon conspicuously evident in British soccer (Redhead 1991; Haynes 1995; Rowe 1995) and American basketball (McKay 1995; Andrews 1996; Boyd 1997). Such developments in the making and meaning of media sports texts reveal the impossibility of separating the different and interacting influences on sports culture. Hence, the economics of sport and media are deeply dependent on cultural dynamics – but no less than, as is addressed in the next chapter, media sports culture is profoundly influenced by economic imperatives.

Further reading

Creedon, P.J. (ed.) (1994) *Women, Media and Sport: Challenging Gender Values.* Thousand Oaks, CA: Sage.

Dahlgren, P. and Sparks, C. (eds) (1992) *Journalism and Popular Culture.* London: Sage.

4 | MONEY, MYTH AND THE BIG MATCH: THE POLITICAL ECONOMY OF THE SPORTS MEDIA

Sporting tradition dictates that whatever the game, it was originally played for pure and honest motives. Money was the servant of the players not the master.

In the 1990s, it's clear that sports tradition has lost out badly to commerce. The sports field is the battleground on which global TV corporations are fighting to test new television technology. The reward is not a gold-plated trophy but the traditional sports consumer. Profile: Male, 18–35, with enough disposable income to attract the sponsors with the big dollars.

(Stan Correy 1995: 80)

Introduction: valuing sport

I have delayed a fuller discussion of the economics of the sports media until the closing chapter of this first 'Making media sport' part of the book, but not because it is of any lesser importance than other influences on production – far from it, as the previous analysis has repeatedly shown. For example, in Chapter 3 we saw how developments in broadcast and print sports journalism are linked to the calculation of their economic value in increasing the size and broadening the base of media sports audiences. The discussion of sport and media economics leads into the second part of 'Unmaking the media sports text' for the slightly perverse reason that, just at the point where many other works in media and cultural studies tend to 'bracket off' the rather unromantic 'business of business' and get down to the more freewheeling task of textual reading and interpretation, it is, I believe, all the more necessary to keep economic concerns to the fore. In this way, no artificial separation can be maintained between the 'light' world of culture and symbols and the 'heavy' world of economics and material objects. Instead, culture, social relations and economics can be seen – as is entirely appropriate under conditions where the economies and social structures of advanced capitalist societies are becoming increasingly dependent on cultural processes – to be inextricably linked in a manner which defies a simple equation involving arrows pointing in a single, determining direction. The sphere of culture is now more than ever where the key economic processes of production, distribution and exchange take place. At the same time, cultural production is always directly or indirectly, currently or potentially, connected to the world of making products, supplying services and generating profits.

I have argued here that the media are both the driving economic and cultural force in sport because they provide (or attract) most of the capital that in turn creates and disseminates the images and information, which then generate more capital and more sport, in an ascending spiral. Booms in capital accumulation are periodically subject to dramatic busts, as the 1987 Wall Street crash and the 1997 'meltdown' of the Asian 'tiger economies' demonstrate. We are yet to see a dramatic contraction of the media sports economy in general, which continues to expand year by year. But the fortunes of individual sports and also of media companies can shift rapidly in response to the involvement of sponsors, crowd attendance and TV ratings, broadcast rights, and so on. It is useful, then, to appraise the major forces in media sport, the ways in which they cooperate and conflict, and the consequences of this economic activity for sport and for the wider cultural sphere. If no single party can be said to dominate the media sports cultural complex or to control its 'image bank', it can hardly be denied that the presence of major economic entities has resulted in far-reaching changes to the sport we see and read about, and to the culture in which it is located.

To illustrate this point, we need only point to the cut-throat competition and multimillion dollar and pound investment involved in acquiring such mega media sports properties as the broadcast rights to:

- the summer and winter Olympics
- English Premier League soccer
- the US National Football League

(McKay and Rowe 1997)

That media sport involves serious money is obvious, but the cultural and economic consequences for media sports texts are less apparent. For this reason, we need to delve further into the place where economic and sporting muscles are flexed.

Sport, media and capital accumulation

In Chapter 2 I provided brief outlines of the intersecting development of sport and media, arguing that each institution had something that the other wanted – and with increasing urgency. The initial reluctance which both parties displayed in forming a deep alliance was, in part, due to the unprecedented nature of the economic and cultural relations which developed speedily from the late nineteenth century onwards (that is, consumer capitalism and national state-sanctioned media were 'feeling their way') and partly because their initial economic base relied on direct exchange. So, when most of the revenue for sports enterprises stemmed from paying customers going through the turnstiles to watch sport in person in highly localized settings, not much in the way of mass marketing and promotion was needed. Word-of-mouth, wall posters and some rather staid newspaper advertisements were the major means of informing the paying public about forthcoming sports events, and the technological means did not exist (and when they did, were not initially welcomed) to record and transmit proceedings for those not present (Stoddart 1986; Whannel 1992). Similarly, for newspapers more dependent on revenue from cover sales than on advertising, and interested more in the great events of state (as in the establishment press) or in scandal-mongering (the province of the 'yellow press'), sport had only limited appeal. With the development of national and international sporting competitions, the 'maturation' of media advertising, and the emergence of broadcast media for which there was no or limited direct payment by the 'consumer', new revenue streams and uses of the sports media were created. In this way, the media sports text became increasingly valorized, a commodity that could be produced, sold, exchanged and distributed. In order to understand precisely how the media sports text becomes such a valuable economic and cultural object, it is necessary to view it in terms of large scale social, economic and cultural transformations (as occurred in Chapter 2), and also to appreciate the specific ways in which that object is desired or can be made to be desirable.

Within the history of capitalist development, the sports media are not 'essential' commodities: they are not vital for the maintenance of life like food, shelter and clothing, or 'consumer durables' which preserve food, wash clothes or transport whole families to work and school. Seen in this way, media sports texts are not very useful goods, but they are, paradoxically, highly prized. This is so because they exist in an economic environment where, as many goods have became easier to mass produce and standardize, only a relatively small proportion of their total price is attributable to the cost of raw materials, labour and manufacture. Hence, the direct production cost of a compact disc or a dress or a child's toy can often be measured in pence and cents rather than in multiple pounds and dollars. Where, then, is the value added and capital accumulated? It is, increasingly, not in the material character of objects that can be reassuringly touched and used, but in the immaterial nature of symbolic goods (Hall 1989). Value in this sense lies in design, appearance and in the capacity to connect different economic processes which exist in a complex interdependence (Hebdige 1989). An extensive and complex theoretical debate (which, readers will be relieved to know, will be elaborated only very briefly here) has been conducted since the late 1980s over the meaning of this development (see, for example, Harvey 1989; Hirst and Zeitlin 1989; Giddens 1991). It is over such questions as:

- Are current circumstances an extension of the same 'logic' and process of modernity (which we might call 'advanced', 'late' or 'high') that brought industrialization, liberal democracy, humanism, and so on?
- Or have we moved on to a new 'condition' called **postmodernity** in which our social, economic, political and cultural life has changed radically from its **modernist** predecessor?
- Has the mass production and consumption 'regime' pioneered by Henry Ford in the car industry (**Fordism**) changed a little (to **neo-Fordism**) or been replaced by a new, more targeted, smaller scale and flexible way of producing and consuming goods and services (**post-Fordism**)?

Posing such questions requires a command of a rather daunting language in which terms like 'flexible specialization' and 'reflexive accumulation' compete for theoretical and conceptual supremacy. In the context of this book it is necessary only to be armed with the glossary of key terms provided and to follow the contours of the following argument that media sport is at the leading edge of cultural and economic development. If cultural factors are emerging as central to economic processes – and most contemporary analyses suggest that they are – then sport and the sports media, as cultural goods *par excellence*, are clearly a central element in a larger process (or set of processes) that is reshaping society and culture.

Of course, goods have always had a cultural character – the 'respectable' appeal of a type of family sedan, the 'reliable' qualities of a brand of vacuum cleaner, and so on – but more and more commodities have nothing else to declare but their status as cultural goods with appropriately high levels of 'sign value' (Baudrillard 1981), as opposed to the more conventional Marxist concepts of use value (what something can do) and exchange value (what something is worth in a direct transaction). As Lash and Urry argue:

[Yet] the objects in contemporary political economies are not just emptied out of symbolic content. They are also progressively emptied out of material content. What is increasingly being produced are not material objects, but signs. These signs are primarily of two types. Either they have a primarily cognitive content and thus are post-industrial or informational goods. Or they have primarily an aesthetic, in the broadest sense of the aesthetic, content and they are primarily postmodern goods (Eagleton 1989). This is occurring, not just in the proliferation of non-material objects which comprise a substantial aesthetic component (such as pop music, cinema, magazines, video, etc), but also in the increasing component of sign value or image in *material* objects. This aestheticization of material objects can take place either in the production or in the circulation and consumption of such goods.

(Lash and Urry 1994: 14–15)

If we consider this argument in relation to media sports texts, then they can be said to be particularly valuable not only because of their 'substantial aesthetic component' (the principal object of media sport is the aesthetics of bodies – their beauty, condition, size, effectiveness – in motion under specified conditions), but also because of their key role in the informational order (cognitive in only a limited sense in terms of 'patented' knowledge about training techniques and regimes, but certainly an informational sign given sport's major role in the news media). Media sports texts, with their almost unprecedented capacity to 'flow' across and around these 'economies of signs and space' in both local and global contexts, their very high levels of 'sign-value', and with their intimate connection to the pervasive '*information and communication structures*' (Lash and Urry 1994: 6), are almost perfect prototypes of signs in circulation, heavily loaded with symbolic value.

To develop this point a little further, Lash and Urry use the term 'reflexive accumulation' to describe a strengthening tendency in the processes of production and consumption of objects and images for the people involved to be in a position not just to be 'buried' in what they are doing, but to reflect on it, criticize it and adapt to it (Rowe and Lawrence 1998). In this way, human subjects can be partially disconnected from the social institutions, structures and identities (including class, gender, work, nation, locality and family) that they inhabit. Or, to put it another way, as the 'automatic' power of traditional social structures over individuals has weakened, new opportunities have emerged to behave, think and identify in less socially prescribed ways. This development, which is sometimes called 'postmodernity', is not so very new (as argued in Chapter 2, it started in earnest with the coming of 'modernity'), but today it is much more fundamental and widespread. It has created, in one sense, a 'market' for collective identification, a vigorous competition between governments, business corporations and social movements for the 'soul' – and, not uncommonly, the discretionary income – of 'cultural citizens' (now described as 'postmodern subjects' – see Miller 1993, 1998a). In more obviously functionalist terms, perhaps a 'values vacuum' has been created whereby many people feel alienated, no longer believing deeply in anything, identifying with anyone, or feeling committed to any cause outside the immediate interests of themselves and their immediate relatives. An opening exists, therefore, for enterprising parties to engage in the 'consciousness' trade (Enzensberger 1976), to help supply the meaning and commitment that rapid social change under late modernity or postmodernity have evacuated from many lives. But what phenomenon has the emotional force to bind symbolically the fragmenting constituents of society, especially where there is abundant critical self-reflection, cynicism and a seeming 'exhaustion' of novelty? Not surprisingly, the answer in the context of this book is media sport.

There is a well known argument (for example, Novak 1976) that sport is a secular religion, having taken over from the church as the primary place of collective and individual ritual, belief, ecstasy, and so on. When sports fans have their ashes spread on the 'hallowed turf' of their favourite sports stadium, the spiritual qualities of sport are very evident. On an occasion like that of a national team receiving a blessing from a religious leader before a major sports event, it may appear that 'sacred sport' is supporting orthodox religion, rather than the other way round. If sport and religion have certain qualities in common, they also share an involvement with business, especially where the religion is, as Max Weber pointed out, the Calvinist form of Protestantism, which he argues supplied many of the values crucial to the formation of capitalism. Indeed, in one (unconsciously) prescient passage in *The Protestant Ethic and the Spirit of Capitalism*, Weber links all three institutions by stating that:

> In the field of its highest development, in the United States, the pursuit of wealth, stripped of its religious and ethical meaning, tends to become associated with purely mundane passions, which often actually give it the character of sport.
>
> (Weber 1930: 182)

If Weber's lifespan had stretched a few decades beyond the year of his death (1920), he would have seen not only 'the pursuit of wealth' in the USA and other capitalist nations given 'the character of sport', but also leisure pursuits like sport take on the character of the pursuit of wealth. He would also have seen sport appropriate many of the functions of established religion, supplying the rituals and deeply held beliefs that have faded in increasingly secular societies dedicated to the worship of the god of conspicuous commodity consumption.

Irrespective of whether sport and its values are religious in the strict sense, in broad economic terms (concerned more with profits than prophets, to use a rather old pun) it is one of the key contemporary sites where the expression of strong emotions is translated into the generation of substantial capital. Or, more expansively, where (following Lash and Urry) aesthetic and informational signs meet popular emotion (which sometimes looks like mass hysteria) in a manner readily convertible into commodified pleasure. Media sport has, as we have seen, a proven capacity to bring potential consumers to the marketplace in numbers ranging from the respectable to the staggering. It is able at particular moments to reconstruct symbolically disparate human groups, to make them feel at one with each other (and perhaps, in the case of the Olympics, the world). When contemporary advertising relies so heavily on making very similar items (such as sugared drinks and 're-badged' computers) appear different, sport's capacity to stimulate emotional identification with people and things is priceless. Sport can connect the past, present and future, alternately trading on sepia-tinted nostalgia, the 'now-ness' of 'live' action, and the anticipation of things to come. Furthermore, even when our human sports 'subject' is being reflexively critical, rather than getting carried away by sporting affect, they can take an ironic, playfully postmodern approach to it, mocking the mangled language of sports commentators (like the satirical magazine *Private Eye*'s 'Colemanballs' section and book series), watching self-consciously bad-taste sports TV programmes (like Australian rugby league's *The Footy Show*), and buying sports newspapers that are parodies of 'straight' tabloid reporting (like Britain's *Sunday Sport*). This chameleonic capacity of contemporary media sport makes it a key aspect of the commodity cycle, its flexibility of form and use fitting perfectly contemporary requirements for speedy change and customization.

Media sports texts are perhaps, then, at the leading edge of this '**culturalization**' of economics: they cannot be eaten or worn yet billions of people desire them in a bewildering variety of types, and media corporations are willing to expend billions of units of currency to supply them, often 'free of charge', to the user. In return, as we have seen, invaluable access is given to audiences, on a global scale, which can be 'cashed in' for large sums of money exchanged between sporting associations, clubs, officials and players, TV and sports management companies, sponsors, advertisers, and governments. Media sports texts are particularly valuable assets because of their flexibility and interconnectedness. A single sports 'live' TV broadcast can be shown in 'real time' and endlessly afterwards, and can be cut up and packaged in myriad ways, with its soundtrack separated from its visual images so that both can be continually manipulated and reproduced. The sports print media, both newspapers and magazines, can help stimulate interest before the event and 'keep it alive' for a lengthy period afterwards, aided and abetted by the celebrity status of elite sportspeople. All manner of goods and services, from sports equipment and 'designer' leisurewear to beer, banking and tobacco, can invoke or be directly associated with media sports events, the associated messages adapted as necessary to the cultural sensitivities of different audience blocs around the globe (Rowe *et al.* 1994). It is for this reason that television broadcast rights to the major sports are often contested more fiercely than the sports events they are seeking to cover – even when those same media companies complain about how much money they lose by winning them. To understand this apparently economically irrational behaviour means delving further into the media sports cultural complex.

How to make money while losing it in sports television

Having set out the broad economic framework within which contemporary media sport operates, more precise explanations of why media corporations are prepared to expend huge sums on securing the rights to television sport are required. Detailing the statistics is not unlike recounting the latest world record time in the 100 metres sprint or the greatest number of points scored in the World Series. Taking the example of the USA's NBC television network, it transpires that in 1995 NBC won the US TV rights to the Sydney 2000 Olympics for US$715 million, as part of a deal in which it paid escalating fees of US$793 million and US$894 million for the 2004 and 2008 Olympics respectively to show the Games to American audiences in (then) unknown locations. Despite its capacity to sell subsidiary rights, charge vastly inflated advertising rates during key events, and make some returns from various 'spin offs' (selling videos of Olympic highlights, for example), the cost of rights and of producing TV coverage ensured that NBC would lose large sums of money on the deal. But this does not mean that the NBC Board has suddenly become philanthropic, and is prepared to carry out a selfless task of public service by subsidizing the delivery of Olympics TV to the people of the United States of America. It has a broader economic motive: the huge audiences for the Olympics raise the network's overall ratings, meaning that it is in a stronger position to negotiate advertising rights across all its year-round programmes. The network is also hoping for an Olympics 'spillover effect' – that viewers will be exposed to and 'stay with' its other programmes or, even better, that it will 'get the habit' of switching on NBC first. Being the Olympics station brings with it a great deal of kudos – evidence that the network can handle with distinction one of the world's largest media events. In an image-saturated age where 'branded sign-value' is paramount, being known as the 'Olympic network' – with all the 'brand recognition' and prestige that entails – gives an important competitive advantage in the media industry. Securing the US broadcast rights to the Olympics also has a 'spoiler effect' – ambitious commercial rivals, such as Rupert Murdoch's FOX Network, can be thwarted (McKay and Rowe 1997), and also forced to expend equally large sums of money on other broadcast rights on pain of being locked out of major TV sport altogether.

There is great symbolic and economic value to be gained, then, from controlling the production and distribution of symbols – and in the case of Olympic sport global images do not come any more desirable. It is for this reason that there is so much antagonism between Olympic rights and non-rights holders – a struggle that also inevitably draws in sports organizations and even athletes. In Australia, for example, the zealous safeguarding of Seven Network's AUS$45 million television rights contract for the Sydney 2000 Olympics has been the subject of considerable anxiety among its commercial and public rivals. At the earlier Atlanta Olympics, where Australian rights were also held by Seven, the Australian Olympic Committee (AOC) helped protect its 'investment' (that is, its opportunity to maximize rights revenue by guaranteeing exclusivity) by breaking up an interview between a non-rights holder (Network Ten) with two athletes, ejecting a Ten employee from an official function and, finally, by being instrumental in the withdrawal of the Ten staff's media accreditation (M. Moore 1997). For the Sydney 2000 Olympics, the AOC has attempted to prevent the 'parasitical' behaviour of non-rights holders (which it sees as making money out of athletes but not contributing to their upkeep) by trading more liberal media access rules for a substantial subvention for its 2000 Olympic Medal Reward Scheme.

In such ways – by negotiating, honouring, helping police and strategically modifying broadcast rights – sports organizations and personnel become economic allies, even colleagues of the media. Hence they need to be well versed in the somewhat arcane rules that govern rights – such as whether non-rights holders should be bound by the 'three by three by three' rule ('three minutes of Olympic footage three times a day in news programmes at least three hours apart') which has normally applied in Australia, or by the stricter variation of it ('two minutes of coverage three times a day in established news programmes, but no events screened less than 18 hours after they took place', and no more than one-third of an event to be broadcast, even if it is the sub-ten seconds 100 metres final) as recommended by the IOC in Atlanta (M. Moore 1997: 4). Such deliberations also involve national broadcast policy priorities and the copyright laws with which any rights agreement must be in accord, and even whether the Olympics come under the rubric of 'news' (and, therefore, should be more fully reported on public interest grounds) or 'sport' (that is, more subject to broadcast restriction). These issues continue to preoccupy the broadcast media and sports professionals because the entire economics of the media sports cultural complex turn on the careful rationing, packaging and sale of media sports texts in different markets. Hence, the idea of the global media sports spectacle is at its heart quite illusory: the images that appear to be so freely 'released' have been subject to extraordinarily stringent pre-selection and control, and the sanctions taken against those who breach such arrangements (by, for example, implying official Olympic endorsement when it has not been negotiated and paid for) powerful indeed.

The summer and winter Olympics, however, occur only over four-year cycles, which leaves large gaps between orgies of Olympic viewing, although after 1992 these were staggered at two-year intervals to ensure that the world did not have to wait so long for its Olympic television 'fix'. Other great media sports events – international tournaments like the soccer World Cup, world championships in sports like athletics and swimming, and major competitions with international involvement like Wimbledon or the US Open – have important places on the sports calendar, but they are by their nature intermittent and out of the ordinary. Filling television schedules is a constant task that cannot wait for the next global media sports spectacular. The 'bread and butter' of sports television, then, is annual competition within nations. NBC (which, not coincidentally, is the top-rating network) has the rights to such major US sports as the National Basketball Association (NBA) competition and the baseball playoffs to supplement its Olympic fare. Yet in 1998 it found itself 'frozen out of football for the first time in 33 years' (Attwood 1998: 39). Given that American football (a game barely played, understood or watched in other countries) is the most important television sport in the USA, with broadcast rights valued in 1998 at US$2.25 billion a season, the scramble for broadcast rights to it is vigorous to say the least. As noted above, their direct economic value is almost overshadowed by the image of being a 'winner' (analogous to that of breaking a world record while winning an Olympic gold medal). As Attwood states:

Several morals can be drawn from this US price war. One is that, more than ever, sport is *the* most important commodity for TV. Another is that the desperation of grown men, most of whom have never played top-level sport themselves, to feel as if they are part of the game should never be underestimated.

(Attwood 1998: 39)

The struggle for television sport can be seen to be more than a fight for profit: it reveals the cultural power of sport, particularly in the higher ranks of large corporate enterprises, where aggressive, competitive masculinity is as evident in the boardrooms as in the locker rooms (McKay and Rowe 1997). For example, the loss by the CBS network of its rights to Sunday football in 1993 to a FOX network prepared to pay over three times the amount for them (US$1.58 billion as opposed to US$500 million), had a demoralizing impact on the entire network that went beyond the concomitant fall in ratings. As Attwood (1998: 39) goes on to say, the four networks which paid unprecedented sums for the right to televise American football into the early part of the twenty-first century 'regard football as so crucial to their credibility and programming that they are prepared to pay almost any price', and that this phenomenon is not confined to the boundaries of the United States, but 'demonstrates how crucial major sporting events are to networks, worldwide, in an increasingly competitive TV market'. Thus, as Singer (1998: 36) notes, 'today's rule of thumb mandates that any viable network must have sports to help raise the profile of its other properties'; here he means literally to 'have sports', listing the direct ownership of sports teams by US media conglomerates including Cablevision, who own the Knicks basketball and Rangers ice hockey franchises, Disney (the Angels in baseball and Mighty Ducks in hockey) and Time Warner (the Braves in baseball and Hawks in basketball). While the cross-promotional possibilities of jointly owned media and sports enterprises are attractive, it is the cultural appeal of sport that ensures that old fears of club owners of 'oversaturation' and that ' "giving away" the product on TV would kill the gate' are as 'misguided as Hollywood's fear of the VCR [video cassette recorder]' (Singer 1998: 36). Such popularity also allays the concerns of media proprietors in countries like the USA that sport is not worth the asking price:

There's good reason why sports is a TV staple: It's human drama at a base level, it's cheap to produce and it's live. One can't minimize the power of immediacy in this time-shifting era when sports are the last remaining live coast-to-coast events – the Oscars, the Emmys, even 'Saturday Night Live' are tape delayed to the West Coast. Only sports has the nation, and sometimes the world, watching the same thing at the same time, and if you have a message, that's a potent messenger.

(Singer 1998: 36)

Once again, the power of sports television to create and connect nations fragmented by space, time and social difference is shown to be its crowning economic advantage.

The 'strategic chaos' of media sport

Network free-to-air television is, it should be noted, not the only player in the sports market; the fierce 'internal' competition between networks is replicated in the struggle between the network and pay television sectors. In some cases, as with Rupert Murdoch's News Corporation (which owns the FOX network and various pay satellite services like British-based BSkyB and the Hong Kong-based Star) or the Walt Disney Company (which owns both the ABC network and the leading sports cable channel ESPN), the enterprise is 'horizontally integrated' (that is, spread across different media and modes of delivery) and so is involved in both free-to-air and pay sports television. The continuing and accelerating realignment of organisations and convergence of technologies (as discussed in Chapter 8) ensures that sports television will continue to be in a dynamic (which is often a euphemism for unstable) condition.

While it is premature to conclude that there is a single, integrated global sport or sports media market – for such a thing to exist much greater cultural homogeneity and economic rationalization would be necessary – there is a marked globalizing trend in media sport which makes it increasingly hard to insulate any aspect of sport and media in any particular country from external, disruptive forces. Just how much power the media wield over sport can be seen through some brief case studies. In Australia, for example, a large country with a medium-sized population (now 18 million – as Turner (1990) has noted, a country with a similar land mass to the USA with a population closer to that of the Netherlands) some distance from the centres of power in media sport, there has been turmoil in sports television as the belated introduction of pay-TV (in January 1995) precipitated a convulsion in the industry which is far from approaching a settled state. The intimidating presence in the free-to-air and pay-TV market of Rupert Murdoch (who was born in Australia but gave up his citizenship in order to purchase key media assets in the USA) and his great commercial rival (and sometime strategic ally) Kerry Packer, owner of the top-rating Network Nine, alongside a host of other 'players' like Telstra (the partially privatized national telecommunications company), Optus (whose major shareholder is the British-based communications company Cable & Wireless), the publicly funded ABC, Networks Seven (partially Murdoch-owned) and Ten (whose largest shareholder is the Canadian CanWest company), and many other interested organizations, has seen a story of almost medieval intrigue unfold. Under circumstances where a new conservative federal government was elected in 1996 on a platform which promised to reform the Australian system of media regulation (especially rules which restrict foreign ownership and prevent organizations having substantial holdings in both the print and the electronic media) sports television has been a cauldron of competing policy recipes and conflicting economic ingredients. As Sheehan (1998) argues in a survey of the global media sports scene:

> Strategic chaos is the one area where Australia is ahead of America. There has been a bloody insurrection against the old order financed by media money (Murdoch and Super League). There has been a horrendously expensive cable war (Murdoch/Foxtel v Optus) and there may be about to be a virtual merging of media and sport product if Seven and the AFL [Australian Football League] complete their mega deal [a free-to-air, cable, radio, Internet and foreign rights agreement until 2011].
> . . . In the biggest game of all, global TV sports, it is already game, set, match, Murdoch. Thank you, players, thank you, ball boys.
> (Sheehan 1998: 5)

Sheehan's assessment of Murdoch's inevitable triumph in TV sport is not universally shared – the *Los Angeles Times* in 1997, for example, described Murdoch's expensive attempt to control the sport of rugby league in Australia, Britain, France, New Zealand and the small number of other countries in which it is played as 'one of News Corp.'s bigger blunders' (quoted in Miller 1998b: 5), but there is no doubt that when a big financial player is sufficiently determined to make a major impact on a sport, the outcome is inevitably far-reaching, and the means by which that influence is exerted always involves media, especially television coverage. Thus, while Murdoch's strategy includes taking a stake not just in the sports media but in sport itself (hence his purchase of major stakes in rugby union and rugby league, and the ownership of individual sports outfits like the Los Angeles Dodgers baseball team), it is always the promise of wider TV coverage and cross-media exposure through his newspaper and magazine interests that forms part of the 'pitch'. Furthermore, when new forms of delivery involving subscription are involved, no media identity understands the importance of sport more than Rupert Murdoch. The turning around of his BSkyB satellite service in Britain (News Corporation is its 40 per cent majority shareholder) from a chronically loss-making to a highly profitable business entity can be traced directly to his securing of prime exclusive rights in 1992 to most of the best and most important games in Britain's national sport – soccer. Since 1992, BSkyB has made several multimillion pound deals in sports like golf (including the Ryder Cup), cricket, rugby union and boxing, sometimes in association with the BBC. Not only have these contracts, with their strong elements of exclusive 'live' rights, had the effect of raising subscription levels, but also they have in some cases (including boxing and soccer) included a pay-per-view element, with its opportunities for the kind of direct economic exchange between sports provider (now via an 'intermediary') and sports spectator that once existed only at the turnstiles of sports stadia.

By turning the television decoding box into an electronic turnstile, pay-per-view and subscription sport are, paradoxically, via new delivery technology, recreating an older cash nexus. But now sports themselves are ceding to the media, for a handsome price, responsibility for the presentation of great sporting occasions to the largest component of the audience. The political implications of this shift are serious (as is argued more fully below), in that the new services – and many of the old ones – are now available only to those citizens with the capacity to pay. As Combe (1997) notes, BSkyB's premium, live and exclusive sports coverage enabled it, by 1996, to gain 5.1 per cent of channel share of audiences in Britain for its two sports channels alone. Combe argues that with free-to-air public broadcasters like the BBC restricted by the political imperative of holding down the licence fee, and their commercial counterparts having to compete in a more aggressive 'audience sale' market, BSkyB has been well placed to win broadcast rights auctions where the principal bargaining tool is the making of an offer which is very hard to refuse, and which few if any competitors can match:

> BSkyB dominates the area of premium programmes with its stranglehold on Hollywood films and sporting events . . . In terms of consumer welfare, the multi-channel industry structure diminishes consumer protection and undermines the fundamental concept of pluralism in a democratic society.
>
> (Combe 1997: 19)

The result of this exercise of economic power in sports television, further, is regarded as less than liberating:

> The stranglehold on sports rights enjoyed by BSkyB has changed the economics of broadcasting such events and transformed the organisation

of the events themselves to fit in with the criteria set by television. The continuing domination of BSkyB is as unsatisfactory as was the old BBC/ITV duopoly. Now, large numbers of viewers are excluded from seeing major events on purely economic grounds. The imminent arrival of digital television will set off another round of negotiations between broadcasters and sporting bodies with the OFT [Office of Fair Trading] casting an enquiring eye over the outcomes.

(Combe 1997: 21)

Murdoch's 1998 £623 million buying raid (subsequently blocked 'in the public interest' by the Blair Government) on Manchester United, the world's best known and richest football club, highlighted the economic desirability of simultaneously owning both broadcast rights to sport and the sports teams that are being broadcast. The changing economics of broadcasting popular sports events – sometimes held in check, as we have seen, by political values or by the desire of major sporting organizations like the IOC to ensure maximum television exposure – continually modify the conditions under which media sports texts are made. For example, the timing of 'live' sports broadcasts is now dictated by the need to stagger them over several days and nights, and/or to give a number of parties the opportunity to show whatever material they have gained access to. Thus, while as recently as the 1970s the majority of professional British soccer matches or Australian rugby league games started and ended on the same weekend day within 15 minutes of each other, the 'festival' of football now stretches over much of the week in the sports media equivalent of continuous process production. As seasons have extended and competitions proliferated in deference to the media hunger for sport – and to sport's appetite for media money – the prospect of creating a media sports cultural complex that defies the constraints of time and space – just as the first factory owners began to do in the eighteenth century – approaches closer. The difference, however, is that much of the population is now watching the production process from the domestic sphere rather than participating within the factory walls. Watching, in this sense, is essential to complete the production cycle of relayed movement, meaning and imagery.

This economy of sports television is, it can be plainly seen, thoroughly representative of the newer 'economies of signs and space' discussed earlier, where power lies increasingly in the control of images and information by means of copyright and associated intellectual property rights, rather than by relying on the slower, more predictable process of making goods or providing 'human' services. Of course, such exchanges do still go on and, somewhere and at some time, capital has to be exchanged. But following the 'money trail', as in contemporary tax and fraud investigations, is an ever more complex task. Television sport can, in strictly economic terms, be seen as a battlefield between media corporations seeking to generate revenue from all manner of sources – from advertisers, sponsors, subscribing viewers, and even from sports themselves (the more unfortunate ones who need TV exposure so much that they are prepared to pay for it). It is not a global sports icon like Michael Jordan or a massively successful leisurewear entrepreneur like Nike founder Phil Knight or an 'imperial' sports administrator like IOC President Juan Antonio Samaranch who now dominates the *Sporting News'* annual list of sport's most powerful people in sport – it is the media mogul Rupert Murdoch (McKay and Rowe 1997). Why such a person is at the centre of power in sport can be explained succinctly by the following opening paragraphs from a newspaper feature article on Rupert Murdoch as the 'champion of world sports':

> Last month [January], American television networks spent [AUS]$26 billion on the broadcast rights for American football games for the next eight years. That is not a misprint. That's $26 *billion*. It works out to almost $1 billion for each of the 30 teams in the National Football League (NFL).
>
> This stratospheric number is a foretaste of the revolution that is about to engulf television, and Rupert Murdoch's global sporting empire is playing a central role in that revolution. The revolution will occur on several fronts, all at the same time.
>
> (Sheehan 1998: 4)

Given that, in 1980, NBC paid only US$72 million for the broadcast for the summer Olympics, the coming revolution in television has clearly already arrived. Perhaps, in Trotsky's (1969) famous formulation, it is in a state of 'permanent revolution'. Sheehan is referring explicitly to the imminent technological changes that are discussed here in greater detail in Chapter 8, but even if we focus on the current 'Jurassic' period of television broadcasting (he refers to current TV networks as 'dinosaurs'), then the sports TV world can be seen to be in the grip of tumultuous 'climatic' change marked by a sharply rising temperature rather than a slow passage into a sportless ice age. What is confusing about these circumstances – and it is typical for the human sciences to have to confront a stubbornly reflexive complexity that is much less troubling for those in natural sciences like climatology – is that they often display counter-tendencies. Hence, for example, as Combe (1997) observes in his appraisal of statistics on channel share of audiences, in Britain between 1993 and 1996, when cable and satellite delivery really began to take hold (reaching over 15 per cent of all television households), the total terrestrial share was at the same level (69.9 per cent) at the end of this period, and the hard-pressed, publicly funded BBC1 channel actually increased its share (from 23.8 per cent to 24.1 per cent). There may, then, be a significant role in an even more differentiated broadcasting market for 'mass' public organizations like the BBC with proven brand identity and loyalty after the digital 'revolution', but perhaps it will be at the expense, as it was in the period 1993–6 in Britain under the old regime, of niche broadcasters (like the BBC's own second channel and the innovative commercial Channel 4) and of commercial broadcasters aiming to appeal to wider audiences (like ITV), who lost ground both to general public broadcasters and to pay television.

From this British instance it can be seen that the global sports television market is, despite attempts to portray it as a single entity following predictable trends, a series of smaller national, regional and local markets occasionally linked by spectacular mega media events or by the more routine circulation of content from core markets to secondary ones. In fact, as O'Regan (1992: 76) points out, there is a tendency to exaggerate the extent to which television programmes, especially from the United States, flow freely around the world. He notes that while the USA was in 1989 responsible for some '71 per cent of the *international* trade' valued at US$1.7 billion in an estimated world television export market of US$2.4 billion (one which, it should be acknowledged, has considerably expanded since), it was in the same year estimated that television 'product' 29 times greater in value (US$70 billion) stayed in its 'nation of origin'. Of course, such raw figures do not take into account other forms of 'cultural exchange' – such as the 'uncompensated' imitation of American programme genres like soap operas and quiz shows in many different countries – but they do indicate that judgements of a smoothly completed 'project' of economic and cultural globalization are seriously premature. Cunningham and Jacka (1996: 40), furthermore, observe that most sports programming does not travel well in the global mediascape, so that 'Of the various genres of television . . . most are locally specific, and are not heavily traded', and genres like sport 'except for major international events like Grand Slam tennis, the Olympics, World Cup soccer, or Formula One Grand Prix motor racing . . . are usually entirely local in character'. The aforementioned example of American football is just such a game that has had little success in its attempts to 'export itself' as popular sports television (Maguire 1990; McKay and Miller 1991). However, as Hollywood film and US network television discovered many years ago, a successful if expensive-to-produce item in a domestic market is doubly successful when it can be distributed and promoted 'fully formed' in other markets.

For this reason there is an unending search for new ways to exploit the same or partially modified economic goods and, as Cunningham and Jacka (1996: 40–1) recognize, 'under the pressure of burgeoning channel capacity and commercialisation, new tradeable international formats are emerging', including those 'prompted by new forms of delivery like pay television', leading to the 'growth of specialist sports channels [which] will lead to the televising of sports not previously considered television fare, in order to fill the demand'. Sports like boxing have been quick to appreciate the international economic potential of 'pay-per-view' bouts involving heavyweight (in more than one sense) stars like Mike Tyson, where all the resources of the broadcast and print media can be used, through staged pre-fight confrontations between the combatants and other devices, to stimulate an urge to pay to see the event on screen as it happens. Avid sports fans have been lured over time in respectable numbers to subscribe to pay-TV, especially when prompted by the siphoning of their favourite live sports onto free-to-air television (as has occurred with rugby union in New Zealand). What is intriguing about much of the content of satellite and other pay-TV delivered sport, however, is that there is no discernibly strong demand for it. Multiple 24-hour pay-TV sports channels are as subject to the scarcity of 'good' (in the sense of 'good enough to pay for') content as are those devoted to film, comedy or drama. Apart from 'blue chip' and some 'emerging' sports (with what in the industry is called a 'cult following'), much of the content of pay-TV sport outside its core markets is simply 'channel filler' – an alternative to the test pattern. This means that the current state of pay sports TV resembles what Raymond Williams (1974) describes in *Television: Technology and Cultural Form* as the prevailing conditions existing during the invention of television (and radio) in the first place – a technology looking for a use.

Sport as screen filler

It is worth quoting the following well known passage from Williams's book, not least because of the central place it gives to sport:

> Unlike all previous communications technologies, radio and television were *systems primarily devised for transmission and reception as abstract processes, with little or no definition of preceding content.* When the question of content was raised, it was resolved, in the main, parasitically. There were state occasions, public sporting events, theatres and so on, which would be communicatively distributed by these new technical means. *It is not only that the supply of broadcasting facilities*

preceded the demand: it is that the means of communication preceded their content.

(Williams 1974: 25, original emphasis)

When viewers, then, in one country switch on a 24-hour TV sports channel and encounter a (to them) obscure sport from another country (receiving the same broadcast, including commentary, as the citizens of that country), it is unlikely that they are receiving a service which they urgently demand. In such instances, it is not so much, as Cunningham and Jacka (1996) suggested earlier, a question of pay sports television growing to fill an emerging demand, but, somewhat curiously in economic terms, to supply the filler for what would otherwise be a newly created but empty space. Where sports are hoping to cultivate a new audience (and often paying or subsidizing the broadcasters for the privilege), what is being offered for exchange is not TV sport for interested viewers but TV viewers for interested sports. The 'market' is constructed around the need to patch the holes created by technologically induced abundance; the opportunity to offer sports which cannot command huge broadcast rights revenue the chance to do so in the future by contacting some kind of television audience; and by accommodating those sports with more modest ambitions of receiving some valuable media coverage in the knowledge that some committed fans are willing to pay for it (D. Moore 1996). This form of sports TV delivery, unlike the networked free-to-air televison that is heavily reliant on 'blockbuster', ratings-based viewing figures, is in principle amenable to smaller scale, targeted, niche marketed, post-Fordist sport, as is indicated by the development of a cable channel for golf in the United States and a women's TV network in Canada. But, at least in Britain and Australia, the pattern to date in satellite and cable sport has mainly involved broadcasting well established national and international sports, accompanied by entertainment-based packaged segments which show snippets of sporting moments (triumphant and disastrous), novelty sports, 'extreme' sports, and material relayed from one country to another for no other apparent reason than it is sport and there is a space in the schedule for it.

The 'bonanza' for minority sports promised by multi-channel pay-TV has not eventuated, with claims of increased broadcast sports diversity more closely resembling political and marketing rhetoric than the actual practice of expanding the range of sports on television. As Crosswhite (1996: 58) has pointed out in the Australian context, for example, women's sports have often been required to pay broadcasters (both free-to-air and subscription) in order to get on screen, and have come under pressure to be more 'watchable', and so have been forced to confront such questions as 'Should athletes go into Lycra outfits, or the sport alter the size of the playing area, or speed up the flow of the game, or change the venue, increase the crowd, etc?' Appleton (1995: 32), however, is less concerned by television changing sport than the need for sports organizations to mobilize in order to secure greater genuine broadcast sports diversity rather than the 'resort to entertainment of the ilk of demolition derbies and mud wrestling rather than "real" sport'. Such arguments indicate that (as will be discussed later in this chapter) the economics of sports television are inextricably bound with up with questions of cultural politics. So, while a more complex mix of coexistent market forms of television sport does potentially exist, and is characterized by very different ways of creating and receiving media sports texts, the (full or partial) realization of that potential – or even its failure to materialize significantly at all – are dependent on political as well economic factors.

Free-to-air mega sports events like the Olympics will continue to exist for the foreseeable future because, as the International Olympic Committee has recognized, their greatest economic (and cultural) asset is the massive popularity that can give billions of people the sense of simultaneously having the same sporting experience (H. Wilson 1998). On the other hand, smaller sports TV audiences can be catered for, targeted or (even if notionally) created through various forms of direct purchase. Whatever the mode of delivery, and even if national public broadcasters manage to keep control over some 'hallmark' sports events, economic processes of varying scale and intensity are inevitably in play. This mutability of the production of broadcast media sports texts explains how they keep emerging, 'hydra-headed', despite some complaint that 'television has taken over sport'. It should be remembered, of course, that television is not the only means by which sports culture is framed, disseminated, peddled and circulated. Radio and print are also integral components of the media sports cultural complex, their products just as pervasive in the everyday world. Yet, while radio rights are contested for popular international and national sports; newspapers are committing greater resources to the sports pages, expanding print and photographic coverage and 'headhunting' their competitors' 'name' sports writers; and new general and specialist sports magazines are launched (and closed) every year, in sports television lies the most compelling expression of naked economic power in the media sports cultural complex. Accompanying this economic power to make media sports texts for vast audiences comes (as noted earlier) considerable political and cultural power. Because the arena is 'only sport', the extent and potential of this power is often underestimated. The rest of this chapter is devoted to drawing out the political and cultural implications of the power to make media sports texts for the national and global citizenry.

Media sports policy, politics and myth

It is probable that many times a day, somewhere in the western world, a talk-back radio host or caller pronounces that 'sport and politics don't mix' or proclaims that 'politics should be kept out of sport'. Such comments are a little curious, given the many ways in which sport and politics interrelate. These include deciding public spending priorities, such as allocations by national, state and regional governments to sporting organizations (Cashman and Hughes 1998) and by local governments for civic sports amenities (Mowbray 1993); anti-discrimination policies (such as Title IX section of the US Education Amendments Act of 1972, which denied 'federal financial assistance' to 'any education program or activity' that discriminated against any person 'on the basis of sex', and so had a substantial, positive impact on women's and girls' sport – see Guttmann 1991); and government restrictions on the advertising and sponsorship through sports such as Formula One motor racing and cricket of unhealthy products like tobacco and alcohol (K. Harris 1988). In order to be really vigilant about keeping sport and politics apart, it would be necessary to ban politicians from using sports metaphors like 'going the distance', 'levelling the playing field' and 'moving the goal-post after the game has started' in political speeches and interviews (Rowe 1995). The task of keeping sport and politics forever apart is, then, not only difficult, but inherently futile. While the sphere of sport (as, among others, John Hargreaves (1982) has noted) can never be reduced to 'pure' politics, neither can it be entirely insulated from it. As a result, the sports media, which it was argued in Chapter 2 are always already implicated in the politics of communication, are necessarily embroiled in the politics of sport – and the 'sport' of politics.

The media, in various ways, are called upon to provide good, wholesome 'family' entertainment through sport; to offer sensationally dramatic coverage that will attract healthy audiences (but perhaps for 'unhealthy' reasons); to describe and show what happened to those who were not present or who want to see it again and differently; to subject sport to intense scrutiny as part of the media's Fourth Estate function; to support local, regional and national sporting efforts; and to further the Olympian ideals of sport by transcending petty, partisan politics in the name of international peace and good will. No single organ of the media can fulfil all of these expectations (some of which are seen as unfortunate obligations), just as different types of media sports text are better suited to the performance of some tasks than others. To develop this logic to its fullest extent absolves the sports media of any general responsibility for their actions beyond the minimal observance ('actionable', in any case) of the laws of defamation, obscenity, and so on. The sports public, it is claimed, is provided with what it wants from the media on ortho-dox, market principles – if a demand exists for a type of sports coverage, then the market will provide it. No single sports programme or publication, from this perspective, need feel responsible for what its competitors currently or might do. The different elements of the sports media, it plausibly follows, do what they do – until it is shown to be unprofitable or illegal to do otherwise. To take the sports media simply at their word and to accept this account of their motives, operations and effects would be as unwise as to confine analy-sis only to the surface properties of media sports texts. By pointing out the latent and sometimes manifest political significance of their practices, it is made more difficult for the sports media to evade the proposition that with cultural power comes political responsibility.

One major contention of this book is that, while the mythology of sport rests heavily on the belief that it is or should be free of the grubby workings of the political world, it cannot escape the less than glamorous struggle, both external and internal, for power and influence. In other words, sports culture – at least its official, 'legitimate' face – is highly romanticized. We have also seen that media have their own romantic myth – that of the fearless watch-dog resisting the pressures of the state, capital and other powerful entities by exposing all and telling the truth. When isolated from each other, these two romantic dispositions pull in different directions; sporting mythology relies on the studied evasion of politics, while media mythology depends on a prin-cipled confrontation with it. The uneasy coming together of myths in making media sport helps explain the problems of professional practice and prestige for sports journalism analysed at some length in Chapter 3. An unsentimen-tal 'take' on how media sports texts are framed suggests that both sports and media mythologies – and so, inevitably, sports media mythologies – are mythological in a rather unfashionable, unspecialized sense. The 'lay' mean-ing of something being a myth is that it is untrue or a mistaken impression (such as, 'it's a myth that watching too much sport on television makes you go blind'), whereas in most recent social and cultural theory, the term does not so much denote a lack of correspondence between what is said and what is 'real', but demonstrates the power of particular symbols and narratives in expressing widely, unconsciously and deeply held beliefs as 'natural' in any given society, irrespective of any burden of 'proof' (like the myths of roman-tic love, the 'perfectibility of man', national cultural identity, and so on). The tension between these two meanings of mythology can be traced in media and cultural studies back to the seminal work of Roland Barthes (which is being discussed here in relation to political economy and not in the 'usual place' where textual analysis happens in order to demonstrate the indissolubility of the making and unmaking of media sports texts).

In *Mythologies*, Barthes (1973) attempts to deal with these different kinds of 'truth' – what is believed and what can be established theoretically, empirically and so politically (in terms of a class struggle and other forms of political action) as true. While in later works (such as Barthes 1978) he was somewhat less definitive about the clear division between truth/reality and falsehood/myth (Rojek 1985), the analytical and political dilemma has not gone away. In particular, the ways in which myths can function to obscure objective judgement and cloak it in mystifying ideology is still troubling if the test of any 'truth claim' is reduced to a choice between available myths (Thwaites *et al.* 1994). In the light of the postmodern and poststructuralist assault on the enlightenment concept of 'truth' (see, for example, Norris 1993), how can we speak authoritatively about the way things 'really are' and so propose rational and progressive political values and actions? Rather than attempt to provide a simple answer to this question (which, if it existed, would mean that it need never be posed), it is preferable to develop and refine our understanding of the multiple phenomena and relationships that make the social world and its culture(s). Earlier in this chapter, for example, we saw the undeniable power of economic forces in the shaping of sport and of media sport, but it was also apparent that the mobilization of economic factors was dependent on cultural forces (including the popular appeal of sport in the first place) which did not simply respond to economic imperatives but also helped shape them (as shown, for example, by the stubborn lack of international 'transportability' of many sports no matter how slick the advertising and promotional campaign). An intellectually respectable political economy of the sports media, therefore, must seek to be aware of the many influences – strong and weak, constant and intermittent, predictable and unpredictable – on the making of media sports texts.

In illustrating this argument, it is useful to examine briefly some instances where the cultural politics of media sport are played out in contrasting ways. For example, in looking at the gender order in media sport above, it was clear that women have been subject to subordination and/or under-representation in two key organizational complexes – media corporations (as owners, senior executives and 'rank-and-file' personnel) and sporting organizations (in governing bodies and as professional athletes). The intimate, longstanding linkage between sport and masculinity has helped secure the dominance of male sport in the media and of males employed to cover sport in the media. This is obviously not a simple question of capitalist logic in operation – male media proprietors and executives are no less than many other men drawn to the expression of heroic, aggressive and competitive masculinity by associating themselves with the popular contact sports of which their fellows are so enamoured (McKay and Rowe 1997; Attwood

1998). Yet, pressure to change this pattern of male predominance in media sport is coming from various sources. Sport is, somewhat belatedly, one of the important fronts in which battles for sexual equality are being waged, with both governments and feminist groups demanding an end to male exclusionism in sport (Jennifer Hargreaves 1994; M.A. Hall 1997). Women workers in the sports media have mobilized to improve their positions within media organizations (Cramer 1994), while women's sports organizations have demanded more air time and column inches, sponsorship and broadcast rights revenues (Crosswhite 1996).

These have not, however, all been external pressures; within the media sports cultural complex itself there has been a gradual realization that it is economically and otherwise senseless to alienate a large proportion of a market which, if segregated too strictly on gender lines, would in the case of some sports (like the football codes) be close to saturation. This is even without mentioning the key decision-making position of women in household consumption. Then there is the potential of new media technologies to provide more diverse sports fare, and the requirement for public and commercial broadcasters who have been outbid for sports broadcast rights by their rivals to make a virtue of necessity in 'signing up' some women's sports like basketball and netball. As a result, sports broadcast programmers and print editors have sought (with signal success in sports like soccer and rugby league) to attract substantial female audiences by adopting strategies such as overtly sexualizing sportsmen (see Chapter 6), explaining arcane rules to the uninitiated, giving greater and more sympathetic coverage of sportswomen, employing female sports commentators and writers, and so on. In other words, commodity logic and cultural politics have interacted in new, intriguing ways – although not always with impeccably 'progressive' outcomes (as evidenced, for example, by the willingness of more women's sports and of individual sportswomen to emphasize sexual attractiveness as a marketing tool in pursuit of greater media, sponsor and advertiser attention). The issue of sex and gender equality in sport and media sport, and the ways in which it is confronted by governments and business enterprises, raises the wider question of the role of media sport in the whole domain of 'cultural citizenship'.

Fighting for the right to watch

The concept of cultural citizenship is a broadening of the traditional idea of the rights and responsibilities of states and citizens in recognition of the increased 'culturalization' of society. The outcome is a greater significance of culture and communication under 'postmodernity' in fostering the creation of informed, critically reflective persons capable of taking an active part both in their own lives and in those of the collectivities of various kinds – families, pressure groups, political parties, and so on – in which they are involved. Just as, say, the idea of what constitutes a necessity and what a luxury has changed over many decades – possession of inside toilets, reticulated plumbing and domestic electrical power was, until well into the twentieth century, the exception rather than the norm for most of the population of the west (and still is in many non-western societies and in indigenous settlements in 'white settler' countries) – so what is considered to be an essential prerequisite for comprehensive participation in all of society's major institutions, debates and processes has been extended. If contemporary citizens are to have ready access to highly detailed information about the values, histories, performances and intentions of the parties engaged in the formal and informal political processes in order to make informed choices, then they must possess the means of ready communication in the public sphere (televisions, newspapers, radios, telephones, computers, and so on) and the appropriate educational means to decode, interpret, adjudicate on and respond to the messages that are circulating in that 'public sphere' (Murdock and Golding 1989; Murdock 1992).

As culture has become, across the past two centuries, industrially produced or provided and governed by the state (Bennett 1998), this entitlement to information to be used in regard to voting or family health, personal hygiene or even product choice (as applied both to commercial advertising and state guidance on safe and healthy consumer behaviour) has progressively spread to the claimed right to certain kinds of cultural (including strictly entertainment) provision in order that the citizen can take part fully in the cultural as well as political life of the nation. Here a model of cultural heritage encompasses quite recent historical developments – like the twentieth-century practice of broadcasting major public events to the entire nation. Because sports events have become the most important, regular manifestations of this national culture (Rowe *et al.* 1998), and despite the move towards their supply to the citizenry by commercial rather than by public broadcasters (H. Wilson 1998), media sport has become a major aspect of contemporary cultural heritage and so is deeply implicated in debates about cultural citizenship.

Once, then, free-to-air television provided major national and international sports events at nominal direct expense to viewers, and these cultural items had been counted among the major rituals of national significance, then they became incorporated into the citizen's cultural 'treasure house'. There would need to be compelling grounds, therefore, if the 'free list' of major television sport were to be fully commodified, yet this is precisely what has occurred – and is increasingly threatened – in sports television. The political value of (virtual) universal entitlement in the west has been challenged by market-based values, with the idea of abundant choice of television sports texts as the overriding imperative – a choice that involves a 'user pays' principle and one which positions sport as simply another commercialized entertainment option in an unforgiving and ideally unfettered cultural marketplace. The only rights which, then, need to be safeguarded are those of sports media consumers from fraud, deception and other crimes of commercial practice, rather than in terms of any higher concept of the protection of significant cultural rights. These debates are played out differently according to national context. In Britain and Australia, broadcast sport was first dominated by public broadcasters, which have gradually lost control first to commercial free-to-air broadcasters and then to pay-TV companies. In the USA, with its much weaker commitment to non-commercial broadcasting, the sports media market developed much earlier (Wenner 1989), although this did not destroy network free-to-air sports television, which has survived and prospered through a combination of anti-trust legislation and the economic power of the networks deriving from television audiences captured for mass advertising rather than for targeted 'cable' subscription and pay-per-view. The intrication (that is, perplexing entanglement) of the economic, the political and the cultural is evident in the determination of how televised sport is to be delivered and to whom.

In Australia, for example, the belated introduction of pay-TV in 1995 enabled the (then Labor) national government to avoid what was seen as the folly of Britain's Conservative Thatcher regime, which (as was noted above) had allowed its political ally, Rupert Murdoch, to rescue his BSkyB satellite television venture by 'capturing' English premier league soccer. Australia embarked on what has been called 'the bravest effort at an effective anti-siphoning regime in the world' (Grainger 1996: 25) by introducing in 1994 under Section 115 of its Broadcasting Services Act 1992 legal provisions which would allow the relevant minister (then for Communication and the Arts) to, in the words of the Act, 'by notice published in the Gazette, specify any event, or events of a kind, the televising of which, or the live televising of which, should, in the opinion of the minister, be available free to the general public'. Hence, in a much more forceable manner than occurred in Britain (where the Blair government, elected in 1997, undertook to review and tighten up the weak anti-siphoning regulations of the Thatcher and Major regimes), the minister may list any event deemed to be of national importance or cultural significance that is usually broadcast on free-to-air television. The listed events exclusively involved sport, including horse and motor racing, soccer, tennis, basketball and golf, and covered events staged both in Australia and overseas. The provisions also allowed the minister to 'de-list' events if:

> satisfied that the national broadcasters and the commercial television broadcasting licensees have had a real opportunity to acquire, on a fair commercial basis, the right to televise the event live [and] that none of those persons has acquired that right within a reasonable time.

Here, then, there is direct intervention by the state in the workings of the sports television market, ostensibly in the interests of promoting the rights of cultural citizenship; in this case, that there is a public right to watch major sports events free and live as part of established national cultural heritage. This political determination, however, was not entirely immune from economic influences. The long-delayed introduction of pay-TV in Australia has been attributed to the political influence of free-to-air broadcasters (Cunningham 1992), while the anti-siphoning regime may be seen as giving an unfair market advantage to the established free-to-air television sector over the fledgling pay sector. Indeed, criticisms of anti-competitive behaviour by government are not made only by pay-TV broadcasters: netball, the only women's sport on the Australian list, quickly asked to be removed from the list because, as the National Executive Director of Australian Netball argued, 'it has not taken into account the fact that we have had to pay to get on free to air' (P. Smith 1996: 69), and pay-TV held out the prospect, paradoxically, of being 'free' (even remunerable) for the sport and 'chargeable' for the viewer. Furthermore, the Australian political apparatus did little more than watch from the sidelines while the sport of rugby league (as discussed above) disintegrated in the mid-1990s as Australia's two most powerful media barons, Rupert Murdoch and Kerry Packer, fought over free-to-air and pay-TV rights to the sport.

Throughout the struggle (which ended in a 'truce' in 1998 after two years of hugely expensive court action, a massively inflated and unsustainable rise in players', coaches' and referees' salaries, and a disastrous split competition in 1997) each side tried to win the mythological war, with the Packer camp stressing class, loyalty, tradition, nationalism and 'blokeish' masculinity, and the Murdoch camp promoting values of upward mobility, flexibility, progressive change, globalism and a more sophisticated, even glamorous appeal (McKay and Rowe 1997). Broadcast and print journalists and presenters charged with the responsibility of reporting these events with objectivity and fairness tended, if employed by the contending parties, to report from behind their own battlelines (Packer TV versus the Murdoch press, with the rival Fairfax company revelling in the role of 'neutral' umpire and honest broker). Yet, the cultural scope and resonance of the issues raised in major sports stories like 'The Super League Saga' (Rowe 1997b) take them well beyond the sports pages, programmes and bulletins into another media realm – the general news story and, especially, the domain of media scandal.

Sport as school for scandal

It is worthwhile to look briefly at media sports scandals because they reveal how the political economy of media sport extends far beyond the production, distribution and consumption of sports reports and live television. We have noted how sport has notable popular appeal for large (especially male) sections of the population, and that media sports texts take many forms, from 'hard' objective reporting to the 'soft' news of gossip, background and 'colour'. However, sport's cultural prominence and the visibility of its celebrities make it a useful vehicle for carrying news stories 'outside' itself and its routine audiences. Some of these stories are positive in nature, drawing, for example, after success in major international competitions like the Olympics, on the nationalist impulse that can be activated in many citizens, irrespective of their usual involvement in sports spectatorship (Miller *et al.* forthcoming). But scandals are particularly instructive because their inherently transgressive quality by their nature raises the possibility of 'contagion' or, as John B. Thompson (1997: 59) puts it, 'a corrosive impact on the forms of trust which underpin social relations and institutions'. As we have seen, sport for its adherents is the bearer of strong mythologies of nobility and fair competition, while even those who are not sports fans are of necessity aware of the material success and high standing of sports stars. Media sports scandals like those involving, for example, Ben Johnson's disqualification after winning the 100 metres at the 1988 Seoul Olympics for taking performance enhancing drugs, or the trial of iceskater Tonya Harding for conspiring to injure her US teammate and rival Nancy Kerrigan, directly transgress the 'fair play' values of sport. A 'scandal' can even be created out of a fairly routine occurrence in a sporting event of great significance – like the public pillorying of the English soccer 'golden boy' and Spice Girl fiancé David Beckham for being sent off in the 1998 World Cup finals.

Yet to qualify as media sports scandals, the transgressive behaviour does not have to occur in the pursuit of sport; the iconic status of elite sportspeople means that, as in the case of the O.J. Simpson murder trial, a retired footballer turned sports commentator and film actor is still associated predominantly with his exploits on the field of play (McKay and Smith 1995), while the prosecution of boxer Mike Tyson for rape is directly connected in the media to his performance in the ring (not to mention his identity as an African American male – see Sloop 1997). In the case of high profile HIV-positive athletes like Earvin 'Magic' Johnson and Greg Louganis, the stuff of scandal is provided by the positioning of sexuality within elite sports culture. The mere fact of being gay can be scandalous within this culture, as Justin Fashanu, the first soccer star to 'come out' and the first million-pound black footballer in Britain, discovered to his cost. He hanged himself in May 1998, largely ostracized by his footballing peers and facing allegations in the USA of the sexual molestation of a minor. Scandal cannot be contained within the sports world even where it directly emanates from sporting activity, nor can the heroic mythology of sport be protected from scandal when the 'extra-curricular' behaviour of sportspeople brings it into disrepute by association. As Thompson (1997: 58) argues, scandals have wider social ramifications than is often acknowledged, being 'consequential not just for the lives and reputations of the individuals immediately affected by them'. In the case of sport, they do not merely damage the 'forms of trust' on which the institution relies, but also permit the use of a powerful and popular institution for the exploration and contestation of significant contemporary social issues. In the cases briefly cited above, these include matters of resort to unethical means in the pursuit of approved goals; concepts of the 'normal' body and the use of drugs; private ambition versus the collective good; norms of conduct among women; the relationship between aggressive sporting masculinity and a propensity to violence; physical and other forms of abuse of women by men both inside and outside marriage; the racialized nature of the justice system; the stigmatization of homosexuality and celebration of male heterosexual promiscuity; gender inequality in sports fandom, and so on (Rowe 1997a).

In coming to an understanding of the political economy of the media sports scandal, it is necessary to appreciate how the hunger for content, the power of celebrity, and the ready transportability of images and information within and across media, create the conditions for a full-blown media phenomenon, but that to prosper they must articulate with social questions that are of importance to media audiences and 'moral entrepreneurs' (Cohen 1980) alike. In fact, the media sports scandal is, ultimately, no more than a spectacular instance of the everyday product of the sports media. Every fragment of sports report, snatch of commentary, still shot and flickering image, and all other elements of sports discourse, are couched in visual and verbal languages whose grammar and syntax, vocabulary and framing, carry within them a kind of politics. These need not be overt, clear or consistent, but they represent a politics of the popular that is pumped out unreflectively every day in the name of sport. As Barthes (1973) has famously noted, it is not when politics is close to the surface and easily recognizable that it is at its most popularly powerful, but when it is strongly present but apparently absent, allowing myths to do their work on the emotions, and ideologies to represent the interests of the privileged few as the natural order for the many. We underestimate the political economic weight of the media sports cultural complex at our peril.

Conclusion: media sport lost and found

In their programme for a revitalized and critical political economy of communications set out in the early 1990s, Golding and Murdock (1991: 17) are critical of the 'romantic celebration of subversive consumption' and the loss of interest in 'the way the mass media operate ideologically, to sustain and support prevailing relations of domination' that they see as marking the work of 'new populist' cultural studies theorists like Fiske (1989a, 1989b). They go on to argue that even if it is conceded that there is value in focusing on 'the moment of exchange when the meanings carried by texts meet the meanings that readers bring to them', it leaves out far too much of the overall story:

> But even if this wider perspective is restored there is still the problem that cultural studies offers an analysis of the ways the cultural industries work that has little or nothing to say about how they actually operate as industries, and how their economic organization impinges on the production and circulation of meaning. Nor does it examine the ways in which people's consumption choices are structured by their position in the wider economic formation.
>
> (Golding and Murdock 1991: 17)

In this first part of the book I have taken seriously the question of how the cultural industries work *qua* industries and their consequent impact on the meanings we derive from media sport, in the process acknowledging (although not deeply analysing) their position in the wider economic and social formations (such as, respectively, the informational economy and the media sports gender order). This chapter has engaged with the political economy of the sports media, addressing and/or anticipating the 'three core tasks' of political economy 'in practice' proposed by Golding and Murdock (1991: 22), analysing the production of cultural goods alongside the political economies of texts and of cultural consumption. In the following 'Unmaking the media sports text' part of the book, the conditions of media sports text production and the properties and uses of those same texts will be simultaneously borne in mind – thereby, it is hoped, avoiding analytical amnesia concerning pivotal components of an integrated approach to the study of sport, culture and the media. In the light of the emphasis given to sports television so far, it might be expected that we would first turn to sport on screen – but before the cathode ray tube came the word and the voice of sport.

Further reading

Lash, S. and Urry, J. (1994) *Economies of Signs and Space*. London: Sage.
Martin, R. and Miller, T. (eds) (1999) *SportCult*. Minneapolis, MN: University of Minnesota Press.
Rowe, D. (1995) *Popular Cultures: Rock Music, Sport and the Politics of Pleasure*. London: Sage.
Wenner, L. (ed.) (1998) *MediaSport*. London: Routledge.

Part II
UNMAKING THE MEDIA SPORTS TEXT

5 | TAKING US THROUGH IT: THE 'ART' OF SPORTS COMMENTATING AND WRITING

Some work in Britain analyzing sports writing in the Sunday newspapers and the language used to report on football matches and football hooliganism, points to its lexical and conceptual poverty. With some exceptions the language, even when compared with usage in the rest of the media, is notoriously stereotyped.

(John Hargreaves 1986: 151)

Introduction: the world of sports speak

In Part I most attention was paid to the question of how media sports texts get made, by whom and under what conditions. Suitably equipped with an appreciation of the forces and processes of varying magnitude that go to produce media sports culture, it is important also to understand something of how its texts are structured, the forms they adopt, and the ways in which those texts work in connecting sport's producers and audiences. This task involves the alternately pleasing and infuriating process of deeply interrogating the wild allusions, frantic imprecations, melodramatic narratives, and hysterical outpourings that comprise much of the dauntingly extensive and intense culture of media sport. Of course, there is no 'typical' sports text as such, but rather a jumble of genres and subjects that can be said to fit under the rubric of sport because they have some connection (often tenuous) with its mythologies, organizations and personnel. Such texts are visual and aural, printed and spoken, taking the form of 'live' commentary on television, radio and the Internet, structured segments of news bulletins, brief 'updates', lengthy newspaper feature articles, descriptive reports of games, 'insider' slices of gossip, novels and (auto)biographies, and so on. Each media sports text creates and adheres to its own rules of **sub-genre** and textual relations, representing the sports world and situating it within the wider world with which, often reluctantly, it must deal.

Media sports texts sometimes take on the quality of subcultural 'anti-language' (Montgomery 1986), a lexicon and syntax that is an offshoot of the 'tabloid-speak' that selects aspects of popular speech and then takes such liberties with it that it becomes unrecognizable as anything other that what is found on its own pages (see Chippindale and Horrie's (1990) study of the *Sun* newspaper, *Stick It Up Your Punter!*). This specialist form of sports discourse binds producer, reader and text by the force of its own conventions and rules, but other textual forms have a centrifugal rather than centripetal propensity, opening themselves and readers to matters somewhat wider than results, injuries and transfers. There is a need, then, to analyse the ways in which sports mythologies 'leech out' into wider domains and are used to invest other subjects with popularly digestible meaning, and also the manner in which the discourse of sport incorporates elements of external discourses in interpreting events in the sports world. In this way, sports texts and social ideologies, mediated through different institutions and discourses, can be seen to be in constant interaction, each appropriating and relinquishing imagery and language in the unending process of representing the social world. Given the cacophonic nature of 'sportuguese', it is difficult to find a quiet, ordered space from which this somewhat abstract project can be commenced. For this reason, we shall go straight to the most overheated, parodied and reviled sports text of all – the 'live' sports commentary.

Live commentary, dead language

There is no other media sports text that is subject to greater ridicule than the live broadcast (especially television) commentary which describes for viewers what they are seeing. There are some obvious reasons for this phenomenon: sports fans who are skilled in 'reading' what is unfolding before them on the screen resent intrusive, inexpert and mistake-ridden commentary. Yet, much commentary is not aimed at committed television sports fans; they will watch 'the match' whatever happens (perhaps with the televison volume turned down or, as is the case with many committed cricket fans, watching without any TV audio in favour of the more sedate radio commentary – and in the case of commercial free-to-air television avoiding loud advertising announcements in the process). Some of the more hyped-up commentaries are intended for those 'unconverted' viewers whose interest has to be stimulated by communicating a sense of high drama in the events on screen. If television sports commentators, then, are irritating a core audience while trying to lure a peripheral one (sometimes with the kind of elementary explanation of rules and moves that is almost guaranteed to infuriate the *aficionado*), then it is hardly surprising that they are so often subject to hostile commentary themselves. Live sports commentators are in any case especially easy targets because, however much they 'bone up' on sports statistics and player profiles, and irrespective of the degree to which they rehearse their patter, if their commentary is going to air at the same time as the broadcast, then they have little opportunity to correct errors and avoid asinine remarks. In this sense, live television sports commentators resemble the athletes and officials whose performances they are describing and assessing. This is a rare working condition in the contemporary mass media, where scripting, pre- and re-recording, drafting, editing, spell-checking and so on limit the error count of the final textual product. It is the performance element that in live television commentary invites critical assessment. Of course, such commentary (as noted earlier) is also a staple of radio sport, but it is a little less subject to vigorous criticism, perhaps because the listener does not usually have the 'corroborative' evidence of their own eyes possessed by their viewing counterparts.

Indeed, it could be argued that making fun of television sports commentators (who are not usually print journalists by profession) has itself become a popular sport. As mentioned in Chapter 4, the London-based satirical magazine *Private Eye* has for many years run a 'Colemanballs' column and anthology book series named after the veteran television sports commentator David Coleman, but covering the solecisms of other sports commentators. In 'postmodern' fashion the main 'offenders' may become cult heroes, with, for example, the British motor sport commentator Murray Walker having his own dedicated 'Quotes' page of 'walkerisms' on the Internet, containing many examples of 'deathless' prose by means of which 'he often entertains viewers not by describing the drama on the track, but by his litany of literal backfires. Few other sports callers are so renowned, and yet so acclaimed for their mouth running in sixth gear while their brain remains in reverse' (Jellie 1998: 3). By selecting some entries in the Murray Walker Quotes Page, the pleasurable appeal of recording errors can be discovered. For example:

1 Mansell is slowing down, taking it easy. OH NO HE ISN'T! It's a lap record.
2 And that just shows you how important the car is in Formula One racing.
3 I know it's an old cliché, but you can cut the atmosphere with a cricket stump.
4 As you can see, visually, with your eyes.

In this short catalogue of mistakes, there is a gross miscalculation of performance (1), an unfortunately banal summation (2), a curious malapropism (3) and a 'virtuoso' double tautology (4). Recording and circulating them is not only, as here, a 'cyber parlour game'. Comedians find rich material for parody, as in the case of the Australian radio show *This Sporting Life* and its television offshoot (a series of which was broadcast by British regional television), hosted by the spoof sports commentators 'Rampaging' Roy Slaven and H.G. Nelson, while British television shows like *They Think It's All Over* are named after and pick over fragments of sports commentary. Novelists (and part-time sports writers) like Martin Amis also apply their dialogically attuned ears to the synthetic speech of sports commentary, as in the case of the 'sportuguese' monologue by the protagonist Keith in *London Fields*, who, when asked in a pub to recall a recent football match, immediately falls into familiar, received speech patterns in 'incanting' sentences like, 'A draw looked the most likely result until a disputed penalty broke the deadlock five minutes from the final whistle' (Amis 1989: 91). That a section from Amis's novel was reproduced in the *Faber Book of Soccer* dedicated to the documentation of 'good soccer writing' (Hamilton 1992: 2) indicates the degree to which caricatured media sports texts now flow freely out of the mouths of broadcast commentators through the patter of comedians and popular speech onto the pages of newspapers and 'blackly' satirical novels, which, on occasions, leads television sports commentators like Murray Walker to engage in self-parody – 'I don't make mistakes, I make prophecies which immediately turn out to be wrong' (quoted in Jellie 1998: 3) – in an increasingly elaborate self-referencing and reproducing system of quotation and caricature.

Ultimately, parody tips over into pastiche, as it becomes increasingly difficult to establish the 'original' that is being made fun of. Media 'sports speak' admirably qualifies, then, as a premier instance of what Baudrillard (1983) calls 'simulacra' (copies of copies whose 'master' was long since lost in a blizzard of reproductions) or of what Jameson (1984) describes as the postmodern product of the 'logic of late capitalism' (an endlessly playful dissolution and recombination of the boundaries of genre and style). Media sports texts can be seen in this way as reflective and partially productive of a wider shift towards what can be called, in rather ugly neologisms, the 'ironization' of culture and the '**mediatization**' of advanced capitalist, postmodernized societies. To put it more plainly, the media sports cultural complex generates texts which, while they may be intended initially to be serious and focused on a sporting phenomenon, can be rapidly appropriated and used for quite different purposes. Further evidence of this trend is presented in the following discussion of sports print texts, with renditions ('straight' or 'warped') of media sports speak appearing not only in the 'professional' media, but also in the amateur and semi-professional sports fanzines (especially emanating from British soccer) published by supporters.

Media sports speak also reappears as a comic component in everyday speech; it is common, for example, for 'park' footballers to give their own imagined, imitated and exaggerated sports commentary when scoring goals or tries, liberally sprinkled with ironic sports clichés about being 'over the moon', 'gutted' and 'sick as a parrot'. By lampooning sports commentators, other media professionals assert their technical, communicative superiority and sports fans present their credentials as experts in decoding games. Just as is the case with the print sports journalists discussed in Chapter 3, 'live' television and radio sports commentators are constantly required to justify if not their existence (although there are media sports fans who wish that they would find a more useful occupation, like selling second-hand motor vehicles) then their qualifications for taking up such a prominent place in sport. What is required of the sports commentator, then, is to enhance the experience of watching by various means – through poetic powers of description and evocation (as is often said of highly regarded cricket commentators like the late John Arlott); to provide supplementary information (as in the case of Murray Walker's 'encyclopaedic knowledge of the sport' – Jellie 1998: 3); or to supply the kind of 'insider', expert knowledge that is gained by playing sport at the highest levels (hence the aforementioned movement of retired and even currently practising professional sportspeople into the media). Each form of commentary is equally open to critique – the poetic regarded as self-indulgent ('pseuds corner'), the informational as 'trivial pursuit' or 'anorak' knowledge, the 'insider' as inarticulate and untrained. The live broadcast sports commentator is subject to exacting demands by fellow viewers and listeners because they (usually he) are in broad terms doing the same thing, and for a separation to be maintained between paid commentator and unpaid media spectator requires a demonstration of the superior (or at least the enhancing) quality of the professional's observations.

One way in which this potential for adverse or ridiculing response from those exposed to sports commentary may be avoided is through unobtrusiveness (low-key description and analysis with plenty of space left for the action to 'speak for itself' – a task rather easier in television than on radio) or an attempt to bridge the gap between commentator and viewer by representing them as one. In much the same way as, for example, politicians regularly deploy the rhetoric of unity to represent themselves as being 'of the people' by using the pronoun 'we', so sports commentators often attempt to install themselves as the eyes, ears and voice of the media sports spectating public. This identification between commentators, viewers and listeners is particularly effective in international sport, where an 'us' and 'them' framework can be easily established. In covering, certainly as national broadcasters, sports competitions between citizens, cities or teams from the same country, commentators are usually expected to display at least a notional impartiality, but when a readily recognizable 'Other' exists in the shape of the representatives of other nation-states (or if covering a 'hometown team'), the broadcast commentator is licensed to dispense with any pretence of objectivity.

McHoul (1997) notes, in reflecting (from the perspective of ethnomethodology and conversational analysis) on the mode of address of sport's television, how the practice of 'doing "we's"' (the selection and deployment of a pronoun) implies significant types of relation between sportspeople, coaches, officials, broadcasters and viewers. The example he uses from the 1988 summer Olympics in Seoul is not, strictly, of a television commentator but is, in fact, of a swimming coach at the time who subsequently became a commentator. None the less, the mode of address and behaviour of Lawrie Lawrence – whose 'antics' are described by Miller (1990: 92) alongside those of the Australian Channel Ten television commentator who, as Lawrence's 'coachee' Duncan Armstrong won the 200 metres freestyle in world record time, expostulated 'Oh my God, Oh my God!' before the cameras – are much adopted by 'live' broadcast commentators in a state of high, patriotic excitement. The Australian sports commentator Norman May (1984: 116), for example, describes his much replayed words in the closing moments of the men's 4 × 100 metres medley in the 1980 Moscow Olympics, '5 metres, 4, 3, 2, 1 – Gold, Gold to Australia, Gold', as 'my best known single commentary in 27 years as a broadcaster'. It is at such moments that sports commentator and audience seem to become one, united in the ecstasy of victory. In analysing who are the 'we' when Lawrence shouted, 'We won! We won!', McHoul (1997) argues, following Sacks (1992), that there are two types of 'we' – a specific 'list' (say a named group of swimmers or runners) and a vaguer 'category' (say of men or women). How, he asks, can disparate individuals with very different histories become 'we'?

> there's always the possibility that nonswimmers such as coach, crew, and even family can get, as it were, on the list. Or else there can be categorical 'we's' available to team fans, or indeed (particularly in the case of the Olympics) to any person with the same nationality as the swimmer.
>
> (McHoul 1997: 319)

What McHoul is remarking on is the extraordinary power of sport – one which would be unique were it not for some instances of intense national identification in times of war or disaster – to encourage a literal identification between 'actors' and 'non-actors'. More even than in the cases of 'subcultural' music or 'projection fantasy' film, the performances of sportspeople are appropriated by sports fans as 'ours'. Live broadcast commentary on major international sporting events is consummately aware of this power, and in this way media sports texts can be seen as actively engaged in the task of 'recruiting' audiences (especially for advertisers) by first 'signing them up' as on the same 'team'. This well established theoretical notion of 'interpellation' – what Althusser (1971) calls 'hailing' subjects in much the same way as people in the street automatically turn around when someone calls out 'Hey, you!' (appropriately here we might add the line from the Madness song *One Step Beyond*, 'Don't watch dat! Watch dis!') – is more than a matter of technical communication. It is also a question of ideology. If media sports texts have the power to unite, temporarily or in the long term, symbolically or materially, disparate audiences into relatively coherent groups of patriots or consumers, then they are potentially deliverable, as Golding and Murdock (1991: 17) noted in Chapter 4, to those who wish to 'sustain and support prevailing relations of domination'. For example, the patriotic fervour generated by Argentina's winning of the soccer World Cup in 1978 (at least temporarily) assisted the fortunes of the oppressive military *junta* whose slogan was '25 Million Argentinians Will Play in the World Cup' (quoted in Kuper 1994: 174).

Ideologies and Olympic extravaganzas

Live sports broadcasts (over which, of course, commentators exert only partial control – see Chapter 6) do not have to be rampantly xenophobic to be the bearers of ideology. Gordon and Sibson (1998), for example, note how the absence of commentary on some of the smaller and more marginal national teams during the television broadcast of the opening ceremony of the 1996 Atlanta summer Olympics had the effect of further marginalizing those nations. Tomlinson (1996), similarly, in his commentary on the commentary at Olympic opening ceremonies, argues that at the 1984 Los Angeles summer Olympics the aforementioned (and much lampooned) BBC commentator David Coleman's:

> welcome to the Coliseum mixed history, myth and politics: 'in the sunshine of this Californian afternoon, ancient Greek rites, Hollywood fantasy and the reality of life in 1984 will find common ground . . .' (Transcription from BBC broadcast). There were more nations and

more competitors than ever before at LA (despite Soviet bloc boycotts), welcomed by a showbiz style of 'pure Hollywood extravaganza on a gigantic scale', as Coleman put it. 'The show must go on'.

(Tomlinson 1996: 590)

In hosting on behalf of a national television audience a ceremony which, during the 1992 Barcelona summer Olympics, Coleman described as being watched by 'half the world's population' (quoted in Tomlinson 1996: 595), commentators, with their combination of scripted and spontaneous utterances, are able to call on the grandest myths of all – those which pertain to universal humanity, and the capacity of the Olympics to promote global 'peace, harmony and progress' (the theme of the Seoul Olympic opening ceremony). Yet, as we have seen, commentators are also in the business of making sure that their audiences differentiate between their compatriots and the other branches of the great human family whom they fervently hope will lose. This universalist–partisan balancing act is a difficult one to perform, and helps to explain the somewhat schizophrenic quality of much media sports discourse, as live commentators try to temper their often hysterical and 'one-eyed' support for an individual or team with a more even-handed appreciation of the skills and interests of their opposition. To return briefly to McHoul's reflection on Lawrie Lawrence, the cry 'We won! We won!' could be all-inclusive only if every potential division was denied, leaving us with the heartwarming but improbable meaning that 'humankind' was the winner. Such sentiments are, in fact, rarely heard outside the more platitudinous pronouncements of commentators during mammoth broadcasts for major sports events or of sports officials like the IOC's Juan Antonio Samaranch, whom Tomlinson (1996: 597) quotes as describing the 1992 opening ceremony in his native Barcelona as 'the greatest festival of our contemporary society'. We should also not forget the transparently disengenuous claim by commentators that sport or a particular sport 'was the winner today' when made after an unsatisfactory result in a sports contest. Solace after a major sporting loss can be found, then, by retreating to the universal and high minded values that much of the time are discarded in the search for passionate, loyal media audiences.

Broadcast commentators, however, get criticized not only for their technical failings and banalities, but also for bringing political issues (usually inadvertently) to the surface. For example, when in January 1998 the British television soccer commentator John Motson remarked in an interview that he sometimes had difficulty differentiating between black players when clustered on the pitch, there were angry allegations that this was a 'replay' of the old racist saying that 'they all look the same to me'. The sheer, relentless availability of media sports texts like live television and radio commentary does, as in the case of the sports celebrity scandals discussed in Chapter 4, also facilitate often heated debates about racial and ethnic stereotyping, gendered denigration and exclusion, the celebration of violence and aggression, discrimination against those who are elderly or not able bodied, and so on. The riposte during such popular debates is often that too much is being read into an offhand or joking remark, or that an injudicious word was chosen in the heat of the moment in the same way that most 'live' broadcasts are littered with errors of grammar and expression, and replete with *non sequiturs* and 'spoonerisms'. Setting aside the question of intention (few live commentators with the responsibility of accurately describing great media sports events wish or are permitted to be provocative, unlike their broadcast and print colleagues who provide the necessarily opinionated 'editorial') what is said or written can be subjected to detailed analysis in order to reveal which views of the world, couched in the language of sport, are being given an airing. As Blain and Boyle (1998) argue:

> And, since being a television or newspaper journalist or editor is a position of privilege, we should bear in mind that the ideologies the mainstream media produce or reproduce when giving us accounts of sports-related matters will tend to be those of socially dominant groups rather than those who may be disempowered: we are more likely to find out what men think about women than the other way round; more likely in Italy or France to find out what Whites think about Blacks than vice versa; more likely on British television networks to find out the English view of the next World Cup than the Welsh or Scottish expectations. Conversely, the accounts which we do *not* hear tell us a lot about the groups denied a voice on TV and radio or the press.
>
> (Blain and Boyle 1998: 371 – original emphasis)

The circulation of discourses of dominance in media sports texts, then, occurs as part of the overall flow of ideologies and mythologies in and out of the media sports cultural complex and the social structures, large and small, to which it is linked. While, as Blain and Boyle suggest, there is an obvious tendency for powerful forces to protect their own interests (and sport, even when it is not wedded to the media, has an institutional disposition towards deep conservatism – see Brohm 1978), this cultural system is not as functionally self-reproductive as it may appear. One of the protections against any powerful group entirely or even substantially 'sewing up' sports meanings is (as I have argued above), a quite deep-seated suspicion of (sometimes even contempt for) the sports media by audience members. The frequent refusal to give high levels of professional respect to many producers of media sports texts (like broadcast commentators and journalists) is, as we saw in Chapter 2, galling for them and often rather unfair (especially when journalistic colleagues take an unduly snobbish view of the 'toy department'). But, ironically, public scepticism about the sports media is also a buffer against those media exercising undue ideological power. This is not to argue that all media sports texts are 'reactionary' and all criticisms of them 'progressive', but rather that resistance to the cult of the sports media expert is also something of an assertion of popular power against one of the most efficient and extensive factories of meaning and value yet devised. If the sports television commentary gabbled by the man (usually) with the bad hair, the pocket vocabulary and the messy private life (reported on with much glee by his news journalist colleagues) is hard to take altogether seriously as an efficient vector of dominant ideology, so, too, is much of what appears under the banner of print sports journalism. Which is not, of course, to say that sports writers lack a large (sometimes compulsive) readership or that what they produce is not also a source of pleasure (sometimes cruel) for what it informs about sport and disfigures in language.

On the page, off the air

Sports texts, as I have argued, have many forms, functions and readerships (see also Rowe 1992). The traditional sports report is intended to bear witness to what has occurred for those who were not present. At the most basic, denotative level this is an uncontroversial (if, depending on the result, by turns exhilarating and depressing for those who care) statement that, for example, Crewe Alexandra drew 0–0 with Burnley in Division Three of the English Football League at the Gresty Road Ground before a crowd of 2816 cold, wet masochists. Not much human intervention is needed here: a few units of data are 'sent down the wire' or entered into a computer database, producing a text that has little more cultural resonance than the shipping or stock market reports (hence the invention of the Zybrainic Sportswriter discussed in Chapter 3). Except that, just as those anonymous units of information have much greater importance and depth of meaning for the seafarers and 'desk jockeys' who depend on them for their livelihood, the relevant sports fan will not only invest these facts (which must be unimpeachably accurate) with significance, but also expect more information. Thus it is unlikely that many sports fans will be satisfied with a simple news digest format.

Beyond the bare outline of what occurred lie questions which break down and elaborate what is known in summary form. How exactly did it happen?

Which were the pivotal moments? Who should be exalted/demonized? What was the atmosphere like? The written sports report text, therefore, unlike the more immediate audiovisual form (which, none the less, is also moulded by producers, commentators, camera-people, and so on), is reliant above all else on connotation, evocation, elaboration, embellishment and interpretation. As was noted in Chapter 3, the electronic media have had a very serious influence on the status of the print sports text. Whereas once the reader had to take the word of the writer concerning the veracity and accuracy of what was written or, at least, the journalist could be challenged only by the relatively small number of people present, it is now expected that the report will be produced at high speed and then must be reconciled with the perceptions of a potentially huge audience which has been exposed to the event in sparkling sound and vision. McGuane (1992), in the introduction to a collection of *The Best American Sports Writing 1992* (a work chosen more-or-less at random from the part of my personal library devoted to books picked up in sales – which may or not be significant for my argument), makes clear just how exacting can be the demand of the reader of the print sports text, especially when access has already been gained to the moving media sports text:

> The reader of sports writing is a strict, occasionally cruel individual. There has never been a modernist period in sports writing, much less a postmodernist spell. Anything beyond telling the sports fan what actually happened requires the heart of a lion, a jeweler's eye. Otherwise, one risks being tossed out by the reader himself [*sic*]. The sports page of any newspaper is truly an impact zone where writers and readers compare impressions of something they often have both seen. No one is taking anyone's word for anything. Opinions are truly earned. Fancy sports writing is some of the worst writing of any kind.
>
> (McGuane 1992: xv)

McGuane is reflecting a very traditional view of sports writing which, it seems, is being superseded in the television (and even the post-television) age. The contributions to *The Best American Sports Writing 1992* are by no means confined to the objective style of 'realist' sports reporting, despite his claim that 'what is shared, foremost, is the event' (McGuane 1992: xv). Among the twenty-five contributions (only three of which are by women, which indicates the existence of traditionalism of a different kind) drawn from a pool of 'more than 350 national, regional, and specialty publications' (according to the back cover) including the *Washington Post*, *Sports Illustrated*, *Los Angeles Times* and *Yale Review*, there are not only elaborate reports of sports events, but also biographical profiles of sportspeople like boxers Mohammed Ali (Gildea 1992) and Sonny Liston (Nack 1992), and more provocative essays like Barry's (1992) 'Why the NBA isn't as offensive as you think'. Some of this writing is, indeed, 'fancy', seeming to aspire, like the 'name' sports journalists mentioned in Chapter 4, to the status of literary art. It is not, then, altogether accidental that the first piece of writing mentioned in the foreword to *The Best American Sports Writing 1992* is a poem by David Rein called 'A Baseball Player Looks at a Poet', which likens the criticism of sports performances to that applied to 'the act of writing' (Stout 1992: ix).

In the absence of the capacity to give the direct sense of 'having been there' offered by television and still photography, the reader is presented with a meaning frame which, in the language of economics, 'adds value' (in this case cultural) to the primary text (the result) by building on its foundation as a secondary text which occupies the infinite discursive space of debate and analysis of what is known and what might be revealed. Print sports texts, then, are not limited to accounts and treatments, however extended, of formal sports events. Apart from what is generally available for scrutiny and open to description is what is open to speculation and revelation. The revelatory print sports text moves in the opposite direction to the 'evidentiary'; instead of taking what is (at least in technical terms) publicly on view and, via the mediation of the journalist, 'translating' it for consumption in the private sphere, it takes what is hidden and then, again after being mediated, makes this 'privileged' information public and so available for private digestion. A further form of print sports text is aware of the politics of sport, taking the sports world as a sphere with its own relatively autonomous politics or relating its internal politics to the wider domain of politics either directly (as in the state's involvement in sport) or indirectly (by seeing sport as a metaphor for politics). Sports writing moves beyond straight reportage and insider gossip in this instance and takes on a campaigning or petitioning role. The final mode of print sports text I shall examine here may be conscious of its own position; it is reflexively aware that it is part of what is being discussed. Here the lived experience of sport meets the aesthetics of sports writing. The text is about sport but it is also a thing in itself – sports writing becomes literature and sport becomes physical culture, even art.

These different modes of sports writing (there are no doubt other forms and hybrids) need to be illustrated for the purposes of recognition and analysis. Working from the short digest form of print text upwards it is apparent that even within very strict word limitations, the text is set in play in a manner that never allows it to be tied to the 'bare facts'. If we take two fairly random recent examples from very different newspapers – the much scorned British tabloid the *Sun* and the highly prestigious *New York Times* – it is clear that similar devices are used to attract the interest of readers and to provide an 'angle' for the interpretation of the sports event. In 'Super Goals', a 24-page Monday *Sun* soccer supplement (sponsored by Ford), there are sports stories of varying length and type: manager profiles, features on significant weekend games, a 'where are they now?' section, a 'lifestyle' segment (asking traditional questions of players like their favourite foods, although now with some less traditional answers than 'steak and chips'), and so on. For many lower division games, there are snippets (sometimes without by-lines) like the report of a match (with the punning headline, 'CHIP OFF THE OLD BECK') between Cambridge United and Chester:

> GRANT BREBNER showed David Beckham is not the only Manchester United man capable of hitting long-range stunners.
>
> On loan with Cambridge United, Brebner got two drives on target only to see Chester keeper Ronnie Sinclair produce two great saves.
>
> Brebner said: 'I couldn't believe he stopped them.'
>
> Stuart Rimmer scored Chester's first before Paul Wilson equalised, but Rob McDonald sealed City's win in the final seconds.
>
> (Sun Super Goals, 26 January 1998: 17)

This is a report of a game lasting a minimum of 90 minutes involving 28 players (including substitutes), various team staff and match officials, and a crowd (admittedly not of epic proportions) of 2473 – all in just 66 words. But in that small print media space, room is found for mentions of an elite team and of a footballer who, as is discussed in Chapter 6, was 'exclusively' interviewed and pictured in the same issue of the newspaper on the occasion of his engagement to a Spice Girl (so enabling a little word play on the '*Sun*-speak' word 'stunner'). Apart from this celebrity association, a theme of thwarted ambition is introduced and the opportunity taken for verbatim comment from the story's main subject, while the final paragraph is a condensed account of the identities of the goal scorers, the order of scoring, and the dramatic resolution to the narrative 'in the final seconds'. In other words, this 'cameo' print news story operates as precisely that – a narrativized account that introduces character, conflict and the passage of events. Yet much of the information contained in it (which teams and players were involved, who scored, and when) is provided only four pages away (p. 21) in the Soccer Results Service section. This duplication of the spare, summary data of match statistics operates as narrative supplementation which contextualizes and elaborates on the sports event. This is a technique that is used just as routinely in august broadsheet newspapers as in tabloids. The following report (supplied by the Associated Press news agency) with the headline 'Bourque Out, Pens Win' of a National Hockey League game in the *New York Times Sports Friday* Scoreboard section is one such example from the broadsheets:

> Jaromir Jagr got Ray Bourque kicked out of the game and then assisted on one of Kevin Hatcher's two goals as the Pittsburgh Penguins beat the host Boston Bruins, 4–2, last night.
>
> Ron Francis became the 11th player in National Hockey League history with 1,400 career points when he assisted on Stu Barnes's goal to make it 1–0 with 7.2 seconds left in the first period. The goal came during a five-minute power play after Bourque checked Jagr from behind, sending him head-first into the boards behind the net.
>
> Bourque also received a game misconduct for the first hit – the first ejection in his 19-year career. Without their top defenseman, the Bruins couldn't hold on, and Tom Barrasso stopped 29 shots to keep the Penguins unbeaten in their last six games (4–0–2).
>
> (*New York Times Sports Friday*, 30 January 1998: C6)

Allowing for some variations in the nature of the two reports – the latter is twice as long (133 words), covers a much more elite sports contest and does not involve direct interview – there are remarkable similarities in approach between two very different newspapers. The *New York Times'* sports section, like the *Sun*'s, contains more elaborate stories than those reproduced above, including several that are not reports of specific sports events. Yet both provide summary data of what occurred (in the case of the *New York Times* directly below the report) accompanied by brief stories which highlight the roles of the main 'actors', the key individual contests, the pivotal moments in the game, and so on – and all in three paragraphs.

Such news story formats can be seen as international print sports media genres (or sub-genres) which accommodate both the sporting preoccupation with statistics and results and the deep concern with the mythological status of sportspeople as heroes and villains, champions and 'battlers' engaged in an eternal contest for supremacy on the field of play. Some of these abiding concerns of sports culture are shared with other elements in the wider media in obeying, as Galtung and Ruge (1970, 1973) have influentially proposed, the dictates of particular 'news values' which signal the presence of 'newsworthiness' (see also Schudson 1991; Palmer 1998). Several of the dominant criteria for newsworthiness – the principles on which only a few of the billions of daily events are selected for media coverage, and, of that tiny proportion, only a minute number are given any sustained attention, with a few matters receiving saturation coverage – are met in the small sports stories I have presented.

This does not mean that the stories are self-evidently worthy of attention, but that they are constructed in a manner that ensures that they observe the usual 'rules' of news media text production and presentation. These include 'personification' (the reduction of large-scale, perhaps abstract events to the actions and motives of recognizable people); 'elite status' (the use of celebrity and, when it is not present, connections made to it); 'consonance' (the events and their treatment are easily fitted into readers' everyday frameworks and expectations when confronting a sports news story); and 'negativity' (the established media wisdom that, on balance, bad news is more newsworthy than good – in our examples frustration at having shots saved in a minor game instead of playing for Manchester United and marrying a Spice Girl; and getting 'kicked out of the game' for the first time in a '19-year career'). Thus, even the most seemingly brief, formulaic and modest print media sports text is surprisingly rich in reaching beyond itself to other games, people, issues and myths. All texts are **'inter-textual'** in that to be effective they must make connections with other phenomena and stories about them. Yet the degree of intertextuality is limited by the amount of media space allotted (it is hard to be too expansive in 66 words, although some sports writers achieve an economy of style to rival Ernest Hemingway) and the tasks that have to be performed in particular types of stories (giving the score, the time of scoring, the identity of the scorer, and so on). Once the print coverage of sport is severed from any requirement to report actual, public events to people who have often seen and experienced them in some way, then the opportunities to 'free' the text from its stricter obligations proliferate.

Revelations, exclusives and 'bungs'

The revelatory print sports text affords greater licence to its creator because it trades on information that is obscured from the public gaze. It relies on privileged access to the sports world which enables it to generate gossip, information that would be mundane if it did not concern sports stars, and unattributed statements and knowledge about the inner workings of sports organizations. A story in the sports pages of a British tabloid newspaper, the *Mirror*, demonstrates how revelatory sports texts work. Entitled 'I PLAY IN THE BIG LEAGUE ... GAZZA DISNEY! Says LES FERDINAND', its main hook involves a reported ' "goofy" exchange' between the English soccer internationals Les Ferdinand and Paul Gascoigne 'as the England players gathered for last summer's European Championship' (Wiechula 1997: 42). It enables readers to eavesdrop on a conversation between two prominent sportsmen in a place inaccessible to the sports public, although it transpires that the conversation has already been recounted in 'the latest issue of Total Sport magazine' and also involves an interview with one of the interlocutors. Thus the story is patched together with a combination of recycled information about a publicized private conversation and direct access to one of the personalities involved (the one who has 'spilled the beans'), made especially newsworthy by its impugning of the standards of Scottish football. The revelatory, controversial tone, reinforced by the tabloid trademark bolded type face and a 'doctored' photographic image of Gascoigne complete with Mickey Mouse ears, nose and whiskers, is central to the attention-grabbing pitch of the story:

> **Les Ferdinand has amazingly told Paul Gascoigne he's 'just playing in Eurodisney' in Scotland.**
>
> The Newcastle and England international responded tongue-in-cheek after Gazza took the 'mickey mouse' over the Magpies' title collapse last year.
>
> Strike ace Ferdy revealed that while Manchester United's double-winning England contingent hadn't rubbed it in before Euro'96, Gascoigne took the p*** a little bit.
>
> <u>Medals</u>
>
> 'He kept on saying, "Aaarrgh, you lot blew it, you lot s*** yourselves, look at my medals".
>
> 'But, as I said to him, "It's alright for you playing up in Eurodisney".
>
> 'I said I could go to Eurosdisney, score 40 a season and get myself a few medals too.'
>
> (Wiechula 1997: 42)

This snippet from the story contains key elements of the genre in its familiar use of dramatic words ('amazingly', 'revealed'); nicknames ('Gazza', 'Magpies', 'Ferdy'), compressed media sports speak ('Strike ace', 'title collapse'), puns ('took the "mickey mouse"'); and authentic seeming – although coyly presented – swearing ('took the p***', 's*** yourselves'). The critical comments about Scottish soccer (likely to appeal to the principally English readership), the inter-textual reference to Disney, and the feeling of being privy to elite football banter, all obey those orthodox principles of news value which promote controversy, celebrity and revelation. The format is varied: some stories carry the tag 'exclusive', relaying information that has been captured by or leaked to the sports journalist, like the following opening to a small item from the sports pages of the British tabloid newspaper *Daily Star*:

ALBION WANT ROYLE
EXCLUSIVE: By Ralph Ellis

Joe Royle is poised to bounce back into football as West Brom boss.

The 48-year-old has leapt to the top of the Hawthorns wanted list in the search to replace Ray Harford.

I understand Albion officials have made checks with Royle's old club Everton to make sure all his contractual ties at Goodison Park have been severed.

(Ellis 1997: 42)

What Ellis 'understands' is unattributed information that he has gained on the sports round – later in the story we are told that 'Royle has told friends he's ready to go back to work'. The sources are mysterious – unnamed friends and club officials – but the story has the authority of insider knowledge to which, by its nature, the readership cannot be privy. Another variation is the interview that generates the highly detailed information that only a dedicated sports fan would be interested in but which the sports journalist has access to through the interview process and by collating and analysing data. For example, an interview-based story of the Yankees' baseball catcher Jorge Posada in the *New York Times Sports Wednesday* is packed with statistical minutiae like 'He said he was leaner after reducing body fat percentage to 6 percent, stronger after adding 15 pounds of muscle and quicker after thousands of sprints and agility drills' and 'Posada (.250 average, 6 homers and 25 r.b.i. in 1997)' (Curry 1998: C2). Such stories, however, stop well short of critique, concentrating instead on the unashamed entertainment functions of the sports media. Others, however, take up the press's more serious, campaigning role, as in the back-page exposé by Harry Harris entitled '**TOP SECRET** – SOCCER BUNG DOSSIER', which appeared in the same edition of the *Mirror* as Gazza and Mickey Mouse.

This type of 'exclusive' affirms and celebrates the media's Fourth Estate role, applauding its own part by breaking a story that exposes the inner, illicit workings of sport. In this instance, *Mirror Sport* claimed to be instrumental in prompting a Football Association inquiry which found that, in contravention of its own rules, hidden payments ('bungs') were paid to various parties in the transfer of players between soccer clubs. Over three pages, the '**3 YEAR BUNG PROBE**' is described, an interview is conducted with the '**FA'S BUNG BUSTER**', readers are told '**HOW WE TRACKED DOWN THE CASH**' and the newspaper's role in the scandal is chronicled under the heading '**VICTORY FOR** *The Mirror*'. Here, the insider knowledge of the sports world (signified by the use of the slang term 'bung') is used in a crusading manner, seeking to 'clean up' sport on behalf of a public suffering from the corrupt use of sports funds. If the *Mirror*'s self-mythologizing seems somewhat excessive, it is perhaps because of over-compensation by sports journalists whose professional and ethical standards are routinely denigrated. Such exposés transform, if only temporarily, the toy department of the news media into something more adult and serious – like the furniture section. At its most ambitious it produces de-mythologizing journalistic books on sport like Simson and Jennings's (1992: x) *The Lords of the Rings: Power, Money and Drugs in the Modern Olympics*, although the authors are at pains to stress that 'We are not sports journalists. We are not part of a circuit where too many reporters have preferred to keep their gaze fixed on the sporting action and ignore the way sport has been destroyed by greed and ambition.' Here, again, the emphasis is on revelation and disclosure. As they state in the introduction:

> This book discloses what you are not allowed to see on TV and what the newspapers do not tell you about the Olympics and world sport. For the last four years we have sought to discover who controls sport, where the money goes and why what a decade ago was seen as a source of beauty and purity is now tacky, anti-democratic, drug ridden and auctioned off as a marketing tool of the world's multinational companies.
>
> (Simson and Jennings 1992: ix)

Critiques like these of the inner workings of major sporting phenomena like the Olympics are usually highly populist in nature. Simson and Jennings (1992: 271), for example, want to remove the 'perks' of the IOC so that 'we might bring sport back down from this wasteful Mount Olympus and into the hands of the ordinary people'. But while performing a no doubt valuable and traditional media role, they tend to confine themselves to problems in sport which need to be fixed according to highly idealized standards (sport as 'a source of beauty and purity'), to leave the relationships between the sporting and other worlds relatively unexplored, and to take a rather unreflexive and unself-critical view of the role of the sports writer. It is a more acute consciousness of sports writing as cultural production which is, in part, producing, reproducing and changing what it is writing about, and a propensity to extrapolate from the experience of sport to wider human experience, that distinguishes the final type of print media sports text that I'm interested in here.

Literary moments

These 'aesthetic' texts deploy the full toolbox of literary devices to invest sport with new meaning and sports writing with new status. They can be found in the newspapers and magazines that tolerate or promote literary style, in novels, poems and short stories that take the subject of sport as a point of departure for the exploration of 'existential' themes. It is this form of writing that is usually to be found in edited sports anthologies (like Coleman and Hornby 1996). Engel's (1986) *The Guardian Book of Cricket*, for example, selects articles published in that newspaper since 1826, describing the ebbs and flows in their quality in the same manner as literary critics characterise the fortunes of literary movements:

> And it seems to me that soon after 1968 *Guardian* cricket writing may have entered a second golden age. There was some vintage stuff in the paper in the early 70s: Arlott in his pomp, Cardus firmly back in the fold for his last years, wit and craftmanship from Eric Todd and Brian Chapman, the young Blofeld and the first brilliant flashes of Keating. After Cardus died, Ian Peebles, for all too short a period before his own death, contributed a series of quite scintillating essays. The paper had a good war during Packer, just as it did during D'Oliveira – and bodyline.
> (Engel 1986: 15)

This 'great tradition' of English cricket writers, it is pointed out above, had handled some of the major sporting controversies of their day that also touched on important social issues: the Packer 'war' with its assertion of the power of television and the commodification of leisure; the 1968 D'Oliveira affair and its bearing on international reactions to South African apartheid (both of which are discussed in Cashmore 1990); and the 'bodyline' cricket series of 1932–3, where 'Cricket's imperial significance, the fragility of Anglo-Australian relations, and the social ravages of the economic depression combined to give the on-field events a sharper edge than might normally have been the case' (Stoddart 1979: 142). In attending to questions that stylishly link sporting and social phenomena, Engel (1986: 15) notes that these sports writers are given 'an intellectual freedom that you sign away in exchange for the pay cheque just about everywhere else in the business'. If we compare the language and form of the following two passages with those quoted earlier from other types of sports writing, it can be seen – even allowing for the elapse of time, changes of style and the expansion of the sports pages to encompass multiple modes of writing – that this type of print media sports text does not sit easily with a highly formulaic and circumscribed approach:

News of sport is, in general, news only inside the small world of sport. When it bursts into the outer world by the weight of its own importance it invariably tends to appear in false perspectives. The vehemence of the protest against the omission of Basil D'Oliveira from the MCC team for South Africa has amazed the close little world of cricket; and its amazement has, in turn, amazed those who live outside it.

> (Arlott, 11 September 1968, in Engel 1986: 168)

Here in an understated and sophisticated way, John Arlott is addressing the relationship between the intersecting worlds of sport and politics without reliance on 'exclusives', 'bungs' – or anyone being told to 'p*** off'. But not all such writing need have such serious intent. As the following nostalgia-tinged opening paragraph of a Neville Cardus article reveals:

Kent v. Lancashire

The distance from Lord's to the Dover cricket field is farther than the crow flies or even than the train travels. Here we find a different habitation than cosmopolitan Lord's: here is Kent and real England. The Dover field is tucked away in hills along which Lear must have wandered on his way to the cliffs. There are green lawns and terraces rising high behind the little pavilion, and you can sit here and look down on the play and see the cricketers all tiny and compact. In such a green and pleasant land as this, with June sunlight everywhere, slow cricket by Lancashire has not seemed quite so wearisome as usually it does. The absence of animated play has gone well in tune with the day's midsummer ease and generous warmth. We have been free to watch the game idly and give ourselves up with lazy delight to the June charm and flavours of a field all gay with tents and waving colours; and we have been free to observe the delicious changes in the passing hour – the full flight of noon, the soft, silent fall to mellow.

> (Cardus, 1, 2 and 3 July 1926, in Engel 1986: 84)

This pastoral, anti-metropolitan view of 'real England', with its allusions to the Williams Shakespeare and Blake, provides a pre-television 'word picture' of a sports event, fleshing out the descriptions of play by communicating ambience. Its lush vocabulary and almost exaggeratedly laidback tone separates it not only from the more upbeat contemporary writing, but also from the plainer prose and more hectic description of much of the sports writing from its own period. This type of sports journalism has the 'feel' of fiction and, indeed, problematizes the distinction between the fictional and the factual which, from the viewpoint of postmodernity, looks somewhat less secure than it once did. As Foley (1992) has argued in reflecting on his ethnographic study of youth and sport, positivist social science and realist journalism both deploy 'narrative devices' borrowed from fiction in representing their subject, selecting disparate events and weaving them into a coherent story. Their naivety and lack of reflexiveness, he argues, leads them to believe that the texts they construct to describe reality do not also to a degree mediate and transform it (because a representation can never absolutely correspond or stand for 'the thing itself'). This postmodern recognition of the pivotal role of textual relations (in which both writer and reader 'produce' the text in a social context not entirely of their making), rather than the text standing alone as an 'omniscient' account of reality (produced by a God-like figure with total vision but without the usual human failings) is distinct from 'the naive realism of new [and, no doubt, old style] journalism and the conscious fictionalization of literature' (Foley 1992: 47).

Print media sports texts which 'play off' notions of the non-fictional and the fictional, the objective and the subjective, the universal and the particular, the real and the artificial, simultaneously take on the character of social science (at least its cultural studies 'wing') and the form of literature sometimes described as 'faction'. A work like Don DeLillo's (1997) novel *Underworld*, for example, takes a real historical but heavily mythologized event – 'the Shot Heard Round the World' in the dramatic 1951 New York baseball game between Giants and the Dodgers (an event which coincided with the Soviet Union's second-ever nuclear test) – and weaves into its narrative a close, journalistic description of the play and an aestheticized observation of the setting, using real people (like Frank Sinatra, Jackie Gleason and J. Edgar Hoover) and invented characters, which melds the fictional and the non-fictional in a manner that threatens to make the distinction redundant. Take, for example, the following passage:

> Not a good pitch to hit, up and in, but Thomson swings and tomahawks the ball and everybody, everybody watches. Except for Gleason who is bent over in his seat, hands locked behind his neck, a creamy strand of slime swinging from his lips.
> Russ says, 'There's a long drive.'
> His voice has a burst in it, a charge of expectation.
> He says, 'It's gonna be.'
> There's a pause all around him. Pafko racing toward the left-field corner.
> He says, 'I believe'.
>
> (DeLillo 1997: 42)

This small extract evokes the excitement of the spectator (who is a radio journalist) and could be an orthodox sports report were it not for some extraneous elements which signify it as literary (such as the description of Gleason's condition). This 'factional' piece, none the less, indicates how many sports reports do, indeed, resemble fiction in their selective assemblage of facts, invention of quotations, and setting of the scene.

I make this point in the closing part of this section in order to avoid too neat a taxonomy of the print media sports text. We have examined various examples of modes of sports writing located in different 'organs' of the media, and it is clear that rigid constraints of content, form, function and length exist which govern the production and reception of many such texts. The presentation of highly technical information, use of formal and informal language that only the initiated can easily decode, and a repetitive, easily recognizable style make the reception of sports stories into an habituated pairing of the familiar author (the sports 'hack') and the implied reader (the sports 'nut'). In Chapter 3 we noted criticisms by some sports journalists themselves of the rather limited scope of sports texts, and various attempts to break out of this writing strait-jacket. But there are also elements of sports culture that can be found in places which are not acknowledged as sporting – for example, in what might be called 'secondary media sports texts' where the language of sport as metaphors and similes permeates non-sporting discourses (including politics and business). Hence, when a political reporter describes a minister as having 'a safe pair of hands' or a business reporter represents an attempted company take-over as a 'race' involving 'hurdles', then elements of sports language and culture are being insinuated into other texts, with the meanings and mythologies of sport invoked. Some print media sports texts – 'amateur' or 'semi-professional' fanzines – are now in circulation which (as noted in Chapter 3) make few claims to technical excellence. Stapled publications like *What's the Story, England's Glory!* (dedicated to the English national soccer team), *Come in No. 7 Your Time is Up* (Bristol City) and *Up the Arse!* ('Arsenal's Premier Spurs-Bashin' Fanzine') have small circulations, poor production values and (to be kind) uneven writing quality, but they form a not insignificant part of a print media sports text 'scene' characterized by multiple modes and expanding spaces – and with spoken live sports commentary for satirical inspiration.

Conclusion: from script to still

In this chapter I have analysed elements of the sports spoken and written word in attempting to understand something of their formal properties and the types of textual relations they generate. Live broadcast sports commentary, for all the enthusiastic lampooning to which it is subjected, is none the less a potentially powerful instrument for the symbolic unification and deni-gration of nations at moments of high sporting excitement. Print media sports texts, however, have greater flexibility of form – from a 'straight' results service to shrill 'tabloid speak exclusives' to tranquil poetic reflection – if less immediacy of impact. Broadcast commentaries and print stories devote much time and space to description of events and places that cannot be or have not been seen, or are seeking to enhance what has been or is simultaneously being seen. The next chapter examines, then, the visual aspects of media sports texts, turning first to the memorable image frozen in time – the still sports photograph.

Further reading

Coleman, N. and Hornby, N. (eds) (1996) *The Picador Book of Sportswriting.* London: Picador.

Haynes, R. (1995) *The Football Imagination: The Rise of Football Fanzine Culture.* Aldershot: Arena.

Plimpton, G. (ed.) (1997) *The Best American Sports Writing 1997.* Boston, MA: Houghton Mifflin.

6

FRAMED AND MOUNTED: SPORT THROUGH THE PHOTOGRAPHIC EYE

In newspapers and magazines images of sportsmen in action proliferate, but we constantly see symbols of sportswomen's femininity (and particularly images that are saturated with sexuality), rather than pictures of female athleticism . . . For example, a female athlete posing with a male athlete where he has a dominant stance and she a submissive one; photographs of male athletes surrounded by female admirers; photographs of female athletes crying with elation or embraced by husbands or boyfriends; in situations and poses that have no apparent connection with sport; in domestic contexts, pregnant or with children; and photographs of female athletes highlighting hairdos, make-up, and clothing.

(Jennifer Hargreaves 1993b: 62)

Introduction: still sport

The epic moments of sport, for all the ready availability of prose, poetry and the moving image, are most memorably captured by still photography. The 'frozen in time' sight of the instant of a famous victory or gesture (such as the 'black power' protest at the 1968 Mexico Olympics – Given 1995) is perhaps the most potent of all media sports texts, able to convey historical weight, emotion, and a sense of the unique. Like all media texts, sports photographs work through a particular ordering of signs and codes which are part aesthetic, part ideological. They are not innocent records of events – through selection, composition and manipulation (cropping, 'burning', 'brushing' and so on in traditional photography and computer commands in digital photography), sports photographs offer up an account of how the world is (or how the photographer thinks it should be). The most important object in sports photography is sport's prime instrument – the human body. The bodies of sportspeople are closely observed through striking images which draw their power not merely from the drama of action, but also by connecting the imaged body to wider social issues and identities. Hence the body in sports photography is always invested with a wider representational role as sexualized, gendered, racialized, and so on.

It is necessary in pursuit of the task of 'unveiling' the media sports text to analyse the 'rules' of sports photography, the kinds of social relations and characteristics offered to the viewer as normal or abnormal, remarkable or banal. Given that the photograph is also usually accompanied by headlines and captions that help 'anchor and relay' the 'photographic message' (Barthes 1977), the text needs to be examined in its totality (it should not be assumed in advance, however, that image, headline, caption and text together form a consistent communicative 'fit'). As with the written sports media, still photographs can be classified according to genres and sub-genres, each with different qualities, motives and implied viewerships. 'Secondary' still photographic sports texts can also be found through the use of images and visual metaphors (such as in advertising) which set popular knowledge of and feeling for sport 'to work' for another purpose. It is the 'primary' still photographic sports text of the captured sporting moment, though, that first commands our attention – the image that transfixes the reader as they go to turn the page through its sheer visual and emotional power, its capacity to make us wish that we were there – and, even if we were, that we, too, had seen it that way.

Caught in the act

Still photography is, as observed above, a form of communication that relies on the notion of 'capture' – frozen for all time is a gesture, an expression, incident or landscape. It is conducted like any other communicative act through processes of selection; many 'snaps' may be taken but only one shot selected out of the multiple variations of angle, focus, composition and light. Even when the image is caught, it can be altered in many ways to improve its 'impact'. Fiske (1982: 109) notes, for example, how a newspaper's picture editor cropped and shaped an incident from a 'riot' in London's Notting Hill to enhance a concentrated sense of confrontation by cutting out 'extraneous' details of houses, trees and bystanders. He quotes the approving comments of the editor of another newspaper, Harold Evans, that the picture 'was the result of perceptive picture editing as well as of resourceful photography' (Fiske 1982: 110) by eradicating signs of domesticity, nature and 'normalcy'. Holland states that the truth claims of such 'photo-journalism' rely on the concepts of 'neutrality and objectivity' which, if handled in a dubious way, may provoke suspicions of viewer manipulation and textual fabrication and to the asking of questions like:

> Was that starving baby separated from its mother so that it looked even more forlorn in the picture? Was that man waving a stick really shouting at the policeman or simply telling the photographer to get out of the way? Was there help at hand for those desperate people just beyond the edge of the frame?
>
> (Holland 1998: 418)

This is not to argue that there is no correspondence between what the camera caught and what was happening at that moment, but merely that many techniques are available to photographers that are ethically dubious and, whatever the motives of the photographer, a framed, two-dimensional image can never be 'the thing itself'. However realistic a photograph might be in style and effective in delivering a feeling of 'having been there', then, it is, like all other media texts, a manufactured representation of the 'real'. Furthermore, as Becker argues, the picture itself is only one component of the text:

> Photographs attain meaning only in relation to the settings in which they are encountered. These settings include . . . the historically constructed discourses in which specific topics and styles of photography are linked to particular tasks or patterns of practice (Sekula 1984: 3–5). The photograph's setting also includes the concrete, specific place it appears and how it is presented. In the newspaper, photographs have no meaning independent of their relationship to the words, graphic elements and other factors in the display which surround and penetrate them.
>
> (Becker 1992: 144)

In 'taking in' a photograph, then, we are also exposed to the caption, headline, the positioning of the item in relation to other items, the reputation of the publication and, importantly, we respond to the subjects with which they deal according to our own 'reading positions' as male or female, black or white, young or old, working class or bourgeois, and so on. In this way, looking at a photograph can be regarded as one social construction coming into contact with another in a perpetual cycle of producing, reading and circulating meaning. It is necessary to make these brief, preliminary comments because the 'action' sports photograph works through seeking to screen out all these reminders of the conditions of its production. The viewer impact sought is to instil a feeling that the sports event can be directly accessed through the photograph by its presentation of a pivotal moment in determining the result (who won and why) or in conveying the atmosphere of the event (what it felt like to be there). The latter type of sports photograph tends to be more self-consciously aesthetic, sometimes making a claim to be taken more seriously as an art object. But it is the action shot that is the staple of sports photography, reinforcing and conferring status on the elite sporting body by showing it doing the extraordinary things that so many people admire and envy.

If the action sports photograph is the premium sports image, and a considerable degree of cultural power attaches to being conspicuous in the sports media, then we might ask who gets to be shown 'doing the business'. It is here that ideology, power and media representation connect; issues of visibility and invisibility, and images of domination and subordination are central to the reading of the media sports text. There is a good deal of

Frozen in time: action appeal and the judgement of history
Picture by Darren Pateman, courtesy of the *Newcastle Herald*

accumulated empirical research on sports photography that has found that it is heavily gender biased in that we see sportsmen much more than sports-women, and that they are often shown doing different things in a manner that confers greater prestige on male than on female athletes. Kane and Greendorfer (1994), in surveying research on gender and sports photography, discover a pattern of, first, 'underrepresentation and symbolic annihilation', and second, of a type of coverage they call 'caricatured femininity'. In terms of the former they find that 'The overwhelming evidence from this literature is that women continue to be severely underrepresented in the highly prestigious world of sport' (Kane and Greendorfer 1994: 36). In coming to this conclusion, they cite a study of the covers of *Sports Illustrated* magazine between 1954 and 1978 in which sportswomen received only 5 per cent of coverage (Boutilier and SanGiovanni 1983) and of photographs in *Young Athlete* magazine between 1975 and 1982, less than 33 per cent of which included female athletes (Rintala and Birrell 1984). If these studies are thought to be in the 'bad old days', they point out that 'Several of the most recent studies [such as Lumpkin and Williams 1991 and Duncan *et al.* 1991] have replicated findings from earlier research' (Kane and Greendorfer 1994: 35). Lest, again, it is objected that these studies are of the USA, similar findings have emerged from studies in countries like Australia (Brown 1996) and Britain (Jennifer Hargreaves 1994).

But the quantity of images is only one aspect of power in the sports media; there is also the second issue raised by Kane and Greendorfer of their quality, concluding that 'the literature suggests that even when sportswomen are depicted in the media, they are consistently trivialized and marginalized through the type of coverage they receive' (Kane and Greendorfer 1994: 36). In supporting this conclusion, they cite such studies as the analysis of the 1979 *Sports Illustrated* Silver Anniversary issue, which found that 60 per cent of all photographs of sportswomen showed them in 'passive, nonathletic roles' compared with only 44 per cent of all photographs of sportsmen (Boutilier and SanGiovanni 1983). If this finding appears to be somewhat surprisingly close in the proportions of males and females shown to be 'inactive' in sports photographs, there are many other quantitative and qualitative studies that produce a starker contrast in the 'gendering' of sports photography. Stoddart (1994a: 5), for example, found that quantity was not the main problem, in that 'Photographs of sportswomen are plentiful in newspaper sporting sections. It is noticeable, however, that the representations are not necessarily about sport and frequently show women as passive rather than active participants.' Duncan (1990), in an analysis of 186 photographs from the 1984 and 1988 Olympic Games, notes the frequently close similarity of images of women in sport and in soft pornography.

There is also a dependent relational element in many images of sports-women which is much weaker for men, with an emphasis on male coaches as authority figures, emotional attachments to partners, and, if applicable, children (whereupon the mother is frequently turned into a 'supermum' – McKay 1992). In other words, the 'pure' power of the action sports photograph can be diffused by distracting attention from the pristine sporting moment and stressing other characteristics of the female photographic sports subject, such as their parental role, how they look after their hair or manage to perform in sport at the highest level while staying 'feminine' and 'sexy'. On this last point, however, it can be suggested that there is nothing inherently wrong with a link between sport and sex. There is something improbable about paying massive attention to the sporting body as an athletic instrument but then rigorously suppressing any notion that it might be or do something else. The image of the sporting body may, then, also be an erotic or aesthetic image, as much concerned with the athletic body as 'sex machine' as the efficient engine of sports accomplishment. We might first canvass possible responses to the sports text in which the photographic subject challenges the viewer with Rod Stewart's pop refrain, 'Do Ya [perhaps, Dare Ya] Think I'm Sexy?'

Sports bodies: hot and hard

In the section above I introduced the action sports photograph in news-papers, and the detected tendency for them to carry hidden ideologies of gendered power through the disproportionate quantity and quality of images of active, ruggedly individual men and passive, dependent women. Action sports photography concentrates on the 'motivated' body: it is doing something to itself and to other bodies. Acres of print are devoted every day to tracking the sports body in motion as it is invested with multiple meanings – the triumphant body, the dejected body, the endangered body, and so on. There is another area of photography which focuses on the body that has a less respectable profile than sports photography. It is called pornography, and is dedicated to the sexual excitation of the viewer. It might be suggested, taking the earlier point further, that there are many parallels between sports photography and pornography, and it is fruitful to pursue questions of the extent to which many sports photographs adopt a direct or indirect mode of sexual address akin to the pornographic, and the ways in which the active/passive dichotomy is played out in both sport and photography. By following this line of argument, I shall not attempt an analytical separation of the erotic and the pornographic. In *The Erotic in Sports*, Guttmann

(1996: 179) concludes that 'the best way out of the definitional *cul de sac* seems to be the frank acceptance of subjectivity' – that is, that one person's 'smut' is another's 'thing of beauty', and vice versa. While it is clearly difficult to provide absolute criteria, I think it is still worth probing the question of the power of both photographic subjects and viewers in the sphere of sexuality. That sport and sexuality have a long association is indisputable, as Guttmann points out in the opening passage of his book on the erotic aspects of sport:

> When Greek men and boys journeyed to Olympia to compete in the great panhellenic festival that honored Zeus, when Greek girls ran races at the same site for an olive branch and a portion of sacrificial cow, everyone seems to have understood that physically trained bodies, observed in motion or at rest, can be sexually attractive.
>
> (Guttmann 1996: 1)

Dutton (1995), similarly, notes the erotic dimensions of ancient artistic representations of the sporting body in sculpture and painting. So, if sport and sex have been constant companions for millennia, the opportunity afforded by the modern mass media (which, according to Cohen and Taylor (1976: 106) included the emergence of an industry devoted to the 'hobby' of masturbation) to develop this relationship must involve some linkage between the photographed sporting and sexualized bodies. Both are fixated on the body, minutely examining its performative possibilities and special qualities. Both are concerned with arousal – either of the photographic subject straining to perform at their best or of the viewer in deriving pleasurable excitement from the image before them.

Pornographic images tend to take two forms. In 'hard' photography, there is plenty of 'action' – a person or persons is doing something to another person or persons. It might be suggested that there is a precise equivalent in sports photography of what is called in hard pornography (both moving and still) the 'money' or 'cum' shot (L. Williams 1989) – the visible male ejaculation that is the culmination of male-oriented pornography which parallels the 'ecstatic' captured moment when a winning goal is scored or decisive play made (Miller 1990). Sometimes (as in the case of most forms of male–female intercourse) the active/aggressive male(s) is represented as exerting power over the passive/responsive female(s), while at other times (such as in the case of fellatio) it is the passive/responsive male who seems to be exerting power over the active/compliant female. In the case of 'hyper' close-ups in 'hard' pornography (where the viewer 'possesses' the very pores of the bodily object viewed) and in more muted form in 'soft' pornography, the power relationship is between the passive recipient of the gaze and the

A win-win-win situation: a temporary triumph of identities of nation, gender and race
Associated Press AP

'controlling' gazer (usually female and male respectively in the case of heterosexual imagery). These issues of power in and of the photographic image apply both in pornographic and sports images. Who is being shown as active and in control, and who is just being 'operated on'? Who is projecting a strong image to the viewer, and who is merely allowing themselves to be ogled?

The main feminist critique of both pornography and sports photography is that women are usually positioned as subordinate in all such tableaux. The image of women in the media is already a heavily sexualized one (van Zoonen 1991), meaning that whatever activity a woman is shown to be engaged in is likely to present her as sexual being first and foremost. The sexuality and appearance of sportswomen of the 1980s and 1990s like the late Florence Griffith-Joyner, Katarina Witt, Gabriela Sabatini and Mary Pearce have often obscured their elite sporting status (C.L. Williams *et al.* 1986; Heaven and Rowe 1990). Often, sportswomen are seen to be performing gender roles rather than sporting ones, and sometimes, as in the case of 'Flo-Jo' (whose early death in September 1998 from a heart attack at the age of 38 was allegedly caused by taking large quantities of the performance-enhancing drugs whose masculinizing, physical effects might have been partially masked by her 'hyper-feminine' appearance), are happy to capitalize on the commercial advantages that follow a highly sexualized profile. Inevitable controversies flow from trying to draw a line between what is seen as the 'legitimate' expression of sexuality in sport and what is judged to be an ultimately repressive and short-sighted exploitation of it which colludes with those patriarchal forces that seek to reduce women to their subordinated sexuality. Such debates are especially intense when sportswomen explicitly play the role of soft pornographic subject on the covers of sports magazines, in calendars, posters and publicity shots.

Probably the best known example of the overt photographic sexualization of the sporting female body (perhaps more accurately described as the sexualized presentation of the female body in a sports-licensed context) has been the annual *Sports Illustrated* swimsuit issue. The use of scantily clad 'proto-sporting' women (that is, models wearing something skimpy that is vaguely associated with sport or leisure) on the cover is a standard promotional strategy of sports magazines like the Australian edition of *Inside Sport*. A representative example (April 1997) is of a model in a leather bikini holding a crossbow, while inside she is featured in various poses and with equipment associated with the pursuits of swimming, diving, archery, roller hockey, baseball, soccer, cycling, skateboarding, water skiing and boxing. In none of these sporting activities is a brief black-and-white two-piece swimsuit the usual apparel. In the same issue there is a '16-page bonus' of the best

Australian sports photography, in which it is claimed that 'Australia isn't only producing world-class athletes. We're turning out the world's best sports photographers too. Here's proof' (p. 40). It is instructive to do more than glance at these images, and also at the photographs published in the previous year in the *Carlton and United Breweries Best Australian Sports Writing and Photography 1996*. The analysis is a little inexact in that only the principal subjects have been counted in those photographs where there are large numbers of (mostly out of focus) spectators and some other media personnel. The 'findings' of this quick content analysis (which can be conducted easily by any viewer of sports photography with, I suggest, similar results in most cases) are presented in Table 1.

Table 1 Analysis of two examples of 'best' Australian sports photography

	Photos	Action no. (%)	Non-action no. (%)	Main subjects no. (%)		Photographers no. (%)	
				Male	Female	Male	Female
Inside Sport	21	20 (95)	1 (5)	37 (100)	0 (0)	11 (100)	0 (0)
Carlton 1996	17	13 (76)	4 (24)	23 (77)	7 (23)	13 (93)	1 (7)

These data, the analysis of which makes no claim to sophisticated statistical representativeness, are instructive in highlighting the gendered nature of the sports photographic text. In the case of the *Inside Sport* feature, not a single sportswoman appears, while almost every shot features action of a mostly dramatic, often violent kind. Most of the images, when examined further, are close-ups or medium close-ups, allowing the viewer to see the strained expressions of the sporting combatant. None of the pictured sports – basketball, athletics, sea and wind-surfing, sailboarding, swimming, cycling, cricket and the football codes – features a performer in a leather bikini. In the rest of the magazine there is negligible coverage of women's sport, thereby creating a deep split between 'serious' sports photographs involving professional sportsmen and 'decorative' sports photographs involving models pretending to be professional sportswomen. Hence, sports magazines like *Inside Sport* (which in this case is part of a publisher's roster that includes 'girlie' magazines) take their place alongside young male-oriented media organs (the term is used advisedly) like *Loaded* and *Ralph* in sedulously resisting what they see as the unwarranted incursions of feminism. As Stoddart (1994a: 8) points out, *Inside Sport*'s 'editors openly admit to using sexual images to sell copy to male readers', by which, of course, he means only 'straight' male readers (and possibly gay women). Short of successfully persuading such publications to change their target marketing strategy to include women and gay men, the only immediate alternative is to follow the sometimes troubled path of women-oriented sports magazines in the USA (Creedon 1994b).

In the case of the *Carlton and United Breweries Best Australian Sports Writing and Photography 1996*, there is a little more variation in what is taken to be a good sports photograph. There are more non-action shots and a small number of women featured but, while there is less reliance on close-ups, it is also the case that all but one of the women (the Australian runner Cathy Freeman, with captioned name mis-spelt 'Kathy') who appear are filmed at long distance. Not coincidental, perhaps, given the paucity of images of women, is the absence of any expressive sexuality and eroticism in the photographs. Little in the way of sexual projection occurs in the action shots, as viewers are encouraged to concentrate on what is being done rather than on how appealing the athlete might look in doing it (although allowance should be made for the full and unpredictable repertoire of human desire which might, for example, extend to finding bloodied faces and painful expressions sexually arousing). There is nothing altogether sur-prising about this observation given the active repression of homosexual desire in male sport (Pronger 1990; Messner 1992). Thus, the 'alibi' for men gazing on other men in sports photographic texts is admiration of their sporting achievements rather than of their musculature (Miller 1998c). Yet there are two images of sportsmen in the *Carlton and United Breweries Best Australian Sports Writing and Photography 1996* collection that do have a sexual quality. In each the sportsman is not active but is receiving and/or returning the gaze. One shot of the Olympic swimmer Kieren Perkins float-ing in a pool has a faintly voyeuristic quality (he cannot see the camera), while another posed shot of the face of 'pin-up' rugby league player Andrew Ettingshausen with shower water pouring down it can be read as a 'smoul-dering' return of the voyeuristic gaze (a photograph of Cathy Freeman, in a similar style and by the same photographic team, has less water, is in extreme close-up, and has a more androgynous quality).

These latter images introduce an important question and development. We may wonder what happens to the image of the sportsman when pos-itioned as the recipient of the gaze in a similar fashion to that of the tra-ditional objectification of the female body. Of course, male bodies have long been gazed at as objects of desire (for both homosexual men and hetero-sexual women) with varying licence to do so (ranging from 'secretive' view-ing of men's sports magazines by gay men (see Miller 1998c) to the open if often sanitized appreciation of male bodies in pop culture). But until recently in sport, there has been a reluctance to objectify sexually the male sports body; this was left to the female sports body, which (as noted above) has tended to be regarded as only tangentially sporting. The gradual freeing up of fixed socio-sexual identities, the influence of feminism and the increasingly overt sexualization of culture and commercialization of sexuality have resulted in a strengthening trend to sexualize openly the male sporting body. Thus, just as some female athletes have allowed themselves to be represented in traditional soft core poses in calendars like that devoted in Australia in the mid-1990s to the Golden Girls of Athletics, so the Men of (Rugby) League Calendar (Rowe 1997c) offered up images of the male sporting body to the sexualizing gaze (Lynch 1993). It even became possible for sportsmen like Andrew Ettingshausen, as we shall discuss below, to feel 'violated' by intrusive cameras in a manner not dissimilar to that of many celebrity women.

Politics and portraits

The increasing eroticization (making sexy) and aestheticization (making beautiful) of the male athletic body does potentially change the gendered dynamics of cultural power that I have analysed in this chapter. For example, *Black + White Magazine*'s (1996) 'The Atlanta Dream Issue' consists of 170 nude portraits of Australian Olympians bound for Atlanta in a non-sexually segregated media context (that is, containing still photographic images of both male and female athletic bodies). Can it be proposed that this is an instance of significant change in the differential imaging of sportsmen and sportswomen? It is useful to examine this case of bringing sports photography out of the sports pages through the 'art' publication to the popular magazine in some detail. A selection of the images was carried in the Australian edition of the popular 'gossip' magazine *Who Weekly* (June 1996) under the front-page banner 'TOP ATHLETES BARE ALL IN A CONTROVERSIAL ALBUM' (the magazine helped to generate part of this controversy by being banned from some supermarket chains). Of the four images presented on page 1, two were of men and two of women, only one of which was an action shot (a male sprinter). Of the three non-action shots, the men's were of torso and head, but the women's involved the whole body (that is, breasts, thighs and so on). In the contents page, nude images of a female athlete (one in silhouette) were used, alongside an inset of four (clothed) women from Leni Riefenstahl's famous film of the 1936 'Nazi Olympics', *Olympia*. Riefenstahl's work is discussed in a short accompanying article entitled 'The Athletic Aesthetic', presumably to demonstrate that naked athletes have been filmed for many decades (in the case of this story, the only nude still images shown are of four distant men). Yet, of the twelve naked athletes selected for the 'photospread', eight are women. The only 'full frontal' shots (although by no means a majority of total images) are of women, with men being carefully posed or cropped, or using the traditional recourse to a strategically placed object interposed between viewer and penis – here a pair of oars in one shot and a large fish in another. Most athletes (male and female) are not shown in motion (although there is a spectacular shot of a female beach volleyballer hanging from a rope above a waterfall), but all the males are standing – only women are shown in reclining positions, with one of a woman water polo player closely resembling 'soft-core style'. Only one image – of two female divers – features any person-to-person contact, in this case with one on top of the other in a manner that connotes lesbian imagery (another soft and hardcore pornographic staple).

In reading, then, this selection for popular consumption of nude images taken from a self-consciously artistic publication, it can be suggested that there are persistent differences (probably largely unconscious) in representation of sportsmen and sportswomen which carry over even into areas of apparently equal treatment. The text that surrounds the *Black + White/Who Weekly* photospread stressed sympathetically that 'Posing nude is not something these athletes do every day – training relentlessly for the Atlanta Olympics in July is more their speed. And with an impressive list of victories behind them, these champions are ready to take on all their equally pumped peers' (p. 30). Yet, while seeming to try to 'do the right thing' in terms of gender equality, more attention is paid to the misgivings of female athletes about posing naked, informing the reader that 'Swimmer Samantha Riley took her mother and boyfriend, Norwegian skater Johan Koss, along for support' and quoting the photographer that 'Sam was nervous . . . I'd do a polaroid and she'd have a look at it and then show her mum and decide if it was OK or not' (p. 20). Even the small inset photographs showing the athletes 'at work' portrayed all the men in active poses but several static shots of women. Thus, as was noted above, media sports texts can be seen to be 'bearers' of social ideologies (in this case of gender) which project meanings that simultaneously draw on already dominant ways of seeing the world (such as, men 'do' and women 'are') and contribute substantially to the maintenance of those perspectives (it always was and has to be that way), which in turn powerfully condition the ways in which the social world operates (men lead and women follow).

This broad, schematic theory of social and cultural reproduction is, however, open to various criticisms on grounds of functionalism, its somewhat mechanical view of how ideologies work within texts, its neglect of the power of the reader, and its inability to deal with contestation, multiple meanings and ambiguities. Were this ideological system to work cleanly and comprehensively, no new ideas and practices could emerge, and the social world would be a much less kaleidoscopic and complex place. The role of media analysts, in particular, would be reduced to reading texts and connecting them to prevailing social perspectives and practices. This is an important task which has continued to provide much of the impetus for a critical approach to the study of society and culture, but it is only part of a much wider 'project' of understanding how culture in multifarious forms is produced under widely different circumstances with a diverse range of outcomes which include both reproduction and transformation. It is important, then, to be aware that all texts have many potential and conflicting meanings according to context and readership, and 'decoding' them may offer up subversive or surprising significatory possibilities. But it would be naive indeed to argue that 'meaning making' is a vast, open game in which every sign has the same chance as every other sign to be taken up and used as definitive of 'how it is'. Sports photographs are no different from any other kind of text in that they are neither the innocent nor the 'natural' products of value-free sport and sports culture. As Duncan (1994) argues in her analysis, using Foucault's (1979) concept of the 'panopticon' (self-monitoring and self-discipline imposed by feeling constantly under surveillance), of women's body images in the body and fitness magazine *Shape*:

> Most poststructuralist media theorists . . . contend that texts carry multiple meanings and that those meanings are constructed by both the texts and the readers or viewers themselves. Although there are 'preferred' meanings invited by texts, all texts contain the possibility of their own subversion, and some readers may find pleasure in resisting those preferred readings. Thus there may be some *Shape* readers who resist the panoptic gaze, or who focus on the strength and power of the body ideal presented therein rather than on the beauty/slenderness motive. My goal, then, is not to argue that every reader uncritically accepts the body beautiful ideology, nor is it to argue that every *Shape* article is potentially disempowering, but I do wish to demonstrate that there are compelling discursive mechanisms that encourage the panoptic gaze and yet conceal its source and motives from 'view'.
>
> (Duncan 1994: 52–3)

Duncan is arguing that it is possible to see the media texts which forge a linkage between women's health, beauty and slenderness and emphasize personal responsibility for achieving it (and culpability for not) as empowering, and it is also possible to reject these demands for women constantly to assess their self-worth in this way. But the merest acquaintance with how many women are on diets, have had eating disorders and have a negative body image (Heaven and Rowe 1990) reveals just how compelling such gender discourses can be and, even for the most critically self-reflexive woman, to escape. Critcher (1993: 234), in arguing that 'textual analysis alone can never deliver anything adequate about audience response', has highlighted the dangers of establishing a theoretical agenda concerning the gendered sports image and then reading all media texts off it as inevitably consistent and straightforwardly understood by all readers irrespective of their social identity. Yet there is equivalent peril in celebrating a 'semiotic democracy' in which cultural power is equally distributed among everyone, so that the political catchcry of 'one person, one vote' is translated into 'one person, as many meanings as they like'. The mutual constraints of the power of the text, the autonomy of the reader and the influence of the social have to be carefully weighed, often with disappointingly inconclusive findings if the aim is to explain all meaning generation according to a single axial principle.

Before this discussion becomes overly abstract, we should return to the image of the sexualized male sports body. We have noted that many feminists have complained about an undue emphasis in the sports media on the sexual and physical appearance of sportswomen. What, then, are the implications of looking at sportsmen in this way? Is this a move towards a kind of equality – every athlete, male or female, gets ogled because for professional sportsworkers this experience just 'goes with the territory'? Is it likely to unite female and male athletes in resistance to being treated like strippers and 'page 3 girls', so that now men know what it is like to be regarded as a sex object, something will be done? Or does the more general power differential between men and women mean that sportsmen find being sexually objectified less oppressive; once they have posed for the calendars and pin-up shots men can still be taken seriously and not identified exclusively with the way they look, but women remain (as Duncan 1994 pointed out above) subject to the 'panoptic' gaze? These issues are complicated further when we take into account the rather heterosexist assumptions of most critical analysts. To what degree do these equations change when we are addressing the homosexual or bisexual gaze? What if the viewer feels homosexual desire (gay or lesbian) for the photographic sports object or, more disruptively, if that object of desire has 'gone public' about their own homosexuality? Thus it can be seen that changes in the way that athletes are portrayed in sports photography and in the relationships between viewer and photographic object/subject (a distinction made on the basis of how much room the person being photographed has to project something of themselves rather than be the 'plaything' of the viewer) have relevance for the whole field of gender relations, sexuality and, as will be discussed later, racial and ethnic identities.

Imaging sporting masculinity

Looking at and imaging the male body is an integral aspect of the culture surrounding post-war popular music. Every year, new pop icons (usually white), from the Bay City Rollers to Hanson, from Bros and Take That to New Kids on the Block and the Backstreet Boys, emerge to take the mantle (usually worn for only a short time) of *the* pop sensation at the centre of current adolescent female desire. More 'mature' audiences are also catered for in various genres through (again, usually white) male figures like Jon Bon Jovi, Chris Isaak and Mick Jagger. So, while we are used to gazing at images of male and female pop stars (such as Madonna and Janet Jackson) and female sports stars in an overtly sexualized manner, this explicit function of the image of the sportsman has been slow to emerge (Rowe 1995). The reasons for this tardiness in exploiting an obvious commercial opportunity have (as noted earlier) often been stated: sport is a traditional domain where men can look at and even touch or embrace other men without homophobic stigmatization. Furthermore, the archetypal 'expert', straight male sports fan 'officially' views the male sports body in technical rather than aesthetic or erotic terms; the body is an instrument of supreme sporting performance rather than an invitation to libidinal pleasure. As we have seen, in order to ward off the vulnerable passivity of the female sex object uncomplainingly and undemandingly receiving the gaze ('take me, I'm yours'), the male image is (hyper)active. He is moving not still, standing not reclining, confronting rather than seducing the camera's eye. In potentially opening themselves up to the 'feminization' of their body image by being portrayed in a sexualized manner, sportsmen seek to counter such a process by doing something – anything – rather than just receive the gaze.

But what happens if, like Andrew Ettingshausen, the male sports photographic subject is caught unawares? Miller (1998a) examines in some detail the notorious defamation case in which Ettingshausen successfully sued *HQ* magazine in 1993 for publishing without permission a picture of him naked in the shower. While he had allowed himself to be featured in other photospreads for women's magazines which clearly capitalized on his sex appeal (readers of the Australian edition of *Cleo* magazine had once voted him 'Sexiest Man Alive'), Ettingshausen (whose popular nickname is ET) argued that the implication that he had connived in the photographic display of his penis to a wide audience showed him in a questionable light and threatened to

Sportsmen licensed to cuddle other men – and to advertise television
Picture by Darren Pateman, courtesy of the *Newcastle Herald*

undermine his reputation as a clean-living family man and his employment as a school development officer for the sport of rugby league. This case highlights three of the key areas of sensitivity that we have seen apply in the area of photographing the male sports body: preventing a view of the penis (an image much less policed in the case of women's genitalia); avoiding any suggestion of passivity or helplessness (as was felt to be precipitated by the 'unguarded' shot); and concentrating on its heterosexual rather than homosexual appeal. Despite the relative novelty of male sports stars adopting an explicit mode of sexual address, however, the case of ET was confined to the 'specular' availability of a heterosexual man to similarly inclined women.

Yet, the very necessity of carrying out such 'hard ideological work' to exclude unacceptable images and meanings of the male sports body confirms its semiotic vulnerability. As Miller (1998a: 107) argues, 'The male pinup draws out insecurity, instability, and contradictions in masculinity. Which kind of gaze is expected to consume it? Contrary to conventional masculine icons, the pinup pacifies the body.' Whereas once the imaging (in television as well as in still photography) of the male sports body was assumed to be only of technical interest to other, assumed heterosexual men, the appeal has been widened to incorporate 'single women and gays, because they have high discretionary income' (Miller 1998a: 107), not to mention the married women who control most household expenditure and constitute a large and, until the mid-1980s, largely neglected audience sector for media sport. The nature of this gaze on the male sports body can be further complicated by the 'seeping' of information into the frame from outside the world of sport. Take, for example, the cover of Guttmann's (1996) *The Erotic in Sports*, which is a reproduction of a striking *Sports Illustrated* photograph of the finely tuned body of US Olympic diver Greg Louganis entering the water in a perfect, aesthetically appealing and, for many, no doubt erotically pleasing dive. The viewer's reading of the photograph is, however, almost certainly changed by being in possession of the information that after retirement Louganis declared his homosexuality and HIV-positive status (a condition which he admitted to having when he bled from a head wound into the Olympic pool). In other words, the still sports photographic image is never entirely 'still'; it is always subject to revision and reformulation according to prevailing social ideologies and the circulation of cultural 'data'.

Similarly disruptive to the 'orderly' containment of images of traditional sports masculinity in the media are cases like that of another rugby league player, Ian Roberts, where the pictured Adonis came out as gay during his playing career after appearing nude in a gay magazine. The appearance of Ian Roberts in the inaugural issue of *Blue Magazine* in 1994 indicates the degree to which, once 'let off the leash', the photographic representation of prominent sportsmen can travel to some previously unexplored spaces. Roberts, a player famed for his formidable physique and toughness (Rowe 1998), had allowed his body to be used as a 'sexual ornament' before, most notably in the heterosexually targeted 'Men of League Calendar' that was part of the modernization and repositioning of the 'working man's sport' in the early 1990s. This marketing campaign included a video of African American soul singer Tina Turner performing 'Simply the Best' and casting admiring glances at the footballers in a manner calculated to induce other heterosexual women to see them in a new, sexualized light (Lynch 1993). Roberts also figured prominently in swimwear in the 'Total Fitness Body' Campaign, his attractiveness to women signalled by his poolside female 'companion' – except that she was his sister, not his implied lover. Roberts, who was in his thirtieth year before he 'came out', had previously hidden his homosexuality from view by pretending to the press that he had a 'girl'.

Considerable consternation was caused for conventional masculine sports culture by a declaration of homosexuality by a rugby league footballer who had played for Australia in the most physically demanding position in the game (prop) and whose muscular body had been much photographed, discussed and admired. His biography, *Ian Roberts: Finding Out* (Freeman 1997), authored by the photographer who had persuaded him to pose for *Blue* magazine, contains a foreword which reproduces congratulatory and denunciatory letters for 'coming out' and copious text on the tribulations of his life. It also contains many photographs of Roberts as child and adolescent, in conventional (and often spectacular) sports action and standard team photos, in an injured state (including being carried on a stretcher and another shot with blood streaming down his face), doing charity work with children who are ill, attending dance parties and other social gatherings in Sydney's 'gay precinct', engaging in the usual 'horseplay' with teammates, and in various publicity, calendar and magazine shots. It is difficult, therefore, to 'pin down' the images of the sportsman to what Connell (1987) calls the 'hegemonically masculine' identity of heterosexuality and aggression (Miller 1998c). It is not difficult to imagine many readers scrutinizing images of Roberts, looking for the 'tell tale signs' of the hidden 'truth' of his sexual identity (Davis 1995).

Roberts' lack of 'camp' challenges stereotypes of the sporting male differently to the presentation of self by African American basketballer Dennis Rodman, whose self-consciously outrageous, 'gender bending' behaviour, which includes 'getting married' in a bridal gown, wearing leather skirts, garish makeup and multi-coloured hair, and the prominent display of body piercing. Like Roberts, Rodman is renowned for his toughness (in the demanding role of 'rebounder'), but his flamboyance and black identity provide new dimensions to his image of a 'different' kind of sportsman. Rodman's image is also a sexualized one, but it is self-consciously 'queer' – that is, it refuses an easy, fixed categorization as 'straight' or 'gay' (see Seidman 1996). Both of his books in the late 1990s, the 'New York Times Number One Bestseller' *Bad As I Wanna Be* (Rodman with Keown 1996) – parodied, it should be noted, in the naked appearance of his ex-wife Anicka Rodman (with Scott 1997) on the cover of her own 'right of reply' book, *Worse than He Says He Is: White Girls Don't Bounce* – and the rather less successful *Walk on the Wild Side* (Rodman with Silver 1997), have bizarre covers of a naked Rodman and contain conventional action photographs of him on the basketball court alongside (especially in the latter book) many outlandish shots of him off it. The images of Rodman that circulate readily in newspapers, magazines and books (including academic works like Baker and Boyd's (1997) *Out of Bounds: Sports, Media and the Politics of Identity*, which has an apparently now *de rigueur* cover of Rodman in vinyl displaying his biceps and biting a metal chain) are clearly a major departure from the orthodox, traditional images of sportsmen that still form the vast bulk of sport photography. Indeed, they raise a question which I shall take up below of what constitutes a sports photograph in the first place.

It is still necessary to ask how such images can be read as an index of the state of sporting masculinity. One obvious response is to adjudge them to be mere effects of the American sports hype media machine, a 'freak show' designed to give celebrity status to a publicity-craving exhibitionist. There is no doubt some validity to such an assessment, but there is also something more culturally disruptive in the figure of a black elite basketballer known for his aggressive approach to the game (and hence gaining approval within traditional masculine sports culture) whose stock-in-trade is projecting an extraordinary visual image of himself while making pronouncements like 'I've fantasized about being with a man many times', 'the sports world is the ultimate prison of macho bullshit' (Rodman with Silver 1997: 179, 188) and 'people have assumed I'm bisexual. I don't do much to discourage that, since it fits into my idea of keeping people guessing' (Rodman with Keown 1996: 211).

'Keeping people guessing' is not the usual function of sports photography, which I have argued has been a rather conservative force that has tended to confirm rather than challenge dominant (especially patriarchal) roles, identities and structures of power. But, as it develops through the proliferation of genres and subjects – moving away from a reliance on action shots of men and 'honey' shots of women to a greater coverage of the aesthetic, 'ambient' and 'flexibly' sexual aspects of sport – it can be expected that the sports still image bank will play a more prominent role in recording cultural change

and challenging prevailing social ideologies. I have concentrated in this section on the sexualized masculine sports image (by way of exemplification
and on account of its dominance of sports imagery), but there are other
unorthodox sports images which form part of the changing discourses of
identity that are a major feature of contemporary life (Giddens 1991). For
example, Ndalianis (1995) has written of the representational tensions
within bodybuilding 'muscle' magazines like *Flex*:

> But, as the old saying goes, 'a picture tells a thousand words', and in
> bodybuilding magazines it tells a story that attempts to bring back into
> play a gendered power structure. While, in one way, the written word
> serves to break down years of a subculture that was dominated by rigid
> boundaries that served to contain and construct gender according to a
> system of power negotiated around sexual difference, the image often
> contradicts the word, aiming covertly to re-establish the status quo and
> set up clear gender demarcations.
>
> (Ndalianis 1995: 19)

In this case, 'serious' debates in the magazine over the issue of 'femininity
vs muscle' were undercut by the use of 'images of these [female] body-
builders posing seductively in conventional "feminine" poses – and most of
them either wear thong backs or high heels' (Ndalianis 1995: 20). Thus the
traditional sexualization and patrolling of the 'socially approved' appearance of sportswomen is still occurring in sports photography just as, in
other areas, some rules are being (at least partially) rewritten for men. Such
issues are made more complex when other social variables are introduced
which demand greater analytical scope in order to go beyond the prime
concerns of white, heterosexual men and women. Little is known about
how gay men and lesbian women respond to sports photography, especially
given that few professional sportspeople have ever 'come out', especially
when at the peak of their careers (Rowe and Miller 1999). Furthermore, in
these 'image stakes' Linda D. Williams (1994) notes the double disadvan-
tage of black sportswomen. On the assumption that 'no feature is so important to a magazine as its cover' (L.D. Williams 1994: 51), she conducted a
study of the covers of *Sports Illustrated* between 1954 and 1989, finding
that while only 114 (6 per cent) of the 1835 covers in the period involved
women, only 5 of these featured black sportswomen (4 per cent of magazine covers with women appearing and 0.3 per cent of total covers), with 4
appearing in the short period between 1987 and 1989 (L.D. Williams and
Lumpkin 1990). When we add this 'quantitative' neglect to the 'qualitative'
question of the manner in which black women have been represented, as

encapsulated in the assertion that, 'Throughout U.S. history, African American women are constructed as inherently sexual and excessively available' (Ono 1997: 86), then the intersection of gender and racial ideologies in sports photographs is revealed to be an area worthy of more detailed analysis and critique. The racialized dimension of photography is especially important in the use of the black male sports body in the advertising of products, where the sexualized component (which is also a key element of the cultural construction of black men – Mercer 1992) is 'bundled' with a more extensive admixture of contemporary style and cool. This prime role of the black male sports image in the selling of products (discussed below) is one of part male pin-up, part style guru. It is reliant on an 'in your face' sexual address that (Dennis Rodman included) as resolutely rejects feminized complaisance as any traditional sports photograph of the tough, unyielding sportsman.

Before moving to a brief discussion of this genre, we might ask, finally, how a sports photograph becomes sexual or erotic. 'Sexiness' may be consciously cultivated in stronger or weaker forms by deploying a titillating mode of address associated with 'cheesecake' photography and pornography. As a corporeal discipline, sexiness can be a bi-product of the inherently sensual expression of the sporting body in some sports. Guttmann (1991, 1996), as noted above, argues that many (especially feminist poststructuralist) critiques of sport have not been sufficiently well informed about the historical linkage of sport and the erotic, and have been blind or resistant to the erotic quality of toned bodies and athletic movement. In making a plea for 'mutually admiring male and female gazes (and for gay and lesbian ones as well)' (Guttmann 1996: 163), he contrasts the 'travesties' of trying to make (in this case sportswomen) sexy to the 'marvel' of the eroticizing effect of 'athletic performances' (Guttmann 1991: 261). Perhaps, then, the most sexually appealing photographic images of sportspeople are not those in which they are playing at being sexy, but where they become unconsciously so by playing their sport well (although, obviously, some sports lend themselves better to 'balletic' moments of beauty than others). But returning sports photography to the field of action leaves vast quantities of images sprinkled throughout newspapers and magazines. These are the aforementioned 'secondary media sports texts' (including some of the images discussed above) which have a less direct relationship with the practice of sport, but none the less draw on sports news, celebrities and mythologies. It might be objected that, in the strict sense, they use sport rather than constitute sports photography *per se*, so calling into question the precise characteristics of the still sports image.

The uses of sport in photography

In this chapter I have concentrated on two types of sports photographs. The first and most unequivocally sporting is the action photograph, but we have seen, second, that pictures of sportsmen and women take many forms, such as pin-up and aesthetic images. These photographs rely on representing recognizable aspects of sport – the body of a famous athlete or 'signs' of sport such as uniform or equipment. There are other types of sports photographs to be examined that do not concentrate on the bodies of athletes in motion or in repose but which take in the wider context of the event by putting to the fore the crowd or the venue. These 'atmosphere' or 'ambient' shots are most commonly found in the sports sections of broadsheet newspapers and in specialist magazines which have the space to present often sumptuous photo-essays of major sporting occasions or sites. Sports images, then, appear both in the parts of the media clearly designated for them and also spread far beyond the sports pages into the realm of general news and human interest stories. The 'sports action' emphasis is reduced to such an extent in such cases that the photograph becomes a hybrid – part sports photo, part 'society' image, part mood shot, and so on.

Let us take, for example, the British tabloid *Sun* newspaper's 'exclusive' front page story 'Our Love', in which pop singer Spice Girl Victoria Adams (professionally known as Posh Spice) and Manchester United and England soccer player David Beckham display their engagement rings and discuss their 'Romance of the Decade' (Coulson 1998). All of pages 2 and 3 – traditionally areas of 'quality' newspapers that carry 'serious' news – are taken up with interviews with the happy couple and several more photographs, while the centre pages are devoted to more photographs and pronouncements on the union by Debbie Frank, '*Sun Love Astrologer*'. Clearly, sport is an important element of this 'photostory' – the engagement of a leading footballer and a member of a world famous pop group is a publicist's dream – but its qualifications as a media sports text are weakened by the lack of direct concentration on sport itself. Such texts, with a stronger or weaker connection to sport, are diffused across the media, sometimes with sport as the focus, sometimes with it as an ancillary aspect that helps to secure interest by association. It is this associative function which is crucial to the imagery of advertisements that use sport as a key element in addressing potential consumers. Sports myths, especially those of heroism, patriotism and teamwork, are readily available to corporate enterprises like banks, computer companies and motor vehicle manufacturers as means to stir the blood of consumers and induce them to feel well disposed towards the product or service because they already feel positive about a national team or champion athlete. Often, the alluring image is of a sportsperson who comes from a social group more commonly associated by the news media with criminal activities, social dysfunctionality and economic dependence than with spectacular feats in sport or in any other field of action.

The use in advertising and promotion of still images of black male athletes was mentioned above as one of the most prevalent practices in contemporary consumer persuasion. Flicking through newspapers and magazines, now retired basketballer Michael Jordan (and, in another Nike advertisement, unnamed Kenyan runners) can be seen endorsing 'air' athletic footwear; his former colleague Scottie Pippen is selling 'Ginsana Capsules and Tonic'; multi-medal-winning athlete Carl Lewis is modelling the Nike 'Apparel' range, and so on. It could be argued that such positive images of a minority group subject to deeply entrenched racism and suspicion within dominant white culture are welcome signs of social progress. Yet, as McKay (1995: 192) observes, the attractive images of highly privileged black men pumping out slogans like 'Just do it' (Nike), 'There is no limit' (Puma) and 'Life is short. Play hard' (Reebok) help conceal the alienation and degradation of so many of their peers, and of the exploited 'people of colour' in the Third and Fourth Worlds who work for miserly wages with no or highly circumscribed rights of labour organization to produce expensive leisure goods for more affluent consumers in other countries. At the same time, important acts of black militancy are drained of their political punch, as occurred when one of the most famous black political statements in sport – the victory dais black power protest by sprinters Tommie Smith and John Carlos at the 1968 Mexico Olympics – was rendered a quarter of a century later as a full-page colour advertisement for Puma sports shoes in a magazine mainly 'aimed at affluent young blacks' (McKay 1995: 192). For Boyd (1997; see also Maharaj 1997), the outcome of selecting and decontextualizing aspects of black male culture, linking it to the appealing aspects of sport, and then fashioning the combination into consumer iconography (extending from the orthodox to the more threatening figure of the 'bad nigga') is not the liberation and enhancement of an oppressed minority, but the commodification and expropriation of their difference and resistance. Perhaps there is a self-reinforcing element in such arguments – racial oppression is both cultural marginalization and 'mainstreaming' – but it is important to remember that there is more to racial equality than a billboard with a sassy image of an athletic, affluent black man selling overpriced leisurewear.

Conclusion: sports images on the move

In this chapter I have not attempted an exhaustive review of every type and genre of sports photographs and ways of reading them, but rather to demonstrate how they have proliferated in the media and are linked to specific viewerships, ideologies, myths and other texts in a way that makes them important components of contemporary culture. The still sports image, perhaps sepia-toned for nostalgic effect, vibrantly coloured for dramatic impact or glowingly lit for full sensual appeal, is important for the tasks of creating sport's social memory ('Do you remember when?'), securing audience attention ('Did you see that?') and extending its appeal ('What a bod!'). The predominant form of sports photograph remains, paradoxically, the body-focused action shot – the subject is in motion but the medium is capable only of stopping the action and freezing the instant. What happens, then, when the static sports image becomes animated? Our attention now turns to the moment when the wall poster comes to life and the still media sports text starts to move.

Further reading

Dutton, K.R. (1995) *The Perfectible Body: The Western Ideal of Physical Development*. Sydney: Allen and Unwin.
Guttmann, A. (1996) *The Erotic in Sports*. New York: Columbia University Press.
Hargreaves, Jennifer (1994) *Sporting Females: Critical Issues in the History and Sociology of Women's Sports*. London: Routledge.

7

SCREENING THE ACTION:
THE MOVING SPORTS IMAGE

In an ideal world, a competitive television environment would strike the perfect balance: gradually introducing non-enthusiasts to the intricacies and pleasures of new and diverse sports, using all the sophisticated wizardry of new technology while remaining faithful to the innate spirit of the game. All the evidence suggests that, while a visual spectacle is enhanced by innovative camerawork, both commentary and contextual artifice is increasingly exploited to entice the uncommitted. In the end, the overwhelming considerations are those which transcend any concern for honest reproduction.

(Steven Barnett 1990: 170)

Introduction: action, drama and narrative

If the still sports photograph seems to lodge in the mind, its neatly defined and structured image easily conjured up in fine-grained detail, the moving sports image often seem to fills up any spare cerebral and perceptual space, crowding out other subject matter with its movement, colour, noise and melodrama. Much critical attention is given (for reasons outlined in Chapter 2) to television, but sport is also the subject of many films and even some theatre (see, for example, Fotheringham 1992). Programmers have devised myriad ways of presenting sports television – 'live' and delayed broadcasts with multiple-camera locations and sophisticated studio technology, sports 'magazine' programmes, quiz shows, dramas, studio comedies and variety 'turns' that appear in different parts of TV schedules. Most sports TV formats are heavily dependent on the recorded 'live' action which, once placed in the vaults of television companies, is permanently (when correctly stored and preserved) available for repackaging as highlights, memories, 'what happened next' questions and funny moments. The core audience for TV sport is traditionally regarded as the male 'sports nut'; however, not only are substantial numbers of women enthusiastic sports participants and viewers, but also television makes available sports texts to men and women alike who do not count themselves among this established fraternity and growing sorority. Given that the logic of all television is to secure and expand an audience, it is necessary to analyse the textual strategies adopted by TV producers to win over uncommitted viewers to the joys of sport on television. While it should be recognized, as Stoddart (1994b) argues, that the many decisions taken and tasks performed in producing live sport may not 'hang together' in terms of a single determining logic, strong attempts are made to give such broadcasts a coherent identity that can be easily interpreted.

'Action-dependent' sports television does not simply rely on an appeal to the senses through the immediate stimulation of sight and sound. Viewers would quickly tire of a TV sport that consisted of much sound and fury which signified nothing (as has tended to be the fate of fabricated, pseudo-sports TV competitions like *Gladiators*) and so must be made to feel that what is happening on screen actually matters. By inducing (or reinforcing) the identification of viewers with sportspeople and teams – for example, as local or national representatives – sports TV producers tap into the affective power of territoriality as it applies to sectors of cities, whole cities, regions, nations, even entire continents and hemispheres. In this way, the unfolding TV sports event – an important component of news, as we saw in Chapter 3 – is also a narrativized construction, with twists and turns in the plot, heroes and villains, and, in the traditions of Greek and Elizabethan drama, a 'serious' purpose of confronting the great public and private moral dilemmas. In the case of fictional film and drama, where the starting point is narrative, character and dramatic tension, sport is used as a means of attracting those already interested in sport and as a dramatic vehicle for those who are not. Fictionalized sports texts, therefore, tend to be highly charged moral tales or allegories in which the state of the nation or gender and racial orders can be glimpsed through sport. How successful such mythologized treatments of sport will be is heavily dependent on the historical, social and cultural position of particular sports and their persuasiveness in making substantial groups of people care about the outcome (in this case narrative resolution) and feel an affinity with the players (character identification). Before interrogating the sports drama text we need first to 'cut to the chase' – for ratings on free-to-air or subscribers for pay-TV. This task involves a close inspection of the premium TV sports text – 'live' action coverage.

The front row seat in the living room

If we consider the activity of going to a 'live' sports event 'in the flesh' as a specific kind of embodied consumption of a text, then watching that same event 'remotely' on television was in the first instance a compensation for the absence of the sensory experience of moving with the crowd, soaking up the atmosphere and all the sights and smells of an event unique in space and time. If the sports fan at the stadium feels part of history and a strong sense of consuming the sports text under superior conditions (often saying something like, 'you just *had* to be there when we won the trophy for the first time in 50 years'), then at least those watching on television at home or in the pub get some exposure to the text (albeit two-dimensionally on a small screen from a vantage point determined by television producers and camera people) in the absence of such an intimate encounter with it. At the same time, some aspects of the sports television viewing experience may be advantageous – such as no (or minimal) entry cost (for free-to-air television), no traffic jams, wet clothes, restrictions on alcohol consumption or violent encounters with rival spectators (apart from family members and bar patrons). When the comforts of home or the pub are placed alongside technical improvements in television broadcasts such as bigger screens, high definition images, stereo surround sound, multiple camera angles and slow motion replays, then it might be concluded that this is no mere compensation for not being there; it is, instead, a more satisfying and pleasant way of experiencing sport. Indeed, a considerable number of people may, as noted in Chapter 2, choose to pay per view as if they were going to the match, especially where they are looking for comprehensive coverage of simultaneous events (or by compulsion if the option of seeing top 'live' television sport for free has, as in the case of British premier league soccer, been largely taken away from them). As Samuel Weber (1996: 113) reminds us, television literally means 'seeing at a distance', a technology that allows us to overcome some of the limitations of the body. But watching sport on television is not a 'disembodied' act: it generally involves one body in a state of excitement watching others performing *in extremis*. Yet the viewing body is also a disciplined one: it has to consent to being exposed at a specified time to the images of the sporting event provided.

Sports viewers, however deeply embodied their watching experience, must first be induced to sit before the screen, to pay directly per view, or to be willing to pay for the option of doing so, even if that option is not always exercised (that is, induced to subscribe to a service). Like any other small screen genre, sports television typically presents itself as compulsive viewing. In the case of 'live' television, part of this pitch connects to news discourse

– real events are unfolding before the viewer's eyes, history is being made, and so on. Such promotions can work only if sports events are imbued with the necessary sense of significance, without which all sport looks like a series of bizarre manoeuvres observing arcane rules for no apparent reason. Sport as news is dependent on conventional news values (Hartley 1982; Critcher 1987), and the consequent placing of happenings in hierarchies and categories. Just as news is sorted by criteria of importance (the assassination of a monarch or president taking precedence over a politician's photo opportunity), then organized and presented to heighten its dramatic appeal, so sport is awarded significance in the media (as well as receiving it from outside). Different media spaces can be utilized to give 'live' sports events prominence and appropriate *gravitas*. Newspapers can endlessly preview the 'big game', radio bulletins update listeners on the lead-up to it, and television news 'set the stage' for the major sports event to be televised live. Once shown, the action sports television text can then be replayed in numerous ways, and act as the subject of a post-mortem which can plug the gap until the next big sports event.

By tracing the features of the communicative apparatus that surrounds the live sports text in the electronic media, it is readily apparent that even the most important sports moments are not permitted to speak for themselves. We have already discussed in Chapter 5 the aural commentary that accompanies and helps direct responses to the visual text alongside the recorded sounds (increasingly within the range of more sophisticated microphones) of the crowd, sports competitors and officials, and ball against bat, body against body, and so on. Beyond the more efficient capture of the sounds and sights (from helicopter shots to extreme close-ups to slow motion replays) of sport is the organization of the action into an intelligible narrative that vastly extends its range of meaning and cultural resonance. In bringing us this action, the electronic media also help to produce it as something greater, so that what appears on screen connects with other cultural and social phenomena in a variety of ways. Tudor (1992: 391), for example, advances this argument in examining British television coverage of the 1990 soccer World Cup. After noting the well known sports TV audience research studies (such as by Comisky *et al.* 1977) which demonstrate how 'it is commentary above all that provides the television audience with a framework through which events can be viewed, interpreted and emotionally glossed', he assesses the coverage of a match between England and Cameroon in terms of the national and racial stereotypes produced by 'British television's commitment to sustaining a partisan and nationalistic England narrative' (Tudor 1992: 407). While Tudor observes that the discursive positioning of English and African people was not always consistent, there was a strong tendency to represent Cameroon as ' "happy-go-lucky" amateurs' lacking England's 'old bulldog spirit', and an unfolding process of 'discursive upgrading' which:

> involves narrators in constructing a coherent narrative by progressively spelling out the system of oppositions on which the account of national (football) character depends, and by reinterpreting these oppositions as necessary.
>
> (Tudor 1992: 410)

Yet, Tudor goes on to argue that distinguishing 'us' as superior to 'them' also lays bare the anxieties that 'we' might feel about the state of the nation, our personal wellbeing, and so on. It is for this reason, perhaps, that there is so much emphasis in television sport and its commentary on the 'final score' in sports contests as an absolute and unquestioned measure of success and failure, so that 'Televised sports allows viewers to take comfort in the possibility of unequivocal decisions, of being able to distinguish winners and losers, as well as in the possibility of "records" that are quantifiable and measurable' (S. Weber 1996: 127). Of course, if the hoped-for victory does not occur, it is also necessary, short of mass suicide, to come to terms with failure. This loss rationalization process opens up other narrative possibilities present in the age-old popular cries of 'we wuz robbed', 'string up the Board', and so on. One particularly prominent element in television sport is its absolute focus on what Turner (1992: 12) regards as the prime object of contemporary anxiety in the 'somatic society' – the body – so that, as Samuel Weber (1996: 127) proposes, 'televised sports reconfirms the individual body as focal point of a reality that television itself calls into question. The body that appears in the televised sporting event is one that accepts its limitations only in order to surpass them, in an infinite progress of record-breaking and record-making.' Here again the anxious viewing subject is seen as scrutinizing screen sports images – especially the extraordinary performances of athletic bodies – for signs of social and personal 'truth' (Davis 1995). In televised sport such linkages are made not only with non-sporting matters (from the state of national morale to the health of the economy) but also between the media sports text and other familiar types of text. As the action unfolds on screen, it becomes recognizable as drama both on and off it.

It is useful, then, to appraise the media techniques and textual uses that turn televised 'live' sports action into television drama. Rose and Friedman (1997: 3), using Siegfried Kracauer's theory of distraction developed in the 1920s, have proposed a particularly strong relationship between television sport and 'a uniquely masculine experience of spectatorship' which questions the gendered segregation of television viewing patterns. They argue that in television viewing hierarchies soap opera (especially of the daytime variety) tends to be denigrated as 'light' entertainment for bored housewives, so that:

> in their very structure, soaps habituate women to the 'interruption, distraction, and spasmodic toil' [Modleski 1983: 71] which is characteristic of housework. At the same time, by focusing the female spectator's gaze on others, encouraging her to read their needs, desires, and intentions from facial expressions and body language, the soap opera reflects and reinforces the cultural imperative which requires women to do the emotional work in their relationships.
>
> (Rose and Friedman 1997: 4)

In contrast to the traditional positioning of women as concerned above all else with emotions and relationships (as is exemplified by the current revival of the 1960s' term 'chick's movie' to describe films which deal deeply with human, especially romantic, relationships in contrast to the spectacular 'shoot 'em up' and car-chase action of the typical 'guy's movie'), Rose and Friedman (1997: 4) describe the traditional 'masculine mode of spectatorship' as one expected 'to avoid the emotional register, emphasizing instead the classical masculine pleasures in voyeurism and objectification, and constructing a more linear, goal-oriented structure of looking'. So, if men are culturally trained not to get too emotional and involved in their viewing activities, we would expect television sport – until quite recently a predominantly male viewing choice and still one dominated by men in terms of which sports get watched on TV and when (Sargent *et al.* 1998) – to be sober and cool, appreciating the technical excellence of the athleticism on show, and balanced in its appreciation of the merits of all competitors and teams. Such a television sports spectator would scrupulously honour the Olympic ideals of fair play and respect for taking part rather than for winning. The familiar picture of the unhinged and hysterical male viewer supporting an individual or team as they engage in 'live' sports competition is hardly in accord with this view. As Rose and Friedman (1997) go on to say:

> The sports gaze depends not on distance, fragmentation, or objectification, but on identification, nearness, and participation. The male viewer's relationship to the image is in fact quite similar to that of the female soap viewer: he is alternately absorbed in multiple identifications and distracted. Rather than emphasizing a voyeuristic and objectifying gaze, television sports seems to invite the viewer to engage in a distracted, identificatory, and dialogic spectatorship which may be understood as a masculine counterpart to soap opera's 'maternal gaze'.
>
> (Rose and Friedman 1997: 4)

In suggesting that male (and, presumably, female) television sports spectators have a similar relationship with the moving sports text as do *aficionados* of screen melodrama (McKay and Rowe 1997), Rose and Friedman could be proposing either that sports fans want their television sport that way or that the practical logic of securing and holding mass audiences in television inevitably impels the text towards a deeply emotional engagement between text, subject and viewer. In fact, both possibilities exist – the affective power of sport is such that few committed spectators who identify closely with the people performing on screen (which include athletes, coaches and other fans) can watch in a cool, detached way. The terms 'committed' and 'identify' are paramount; as we saw in discussing sports photography in Chapter 6, it is perfectly possible for male spectators to objectify sportswomen in a sexually voyeuristic fashion when they have no respect for their activities as athletes. But once sporting qualities come to the fore – as in the case, say, of female Olympic swimmers involved in close races against rival nations – then it is likely that the emphasis on 'just looking' will recede (at least temporarily) in favour of an active engagement in the sport itself.

Second, the logic of (especially commercial) television is deeply reliant on fostering a sense of audience involvement. If men and women care about their sport, then that level of emotional commitment will have at least to be matched, if not stimulated and exceeded, by sports television. The huge general popularity of sport does not of itself deliver audiences in specific instances. There is constant competition between individual sports (like basketball and football) and between sport and other forms of popular entertainment (such as music or film) for audiences. Television sports audiences have to be 'primed', therefore, and can always be profitably expanded. But first the missing millions must be found.

Audience hunting

As I discussed earlier, it makes little sense for a mass medium to exclude or alienate men who do not regard themselves as 'sports nuts', or gay men or women who like sport, or women who could be encouraged to develop an interest in it by various means. Miller (1998a: 107), for example, notes the fact that half of the British television audience of 24 million for a match during the 1990 soccer World Cup were women, which led one newspaper to speculate that 'TV production houses and female viewers were both engaged by the "bum not the ball" '. Playing up the human interest or broader entertainment side of sport (normally associated with 'soft' news and 'low' drama) in order to appeal to larger television audiences can, of course, annoy the purist sports spectator. While the application of new camera and sound technologies (such as miniaturized lenses and microphones on the field of play) are likely to be much welcomed by regular viewers who are looking for an ever closer simulation of the actual event, the explanation of rules or moves or various comic innovations are anathema to the 'expert' viewer. As Barnett (1990) has noted:

> When [Kerry] Packer's Channel Nine finally wrenched Test cricket away from the Australian Broadcasting Corporation, it invested considerable financial and technical resources into coverage. Some of the innovations – aerial shots of field placing, split-screen comparisons of respective bowling actions – were valuable contributions to a better view and a better understanding of the game. Others were little more than cheap production tricks which had little to do with explaining a complex game to the uninformed. At the most banal level came the introduction of a ridiculous cartoon duck, which tearfully accompanied a batsman dismissed for nought (in cricket terminology a 'duck') to the pavilion . . . Cartoon characters in live sports have only one objective – to keep those with minimum interest in the game (particularly children) tuned in. This is, no doubt, precisely why Sky imported the same triviality into their coverage of the 1990 West Indies–England Test series (along with the excitable commentary of Tony Greig).
>
> (Barnett 1990: 169)

Barnett (1990: 169) also notes the use of 'honey shots' of 'scantily clad young women in the stands' to dissuade heterosexual men not 'riveted' by the sport from changing channels, the equivalent tactic to the sexualization of male sports performers for heterosexual women. But the dramatization, 'cartoonization' and sexualization of television sport do not exhaust the repertoire of techniques for keeping and holding large audiences. Sports authorities and television companies have also devised new 'telegenic' forms of sport that lend themselves well to fixed television schedules and reshape sports contests in a manner that accentuates even more the melodramatic character of live sport.

Looking further at the game of cricket, for example, we can see that the 'one-day' form has been moulded well to the demands of television in terms of its structure and guaranteed result; unlike Test cricket, impatient audiences with busy lives will not be required to watch at least 30 hours of live action over five days only for the event to end inconclusively as a draw. The one-day game, unlike its traditional three, four and five-day counterparts, allots a fixed number of overs for each side to bowl. The side with the lower score after this allocation or which is dismissed before the other's score is reached loses. Draws are extremely rare, as they rely on the improbable outcome of 'tying' the scores rather than the passage of time, and, even then, a victor can if necessary be declared on a 'count back' (such as the number of wickets lost). The rules are also varied to encourage more spectacular action, such as hitting the ball adventurously in the air rather than more cautiously along the ground; through the imposition of fielding restrictions (especially during the first 15 overs, which in the traditional game often involves a careful jockeying for initial advantage) that make it less likely that an ambitious, big-hitting batter will be caught in the 'deep'; the limitation of the length of run up for bowlers in order to speed up the game while reducing the speed of the deliveries batters have to deal with; operating a quota for the number of overs allowed to be bowled by any one bowler, in order to give batters the opportunity to face some less specialist bowlers and so score more runs; applying a much stronger test to the assessment of 'wides' and 'no balls', the illegal deliveries that must be repeated and are penalized (in this form of the game more heavily) by the awarding of extra runs. All these tailored changes to the game (no doubt unfathomable to those who do not have an intimate knowledge of the game of cricket, but the source of endless disputation for those who do) are designed to ensure that the televised one-day cricket match is fast and furious, encouraging high scores and high drama.

Harriss (1990: 118) has observed how making cricket more television friendly through these changes aligns it with the dramatic form (even before the contribution of commentators and producers is 'factored in'), so that in 'the age of late capitalism based on mass consumption, cricket becomes a postmodern, decentred spectacle that emphasises a glossy surface without depth'. Television is seen here to be part cause, part effect of the transformation of cricket (and, no doubt, other sports like tennis and golf) from the controlled and stately progress towards victory based on a rationalized 'cost-benefit analysis' to a much flashier spectacle dedicated to instant gratification by seizing the ephemeral attention of a media-saturated and more diverse audience:

> The one-day spectacle is packaged in much the same way as a one-hour television melodrama. There is some variation in each individual episode, but the conclusion is inevitably a hectic chase sequence. The paradox of one-day cricket is that, like the television melodrama, while it emphasises action it does so only within the framework of a formula. Also like the television melodrama, the plot of each game is circumscribed by the structure of the series as a whole. This eliminates complexity and allows the viewer to be immersed quickly and easily in the immediate plot.
>
> (Harriss 1990: 118)

It might be suggested that the kind of melodrama described by Harriss is much more action dependent (in the manner of 'cop' and 'mystery' shows like *X Files*, *NYPD Blue*, *Water Rats*, *Blue Heelers*, *Prime Suspect* and *Cracker*) than that discussed by Rose and Friedman (which is closer to day-time and evening 'soaps' and dramas like *Days of our Lives*, *The Young and the Restless*, *Neighbours*, *Home and Away*, *Melrose Place* and *ER*). This specific point – which, while valid, requires a more detailed analysis of the concept of melodrama (see Brooks 1976) than is possible here – does not rebut the more general proposition that live television sport moves well beyond the territory of describing action on the field and into the space of narrativizing and mythologizing its subject. In fact, it plainly draws on both the action and 'feeling' oriented sub-genres of melodrama to construct a media text that we could typify as combining the spectacular physical, often violent elements of 'action' dramas with the detailed characterization, emotional concentration and relational emphasis of 'human' dramas. The outcome can properly be described as 'inter-textual' and multi-genre in nature, not always satisfying individual viewers but ceaselessly working to link what is on the screen in a meaningful and attractive way to other media texts and life experiences.

Because television sport is a moving spectacle of varying pace (golf, for example, is positively pedestrian when compared to ice or field hockey), it relies on capitalizing on the visual drama of movement when it is readily accessible and producing a sense of rapid momentum when it is not. Even sports that already seem frenetic are 'sped up' by television in the pursuit of the uncommitted viewing eye, yet this constant acceleration of the rhythm of the sports TV text is to some degree in tension with the impulse to slow it all down and see it more clearly from numerous angles and in minute detail. By making the spectacle of sports television louder and more frenetic in a drive to interpellate, in Althusser's terms, potential viewers ('Oy! Look!') and then distract (in Kracauer's terms), even transfix them ('Don't Look Away For A Moment!'), programmers are attempting to occupy the exterior and interior spaces of homes and minds. This urgent mode of address is also associated with a traditional split between British and American styles of sports broadcasting. It is useful to trace some of the major changes in the way that images of sport are presented on the small screen. In order to do so, it is necessary to know something of the history of the principles governing the capturing of 'reality' for television and, in particular, of recording and transmitting sports events. As Whannel (1992) points out, in the earlier part of the twentieth century, when protocols for the reflection of the world by television were being developed:

television merely took over a lot of standard realist conventions from film-making – the 180-degree rule, the principle of complementary angles, and so on ... These conventions aimed at transparency, strengthening the claim to television to reflect events and minimising its own active construction of representations.

(Whannel 1992: 32)

Thus the television camera was thought of as an unseen eye, its 'sweeping' of what was before it from a single, static position simulating the experience of the spectator watching from a particular vantage point. The key to this form of television, as in all forms of realism, was to make the infrastructure of communication invisible, turning two-dimensional (and initially mono-chrome) perception into three-dimensional (colourful) experience. When single cameras were supplemented by others, the consequent shifting of per-spectives made it harder to hide the production decisions being made on behalf of the viewer, sacrificing a degree of 'reality effect' for a technologi-cally enhanced view of the action. A tension quickly emerged between a rather 'Olympian' view of the sports action (watching from a suitable dis-tance in a detached, objective manner) and a more 'dramaturgical' approach reliant on close-up shots that engaged the viewer much more closely with the personalities of the participants. To some degree, this was also a struggle between those who took a high minded, serious approach to the visual reportage of sports events and those who saw it merely as one form of popu-lar entertainment which, like others, should be presented using all the avail-able, audience-pleasing techniques (Whannel 1992: 33). The development of such techniques included the possibilities of the rapid-fire editing which could give to even the most ponderous sports contest the appearance of a series of lightning strikes.

One way to establish the existence of such shifts from slower to faster styles of sports television presentation is to quantify for comparative pur-poses the length and duration of shots in individual live sports programmes. The variables measured include any changes that might occur over time and differences between countries influenced by one or other of the major sports broadcasting traditions. Fiske's (1983) case study of televised cricket in Aus-tralia revealed that average shot-length was 6 seconds out of a total average of 46–9 shots per over. When Whannel (1992: 99) replicated the study in England in 1991, he found considerable differences – an average shot length of 8 seconds (one-third longer) with an average of only 32 shots per over (29–30 per cent fewer). This variation can be explained, as suggested earlier in the mention of the Packer Cricket 'Revolution', by a change of broadcast philosophy (mirroring a wider historical shift as the first colonial power, Britain, was superseded by the second dominant force of media and cultural imperialism – the USA) that saw some commercial television stations in Australia depart from the patented BBC model of broadcasting restraint and embrace the more upbeat American style (Barnett 1990). In 1998, my own update of these studies revealed some similarities and variations. An October one-day match between the unobtrusively named Queensland Bulls and the Tasmanian Tigers revealed an average shot length of less than 6 seconds (5.7), but an average number of shots per over of only 29. The explanation of this uneven finding is that the average over length was only 166 seconds, barely half that of those sampled by Fiske. The Australian cricketing audience's assumed attention span, it seems, shrunk markedly in those 15 years. A comparative study in September of a one-day game between Essex and Nottingham revealed an average shot length of a little under 8 seconds (7.95) and an average number of shots per over of only 24 (23.66). The English, it seems, have maintained their reputation for a more sedate brand of TV cricket. But, with an average over length of only 188 seconds, the screen action is positively frenetic by earlier standards.

Goldlust (1987) also carried out a limited empirical study of the different forms of sports television by performing comparative visual component and shot analyses of tennis, baseball and football in the USA and cricket in Australia. Goldlust, like the aforementioned writers, operated with the:

> somewhat artificial, but still meaningful, distinction between an emphasis on commercial *entertainment* values best represented by the American networks and *journalistic* values emphasising accuracy and 'objective' reporting of events that has become the established ethos within the BBC and a significant element of its institutional self-image.
> (Goldlust 1987: 98)

While he did not do any quantitative analysis of British sports television, recording only 'his impression that the distinction would still hold' (Goldlust 1987: 100) on the basis of viewing British TV soccer for three weeks on both the public BBC and the commercial channels (and finding that the average shot length in West German TV coverage of the 1974 soccer World Cup was almost double that of the BBC), Goldlust found general evidence of a move towards 'a "high tech" form of "snap, snap" television typified by contemporary American network coverage of sports' (1987: 100).

Of course, variations in the structure and form of very different sports like tennis and American football impose constraints on how television will cover them (for example, the average length of a segment from the Masters tennis match sampled was over twice that of the Super Bowl), and there are cultural variations of various kinds – the amount of commentary 'hype' tolerated, the quantity of background information provided, and so on. Gordon and Sibson (1998) have also shown in their comparative analysis of US and Australian television coverage of the 1996 Atlanta Olympics that there are perceptible differences in how broadcasters from different countries handle the same live sports 'feed' (that is, in how they process the same raw textual material). But the most significant finding is that the now entrenched methods of television, much imitated or directly imported from the USA in countries like Australia, have the impact of eroding the differences between sports with wildly varying histories, tempos and spectatorships. Above all, this is an impulse constantly to shift the viewer's perspective and to provide a barrage of sights and sounds in order to prevent their attention from wandering and their hand straying to the remote control button, so that:

> illustrative of the overall tendency towards fragmentation of viewpoint is that the longest shot of any kind over all four telecasts lasted 51.2 seconds and this was a close-up of a baseball pitcher warming up before an innings, while graphics listing the team line-up were superimposed over the picture. Overall, rarely did any shot exceed twenty-five seconds in length – in the [one-day] cricket the longest was only nineteen seconds.
>
> The multiplicity of viewing perspectives provided by the television coverage is further increased in that the slow-motion replays are often from one or more camera positions different from that shown in the live segments.
>
> The analysis above sensitises us to the extent to which the sporting event is transformed through the dictates of what is considered to be 'good television' into a form of rapidly alternating images and visual perspectives that has much in common with the editing style of many other contemporary commercial television programmes.
>
> (Goldlust 1987: 105–6)

Furthermore, in noting Fiske's (1983) calculation of the rough approximation of average shot length in sports, adventure and news programmes, it can be suggested that the logic of television is towards a homogeneous rendering of its subject – any subject, from sport to strikes to soap opera. The more traditionalist lovers of sport worry about the power of television to make sport in its own image – that is, for sporting traditions to be discarded in favour of the *Sturm und Drang* (the flashing, thunderous spectacle signifying not too much when the billows of dry ice have cleared) that viewers have become conditioned to expect and demand. In the world of free-to-air, network television at least, where there is little toleration of specialist, minority interest, the moving media sports text also seems to be a convergent and more uniform one. In theoretical terms, this trend exposes one of the paradoxes of postmodernization (Crook *et al.* 1992) – as differentiation (say, of news and entertainment media functions) gives way to hyper-differentiation ('hard' versus 'soft' news within the genre of journalism), the result is often de-differentiation (the collapse of boundaries between functions and genres). So, as Real (1996) points out in his analysis of the televising of the Olympics:

> The fast-paced Olympic television presentation of multiple events with on-screen graphics and announcer commentary is the opposite of the classical coherent, single-authored, focused artistic experience. Underlying this postmodern presentation is the commercial incentive to maximize viewing audience by promotion and titillation, by superlatives and historical allusions, by giving the audience what it expects but in an even fancier form than it had hoped.
>
> (Real 1996: 242)

In likening the experience of watching the TV Olympics to that of taking in pop video channels like MTV and the strange films (and, in the former case, television series) of directors like David Lynch and Quentin Tarantino, Real is proposing that sport has joined many other mediated cultural forms in being overwhelmed by a (post)culture of fragmentation, pastiche and promiscuous borrowing from any style or genre at hand. Following Jameson's (1984) characterization of postmodernism as the 'logic of late capitalism' (noted above), such arguments taken to their fullest extent foresee the complete collapse of all the divisions between texts. This is an improbable development given that the media sports text is still recognizable as such; few in full possession of their faculties would mistake it for a children's programme or a soap opera, yet this does not mean that elements from them (the infantilization of the audience or the dramatization of the action) have not infiltrated the sports text (and, presumably, vice versa).

What we have seen is something not altogether surprising given the nature of sports mythologies and the reliance of the popular media on narrative – the deployment of different styles and genres in order to transform what could be the 'spartan' act of sports viewing into a luxurious wallowing in spectacle. In the process, the 'real' events on screen are coupled with the 'fictional' elements of story telling and myth making. As Cunningham and Miller (1994) point out, a key element of this narrativizing impulse is, as in other entertainment forms, the creation and promotion of sportspeople as celebrities. Hence, it can be said that 'TV sport is an individualising genre,

announcing, auditing and ending the careers of stars' (Cunning
Miller 1994: 77). In accentuating the specific character traits of ath
collective aspects of sport (especially uncomfortable questions of so
politics) are often strategically played down (Hilliard 1994). Th
national or city teams routinely have group traits ascribed to them by television commentators (tough, flamboyant, sneaky and so on), the simplest
and most direct way of developing drama through character is to focus
closely on single sportspeople. It is not a very long step from creating sports
stars through television to their appearance (as either themselves or another
character) on film and then to film stars playing them on the big screen. Feature films that are not documentaries or biographies are moving media
sports texts which obey a different logic to live action in starting with the
'fictional' (or fictive) and working backwards to the 'real' practice of sport.

Screen of dreams

We have noted above how actual sports action, when caught on screen, is
invested with the quality of dramatic fiction. What happens, then, when sport
appears on screen as fiction? If 'unscripted' screen sport already has recognizable actors, plots, sets, and so on, then its fictional counterpart might be
expected to develop these into an even more structured and mythologized
cultural entity that operates in the space between the 'real' and the 'imaginary'. Fictional moving media sports texts are subject to different imperatives
than those which operate in the non-fictional. Miller (1996) suggests that
more attention should be given to documentary and instructional films which
are not discussed in any detail here (for an example, see Robbins's (1997) discussion of the basketball documentary *Hoop Dreams*). For media texts
regarded as 'actuality', the drive is to get up as close to the sporting subject
as possible, to reveal its 'reality' in ever more finely grained and multi-
perspectival detail. Once the veracity of what appears on screen is established, it is possible to build up the fictional and mythological qualities which
turn sport from a series of physical manoeuvres into a meaning-laden cultural
practice. In the case of fictional works, it is necessary to move in the opposite
direction – from the 'invention' of a fictional world to the 'truth' of sport and
human existence. As in the case of photographic images and literary texts, the
place of sport varies widely from being about sport above all else to deploying sport in order to reach a large audience or in combination with other subjects in the service of narrative, character, and *mise-en-scène*. I am more
interested here in the films such as *The Loneliness of the Long Distance
Runner* (1962), *This Sporting Life* (1963), *Rocky* (1976), *Raging Bull*

(1980), *Chariots of Fire* (1981), *Field of Dreams* (1989), *White Men Can't Jump* (1992), *Jerry Maguire* (1996) and *Fever Pitch* (1997) in which sport is integral, rather than those in which it is incidental. An example of such an incidental use of sport on film is the scene in *Men in Black* (1997) where the baseball crowd in Queens, New York, is seemingly so caught up in the sports action that the only person to see a spaceship flying overhead is a transfixed outfield catcher searching the night sky for a descending ball. Many films use sports stadia as locations because of the narrative possibilities of large crowds (usually a desperate search for a 'needle in a haystack' and/or a threat of carnage). Others feature prominent sports stars like O.J. Simpson in the *Naked Gun* (1988) series, Kareem Abdul-Jabbar in *Flying High* (1980) and Michael Jordan in *Space Jam* (1997). But bona fide fictional sports films put sport and the social relations and mythological constructions that surround it at the heart of the film (Bergan 1982; Rowe 1999).

When we set about reading a sports film, the same questions apply as to the analysis of any text – what is its message at manifest and latent levels, to whom does it hope to appeal, why has this subject and this approach to it been selected? Some of these questions may seem deceptively simple to answer. For example, it is obvious that sport will be chosen as a subject for film because sports fans constitute a readymade and willing audience for such films. Yet if sports fans are so eager to conduct a pursuit of the 'real' in and through media sport, how tolerant will they be of a Hollywood studio or any other production housing using sport to 'tell stories'? Sarris (1980: 50) is unequivocal on this matter: he likes sport and film but not together, because 'Sports are now. Movies are then. Sports are news. Movies are fables'. It might also be that a prominent place for sport in fiction film will deter non-sports fans at the box office. Thus, sport on film, unless it is to be very carefully targeted at relatively small, specialized audiences, needs to be tailored to the needs of sports and non-sports fans alike by doing justice to the sporting elements of the film for the former and expanding its concerns to the satisfaction of the latter. In order to be a broad 'audience pleaser', the issues confronted in the fictional sports film must simultaneously illuminate the sporting world, the other worlds with which it comes into contact, and the relations (actual and metaphorical) between them. For this reason, fictional sports films tend to be allegorical (Rowe 1998) – that is, they are grand moral tales in which sport is represented as a metaphor for life and, not uncommonly, life is represented as a metaphor for sport. In order to demonstrate this point, it is instructive to examine some well known sports films and to tease out the themes that link sports mythologies to the concerns of everyday life.

One of the definitive sports films of the early 1980s (not least because of its sweeping, stirring electronic soundtrack by Vangelis) was the British film *Chariots of Fire*. Released in the early years of the Thatcher government, it was a popular choice for exhibition at fund-raising events for the Conservative Party, who had their own 'prototype' champion elite athlete seemingly drawn from the frames of the film – Sebastian Coe (later to become a Conservative Member of Parliament). *Chariots of Fire* is a quintessential sports film (in this case based on real historical events and characters) in that it deals squarely with the mythological possibilities of transcendence of class, ethnic prejudice and human selfishness through sport. The main featured runner, Harold Abrahams (played by Ben Cross), has to overcome the snobbishness and anti-Semitism of the masters of his Cambridge college; deal with the problem of being at the same time teammate and competitor with other athletes, including one drawn from the same aristocratic class that has ridiculed him; compensate for his own lack of material resources, and so on. In the most famous scene from the film, he is shown on a training run on the beach, the rhythmic pulse of the soundtrack (overlaid with a grandiose melody) matching the pace of the runner striving against the odds for sporting victory. The 'feel good' quality of his final success, the patriotic fervour induced by international sporting competition, and the nostalgic atmosphere of a film (including an evocation of the Olympianism of antiquity, as the title indicates) set in a time before big business had penetrated to the core of high performance sport, made the Oscar-winning *Chariots of Fire* appeal to sports fans and to others. Sport has (as we have seen) extraordinary affective and connotative power, making many people feel deeply moved and also encouraging them to translate sporting values and measures of success and failure to other spheres. Hence, not only are sport and sports metaphors deployed in advertising, but also they can be used readily as the vehicle for the fictional handling of many pivotal social issues.

If we take a very different film from *Chariots of Fire* like *Jerry Maguire*, the 'cut throat' world of US sports agents provides a very effective setting for an exploration of the ethics of capitalism, the necessity of balance between working and personal lives, and the nature of alliances (economic and friendly) between black and white. In the film, Jerry Maguire (played by Tom Cruise), a successful and ruthless sports agent, momentarily penetrates the amorality of his occupation and embarks on a brief crusade to restore more altruistic values to the duties of representing athletes in contract negotiations. Instead of chasing more money and clients, he decides to safeguard their interests by limiting the number but improving the quality of his business relationships, even making room to consider the broader health of sport itself. By the time he 'comes to his senses', realizing that his newfound and publicly expressed ethical commitment was no more than a passing fancy, he is sacked from his firm and abandoned by most of his clients (including those who had professed their unshakeable loyalty to him). Cut adrift by his usual class allies, Jerry Maguire is supported only by Dorothy Boyd, a single mother from a working-class background (played by Renee Zellweger) with whom he becomes romantically involved, and Rod Tidwell (Cuba Gooding Jr), an African American footballer with a rather uncertain career trajectory who keeps demanding 'Show me the money!' Ultimately, Maguire becomes successful through the ascendancy of his once doubtful but loyal client and saves the marriage that he has placed in jeopardy, which, as Miller (1997) points out, is somewhat unusually represented as more fragile than his client's own conjugal relationship – the black family generally shown to be in crisis because of the lack of commitment of the black male.

The pivotal scene in *Jerry Maguire* is when his client appears to have broken his neck during an important football match, only to become a sports celebrity through the degree of showmanship he displays as he rises from his prone position to 'milk' the applause of the crowd. Sport is shown, finally, to be about 'caring', commitment, forging alliances between unlikely people of different race and class in the pursuit of dual successes in sport and commerce. Hence, the tension between capitalism and sport is resolved by reassuring the audience that ethical and humane business practice in sport brings more rather than less financial success, while also guaranteeing that sport is never reduced to mere capital accumulation. The relationship between new capitalist and old sporting values in the USA is a constantly recurring theme in films about the quintessential American sport – baseball. *Field of Dreams*, with *Bull Durham* (1988) a key text in the sub-genre of the baseball film in what Sobchack (1997) calls 'Post-American Cinema' (by which she means a nation that has fragmented and lost any sense of common cultural identity), is preoccupied with the problems of (in this case rural) capitalism and the erosion of authentic feeling and cohesive, self-sustaining community. In the film, a struggling mid-West farmer, Ray Kinsella (played by Kevin Costner, who also appears in *Bull Durham*, presumably on account of his all-American boy image) hears a mysterious heavenly voice whispering 'If you build it, he will come'. The 'it' is a new baseball field on his farmland and the 'he' is a long dead and much-wronged player 'Shoeless' Joe Jackson. *Field of Dreams* invests sport with the magical power not only of bringing back the dead, but also of reviving collective memory and the values of a society which had sold its precious assets – like sport – to the highest bidder. Kinsella, reluctantly at first, takes up the challenge, and sustains his faith despite objections from his bank and family, recruiting an unlikely ally in Terence Mann (James Earl Jones), a reclusive elderly black writer and former activist who shares his belief in the redemptive power of baseball. Finally, the field is built, the ghostly players return to earth, the family farm is saved by charging tourists and baseball nostalgia 'buffs' to visit this ethereal sports theme park, the wrongs done to 'Shoeless' Jackson are righted, Kinsella's family stays together, an old man is made happy, the racial divide is bridged – and the golden age of America restored in Iowa. The allegorical role of sports film – so strong in the baseball sub-genre given its reputation as the USA's national pastime – is clearly demonstrated in *Field of Dreams*, with the condition of sport being presented as both symptom and solution to the dilemmas of social and personal life.

If this is an overtly mystical vision lacking in irony and scepticism, then *Fever Pitch* (1997), a film of a bestselling autobiographical book by the British writer Nick Hornby (1992), provides a much more down-to-earth and self-critical take on sports culture which is no less aware of the power of its romance. In the book and film (for which Hornby wrote the screenplay), Paul (Colin Firth) a middle-aged man recalls how soccer helped salvage an unhappy childhood by giving him something to do with his father during 'weekend visits', initiating him into masculine culture, and providing him with something to be truly committed to – Arsenal Football Club. This was no childhood fad, however, as support for Arsenal became an all-encompassing, adult obsession. The film sets up an antagonism between the immature world of football supporting and another, more 'grown-up' world symbolized by his girlfriend, Sarah (Ruth Gemmell). In a pivotal moment in *Fever Pitch*, the male protagonist breaks up with his (unknown to him, now pregnant) girlfriend after taking her onto the rowdy, male-dominated terraces of Arsenal's Highbury Stadium. On the same day in 1989, in Sheffield's Hillsborough Stadium, 95 football fans were crushed to death (when police allowed too many people into too small an area from which no escape was possible because of security fencing). Paul's response to these horrific events is matter of fact: football fans all over Britain will go back to unsafe grounds because they are compelled by their passion to do so, a fatalistic attitude that his girlfriend finds unfathomable, especially when it applies to a pursuit as 'trivial' as watching a football team. In reflecting on his life through the bottom of a vodka glass, Paul weighs the competing claims of the sports world in a lengthy soliloquy, confused about 'whether life's shit because Arsenal are shit, or the other way round'; considering the time and money spent and the relationships neglected in his pursuit of sports fandom; relishing moments of fans' absorption when 'everything else [has] gone out of their heads' and they feel at 'the centre of the whole world'; savouring the predictable structure of a life organized around the yearly soccer season; and then finally acknowledging that 'some stuff' – like having a partner and becoming a father – is more important than Arsenal.

Living room legend: fantasy football for the confused adult male
Still from *Fever Pitch*, a Wildgaze Films Production for Channel Four Films

Here the familiar filmic preoccupation with the relationship between the sports and wider worlds is evident, albeit in a much more knowing and self-critical manner than an heroic, nostalgic baseball film like *Field of Dreams* (no doubt also reflecting a cultural difference between a modest British film with no superstars and a shambling schoolteacher 'hero' who wears Arsenal boxer shorts, and a Hollywood 'blockbuster' with a mega-star male lead who has injected a stylish, late 1980s element into the rural struggle memorably depicted in John Steinbeck's *The Grapes of Wrath*). *Fever Pitch* is, ultimately, a rite of passage film, with the male protagonist negotiating the transition from a life dominated by football fandom to a richer, more varied and responsible existence. The cathartic moment of a dramatic and unexpected Arsenal victory that provides the film's climax is also the instant of liberation from obsessive football fandom, when sport's place in the world comes into perspective. The allegorical quality of *Fever Pitch* is apparent, even if its tone is reflective and quizzical. Sport's screen of dreams perennially returns to the place where the magical world of sport is compared to the prosaic existence beyond – with the latter usually found wanting. This time, it is sport – and Arsenal Football Club – that loses out.

Conclusion: 'there's always the sport'

The above discussion of sport in fictional film demonstrated its richness as a source of mythologies, allegories and narratives. The rise and fall of the 'standard' sports career lends itself particularly well to narrative film. In a short time-span there are exultant and despairing moments, with the inevitability of athletic decline and the likelihood of personal trauma offering many emotional possibilities. The seeds of the filmic treatment of sport, however, are already present in sports television, with its affinity with melodrama both in its presentation and reception. It is sport on television that has preoccupied cultural critics and business analysts alike. The academic canon on sports television that has been built up since the mid-1980s (including Rader 1984; Chandler 1988; Klatell and Marcus 1988; Barnett 1990; Whannel 1992; Wenner 1989, 1998) has reflected changes in society and culture that have been filtered through sports TV, as well as marking those trends in visual broadcast sport which have echoed across society and culture in a continuous feedback loop.

When we take into account all the other print and broadcast media sports texts, from documentaries to full-length feature films to radio commentaries and newspaper sports columns, sport's amoeba-like cultural capacity to divide and re-form is formidable. Finally, to avoid repentance for the cardinal social scientific sin of 'presentism' (thinking that conditions will always be thus just as they undergo a massive shift), in the next, closing chapter we shall take a short detour into a future showing urgent signs of waiting to be born. In 1970 Raymond Williams (1989: 95) opened a television column with the statement 'There's always the sport. Or so people say, more and more often, as they become sadder about what is happening to the rest of television'. Three decades later, it is necessary to ask whether sport on television is perhaps in decline and a source of angst rather than eternally buoyant and a relief from sadness.

Further reading

Barnett, S. (1990) *Games and Sets: The Changing Face of Sport on Television*. London: British Film Institute.
Bergan, R. (1982) *Sports in the Movies*. London: Proteus.
Real, M. (1996) *Exploring Media Culture: A Guide*. Thousand Oaks, CA: Sage.
Whannel, G. (1992) *Fields in Vision: Television Sport and Cultural Transformation*. London: Routledge.

8

AFTERWORD: SPORT INTO THE ETHER(NET): NEW TECHNOLOGIES, NEW CONSUMERS

Introduction: the coming of cybersport

One fear of every academic author is the instant obsolescence of their work occasioned by a sudden cultural or technological shift. In a dynamic area like media sport this is a reasonable concern, although we can have absolute confidence that there will be more rather than less of it in the future. What we need to consider is not whether media sports texts will disappear or decline, but how their form, content and uses will change. The media will have to deal with transformations in sport (the rise of new sports and the decline of old ones) and sport must handle new media technologies that will provide, through digital compression and the like, not only many more sports TV channels, but also the opportunities for viewers to use interactive technologies and to design their own sports programming. The institutions of sport and media will also have to come to terms with changes in each other's administrative structures and patterns of ownership, and with new (perhaps supra) state policies on sport and media.

It is easy, in an orgy of 'technophilia', to imagine that new machines and capabilities will sweep away the old, but historical knowledge teaches that technological changes have been a constant feature of the media sports cultural complex, and that these are always moulded by social, cultural, economic and political factors. We have also learnt not to underestimate the importance of the sports media as a force within culture, or the wide-ranging repercussions of the cultural items which pass within and through the force field of sports texts and their associated meanings. The sports media are both an index of wider changes and an influence on them, part of the eternal dialectic of social production, reproduction, and transformation. A brief discussion of the 'future present' of sports media will aid, finally, in an understanding of the direction, pace and nature of cultural change.

From consumer to *auteur*

In most of the foregoing discussion it has been recognized that whatever the uses, meanings and gratifications of media sports texts, the process has generally revolved around the acceptance or rejection of already created material for persons constructed as audiences by professional media organizations. I have already discussed (in Chapter 5) the use of existing print technologies to produce the amateur or semi-professional print sports texts called fanzines. Analogous activities may involve the video recording of sports contests for training and/or entertainment purposes, taking photographs for sale to team members and their families, phoning in sports reports and results of events not covered by the professional media to radio stations, as well as the perennial sports club newsletter (and not, of course, forgetting the formidable powers of the Zybrainic Sportswriter). New media technologies, however, aided by the convergence of telecommunications, computers and broadcasting, expand the possibilities of cultural production into areas normally associated with consumption, enabling fans to produce their own custom-made texts out of the 'raw' material supplied. The passive sports media consumer may become both all-powerful media *auteur* and athlete 'replicant'. As one men's magazine contributor (with a rather depressingly predictable focus) puts it:

> Imagine you're watching one of your favourite sports, like female mud wrestling. With the Internet, you'll be able to zoom in on a contestant, bring up her statistics (including bust size), and even monitor her pulse and body temperature (so you know just how hot she is) . . . But the biggest advantage the Internet will offer is viewer shot selection. While we already have things such as race cam, you're at the mercy of the program director as to when it's shown.
>
> With Internet broadcasting, however, you'll be able to choose which camera you want to look through at any one time, meaning that when a car crashes and burns during the Grand Prix, you will be able to look through the race cam to watch the medics arrive.
>
> If that doesn't tickle your fancy, then there's set to be another development within the not too distant future – athlete cam. Thanks to

miniature cams strapped to the athlete's body, you'll finally get close enough to the action to almost smell the sweat.

And when virtual reality arrives, you'll also be able to feel the blows of a hard tackle in a rugby match, provided both you and the footballer wear virtual reality bodysuits.

(Kaufman 1998: 139)

Using digital technology to be 'able to see the replay from any angle you so choose, or [you might want] to flip between two simultaneous matches' (Shipp, quoted in Austin 1998: 5) and to create the home virtual stadium, 'when anyone will be able to buy a headset and decoder and actually feel like they are part of the game' (Cockerill 1997: 52), combine the partial appropriation of the media technology once the preserve of media professionals with the simulation of the experience not only of attending sports events 'in the flesh' as spectators, but also of participating as 'cyber' athletes. Hence, we are taken well beyond the 'seeing at a distance' that (as noted in Chapter 7), Weber (1996) views as the characteristic feature of television. Paradoxically, the new media technology is artificially trying to produce the 'feel' of 'having been there' as participant or spectator long after television first lured sports players and fans away from stadia towards the armchair. Of course, only a tiny proportion of potential athletes and fans can ever be 'actors' in the unique space and time of actual sports events. Digital media technology, therefore, delivers 'actuality' in place of the impossible.

Less ambitiously, those same technologies feed the other huge appetites of followers of sport – for information and dialogue. Web sites like Soccernet receive approaching 100,000 'hits' a day (up to 800,000 during peak events), providing 'news and analysis of games in the English and Scottish leagues as well as World Cup pages, a soccer store, newsletter, spot the ball and indexes in Argentina, Chile, Colombia, The Netherlands, Spain and Uruguay' (Austin and Harper 1998: 4), and planning to 'introduce animated action replays – running a television image through software that converts it into a graphic representation of the game. It's the next best thing to television, and allows fans to replay match action again and again' (Hadfield, quoted in Austin and Harper 1998: 4). A cursory check in July 1998 through the Yahoo! search engine's UK and Ireland sites found 4271 categories and 14,591 sites devoted to sport. All major and many minor sports now have Web sites dedicated to merchandising and marketing (among other functions), just as all major media organizations have online information services. As Tom Loosemore, a senior producer of BBC Online states:

On the Web, the live is much less important than the nearly live – the real value is the Monday morning syndrome, when you come into work and catch up with the goals you missed at the weekend. The secret, in my opinion, is a comprehensive and up-to-the minute news sports offering that gives you all the background that TV and radio can't give you, when *you* want it.

(quoted in Austin and Harper 1998: 4)

This conception of the (mostly male) white-collar worker logging on in search of the latest sports news points to a future of ever more abundant and readily available media sports texts. Rather than, as is often the case, this being seen as a 'zero sum' game within and between media, as new forms inevitably supplant others, it is instead the coexistence and constant supplementation of the existing sports media. Assuming that saturation point is not reached – and on current indicators it seems far distant as sports fans absorb more media content and the media recruit more sports fans – the only likely outcome is maximal media sport, more minutely targeted. For the diminishing ranks of the sports resistant global population, the only alternative, as implied in the Preface, may be solitary confinement.

The Internet has enabled an extension not only of the ways by which the professional media can contact sports fans, but also of those same fans' opportunities to communicate with each other. Newsgroups like 'rec.sport.soccer' allow sports fans to debate issues like ground safety and the merits of different teams and players, while netzines operate as both sports forum and shrine. Fan's Web sites are particularly useful for non-elite sports clubs neglected by the mainstream media. For example, a devotee of Plymouth Argyle Football Club living in an alien location (London, perhaps, or Australia) make take comfort (if that is the word) every Monday morning during the soccer season in accessing 'www.argyle.org.uk'. It is such syntheses of the speed-fixated global and the stubbornly local that characterize the condition of postmodernity.

Conclusion: look and learn

The excitable hype-speech that pours out of the purveyors of new media sports technologies (and not a few cultural analysts who trade in theories of 'the people's' effortless ideological autonomy, resistiveness and capacity for progressive textual decodings and uses) is perhaps counterbalanced in some way by the rather pessimistic academic assessments of the influence of the media on sport. Stoddart (1994c: 280), for example, in reviewing the tendency of 'Many critics [to] regard television as the greatest of all change agents in twentieth century', judges (in the Australian context) that:

The overwhelming thrust of academic analysis of all this has been gloomy, to wit, that television has ruined sport. These findings represent a misshapen view of what sport was like BT (before television), and an assumption that Australian society (and its foreign counterparts) had produced a sports form in syncromesh with its broad social patterns. Those assumptions are flawed seriously and will be redressed only by a full-scale analysis of Australian sport's [and that of other countries'] historical interaction with the media.

(Stoddart 1994c: 281)

It is, I think, reasonable to be critical of the *a priori* assumption of the malign influence of the media on sport, and of the sports media on the wider culture and society. What is incontestable is that media coverage – its presence or absence – has had an incalculably large impact on sport, and that the sports media are a key component of the fabric of contemporary culture. Historians like Stoddart are right to caution against grand generalizations about how sport has been devoured by the media; each sport has its own distinctive history, its own way of negotiating how it is represented in the print and broadcast media, just as individuals and social groups interpret and use the sports media according to their own reading positions and relations within and across texts and social institutions (over which they can, as socially produced subjects, exert only limited control). But where sociologists (even those convinced, like myself, of the importance of properly grounded historical analysis) tend to part company with historians is over the necessity of theorizing social change and unravelling the connections between apparently disparate social phenomena (Rowe and Lawrence 1998).

The contention of this book has been, indeed, that media sports form is to a substantial (though by no means absolute) extent in 'syncromesh with its broad social patterns'. Those broad social patterns are the major social structures (class, gender, racial/ethnic) and processes (capital and other forms of accumulation, postmodernization, 'mediatization') that, once apprehended, make it possible to distinguish between common or unique, connected or distinct phenomena in sport, media and culture. As this book's title suggests, the relationships between these two large institutions, the textual outcomes of their union, and the vast universe of culture which makes them and which they help make, do not obey 'iron' laws of cause and effect, supply and demand. The unruly trinity of sport, culture and the media is not, like its spiritual counterpart, three facets of the same, stable entity. Instead, it is a more dynamic metaphor of contested power and protean forms.

Everyone is connected in some way to the media sports cultural complex

– all those words and images spewing forth, all that money, technology and personnel set to work to give us more. Beginning this conclusion during the 1998 soccer World Cup Finals in France alongside a cumulative audience of 'an estimated 37 billion people worldwide' (Austin 1998: 4) and, like most of them, a long way from the action on the pitch, it is hard not to feel the cultural power of 'this sporting life' seemingly so effortlessly presented for us by an avalanche of voices, words, sounds and images. Pondering the sudden demonization of the sent-off David Beckham (now 'Posh Spite!' according to the tabloids), the rumours of a new European soccer Super League which will further blur the boundaries of national cultures, and the latest drugs scandals in athletics, swimming, rugby league, basketball and cycling (the 'Tour de Drugs!'), the sheer, relentless presence and force of media sport sometimes feels (in, I hope, not too tasteless a simile) like the cultural counterpart of a tsunami. The corruption scandal that gripped the International Olympic Committee in 1999 may have saddened some of the more terminally naive sports romantics, but it provided fantastic quantities of front-page copy and 'shock horror' lead stories. By learning a little more about how media sport is set before us and what media sports texts can be made to mean, perhaps we can take back a little of the cultural power that we have ceded to it.

GLOSSARY OF KEY TERMS

Capitalism: the form of social and economic organization most consistently associated with the pursuit of private wealth; the defence of private property; the creation and exchange of commodities for profit; and the direct 'sale' by workers (the working class) of their 'labour power' to employers (the ruling class). Over the past two or three centuries of its existence, capitalism has gone through various stages. The current 'late' or 'advanced' phase of capitalism is characterized by marked shifts in class relations and identities linked to changes in the organization both of paid work in the 'public' world (such as the shift from manual to non-manual labour) and of unpaid work in the 'private' world (like the large-scale movement of women into the workplace and pressures for gender equality at home and at work).

Code: see **text.**

Commodification: the process by which people and things acquire value which enables them to be exchanged for profit. In sport, for example, amateur play and players have been turned into exchangeable services and products.

Communication: see **media.**

Culturalization: the process by which *culture* – the *signs*, symbols, meanings and values circulating within and between societies – has become increasingly central to the operation of all social institutions, including the political apparatus and economic structures (see *mediatization*).

Cultural economy: a term used to describe both the cultural industries (such as publishers, music companies, and art galleries) and the manner in which forms of culture (like films, books, music, and even ideas and values) take on the appearance of ordinary commodities, with their value rising and falling according to critical reception, status, scarcity, public demand, and so on.

Discourse: the social and cultural framework of institutions and (often unacknowledged) assumptions that organize everyday language, thought and behaviour.

Because multiple discourses exist and are connected to structures of power, social life is characterized by competition between discourses for legitimacy (for example, monarchism versus republicanism) and, consequently, 'sovereignty' over groups in society.

Fordism: the highly organized method of mass production typified by the assembly line and reliant on a corresponding level of mass consumption of vast numbers of the same product. Limited and more flexible production and greater product choice that does not disturb this overall 'regime' is known as *neo-Fordism*. A substantial change in the direction of small-batch production, rapid response to shifts in consumption patterns, and more discerning, demanding consumers is often described as *post-Fordist*.

Genre: the recognizable and predictable qualities of *texts* (see below) which allow us to classify them into types (for example, horror films, rap records and detective novels), and so represent an implicit 'contract' between text producer and consumer. Smaller categories (such as different types of 'techno music') are known as *sub-genres*.

Ideology: the element of discourse that applies most directly to a group's interests. For example, competing ideologies like 'the free market must decide' versus 'the market must be controlled in the interests of everyone' are likely to reflect the degree of benefit which individuals and groups can derive from the different arrangements for distributing wealth which they promote.

Inter-textual: see **text.**

Media: all the organizations, large and small, through which pass various types of message in the process of *communication* (by which meaning is exchanged). The term is increasingly restricted to specialist organizations with the substantial technology, knowledge, information and capital at their disposable to enable large-scale or 'mass' communication.

Media sports cultural complex: a concept which embraces all the *media* and sports organizations, processes, personnel, services, products and *texts* which combine in the creation of the broad, dynamic field of contemporary sports culture.

Mediatization: refers to the extension of the influence of media into all spheres of social life in a manner linked to the larger process of *culturalization* (see above).

Modernity: see **postmodernity.**

Myth: wide-ranging cultural beliefs and meanings that are usually so familiar that they appear to be natural, universal and eternal elements of society. Sport, which generates strong emotions, antagonisms, hierarchies and romantic ideals, is particularly prone to be *mythologized*.

Narrative: the outcome of the organization (or *narrativization*) of events which might be turned into a 'story', involving a plot, scenes, characters, narrators and so on.

Neo-Fordism: see **Fordism.**

Political economy: an analytical approach which links socio-economic power (for example, ownership of a major newspaper chain) with politico-cultural power (such as the promotion of conservative values through the owner's newspapers or the shaping of newspaper stories by commercial rather than cultural or ethical considerations). The master concepts in *political economy* are *class* and *class conflict*, although there is often substantial departure from elements of *Marxism* that have often underpinned it (such as the inevitability of a proletarian revolution).

Post-Fordism: see **Fordism.**

Postmodernity: logically, the 'condition' that has superseded *modernity*, the rather imprecise term for societies that have undergone the process of *modernization* (which includes the development of industries and markets; political institutions that represent the citizenry; tolerance of dissenting opinion and different values, and so on), usually on the basis of a general belief in 'progress'. *Postmodernity* arrives after *modernity* has become 'exhausted' or begins to disintegrate under the weight of its own contradictions, which include the accelerating pace of global economic change, the fragmentation of social experience and identity, and a loss of faith in 'grand narratives' (like socialism, free enterprise and technological liberation). The more restricted terms *modernist* and *postmodernist* are applied to the cultural trends and *texts* (see below) of their respective epochs, although there is disagreement over the extent to which they might coexist, and also over how they may reflect or affect the entire condition of society.

Sign: see **text.**

Sport: recreational and professional competitive, rule-governed physical activity. While physical play and game contests have clearly existed in many societies and epochs, sport of a regular and organized kind is the product of a *modernist* (see above) social institution with its origins in Victorian England.

Sub-genre: see **genre.**

Text: the outcome of a specific combination of elements (*signs*) which takes on or produces meanings (through the process of *signification*) governed by systematic rules (*codes*). The concept of *text* was once dominated by the written form, but it is now common to describe and analyse a wide variety of visual, musical and other textual forms. References to other texts or relations between *texts* are known as *inter-textual*.

REFERENCES

Althusser, L. (1971) *Lenin and Philosophy and Other Essays*. London: Monthly Review Press.

Amis, M. (1989) *London Fields*. London: Jonathan Cape.

Andrews, D.L. (1996) Deconstructing Michael Jordan: reconstructing postindustrial America, *Sociology of Sport Journal*, 13(4): 315–18.

Anon. (1992) Obituary: death of the Right Honourable Game Football, in I. Hamilton (ed.) *The Faber Book of Soccer*. London: Faber and Faber.

Appleton, G. (1995) The politics of sport and pay TV, *Australian Quarterly*, 67(1): 31–7.

Arlott, J. (1968) Untitled article, 11 September, in M. Engel (ed.) (1986) *The Guardian Book of Cricket*. Harmondsworth: Penguin.

Attwood, A. (1998) Football crazy, *Sydney Morning Herald*, 17 January.

Austin, K. (1998) The main game, *Sydney Morning Herald – The Guide*, 8–14 June.

Austin, K. and Harper, C. (1998) Have a ball, *Sydney Morning Herald Icon*, 6 June.

Baird, K. (1994) Attitudes of Australian women sports journalists, *Australian Studies in Journalism*, 3: 231–53.

Baker, A. and Boyd, T. (eds) (1997) *Out of Bounds: Sports, Media, and the Politics of Identity*. Bloomington, IN: Indiana University Press.

Bakhtin, M. (1968) *Rabelais and his World*. Cambridge, MA: MIT Press.

Barnett, S. (1990) *Games and Sets: The Changing Face of Sport on Television*. London: British Film Institute.

Barry, D. (1992) Why the NBA isn't as offensive as you think, in T. McGuane (ed.) *The Best American Sports Writing 1992*. Boston, MA: Houghton Mifflin.

Barthes, R. (1973 [1957]) *Mythologies*. London: Paladin.

Barthes, R. (1977) The rhetoric of the image, in *Image-Music-Text*. London: Fontana.

Barthes, R. (1978) *A Lover's Discourse*. New York: Hill and Wang.

Baudrillard, J. (1981) *For a Critique of the Political Economy of the Sign*. St Louis, MO: Telos.

Baudrillard, J. (1983) *Simulations*. New York: Semiotext(e).

Becker, K. (1992) Photojournalism and the tabloid press, in P. Dahlgren and C. Sparks (eds) *Journalism and Popular Culture*. London: Sage.

Bell, J.B. (1987) *To Play the Game: An Analysis of Sports*. New Brunswick, NJ: Transaction.

Bennett, T. (1998) *Culture: A Reformer's Science*. Sydney: Allen and Unwin.

Bennett, T. *et al.* (1977) *Mass Communication as a Social Force in History (DE353 – Unit 2)*. Milton Keynes: Open University Press.

Bergan, R. (1982) *Sports in the Movies*. London: Proteus.

Bittner, J.R. (1983) *Mass Communication: An Introduction*, 3rd edn. Englewood Cliffs, NJ: Prentice Hall.

Blain, N. and Boyle, R. (1998) Sport as real life: media sport and culture, in A. Briggs and P. Cobley (eds) *The Media: An Introduction*. Harlow: Longman.

Blue, A. (1987) *Grace Under Pressure: The Emergence of Women in Sport*. London: Sidgwick and Jackson.

Boreham, T. and Pegler, T. (1998) Idlers deny industry a sporting chance, *The Australian*, 4 March.

Bourdieu, P. (1978) Sport and social class, *Social Science Information*, 17(6): 819–40.

Boutilier, M.A. and SanGiovanni, L. (1983) *The Sporting Woman*. Champaign, IL: Human Kinetics.

Boyd, T. (1997) The day the niggaz took over: basketball, commodity culture, and black masculinity, in A. Baker and T. Boyd (eds) *Sports, Media, and the Politics of Identity*, Bloomington, IN: Indiana University Press.

Brierley, S. (1998) Advertising and the new media environment, in A. Briggs and P. Cobley (eds) *The Media: An Introduction*. Harlow: Longman.

Brohm, J.M. (1978 [1976]) *Sport: A Prison of Measured Time*. London: Pluto.

Brooks, P. (1976) *The Melodramatic Imagination: Balzac, Henry James, Melodrama, and the Mode of Excess*. New Haven, CT: Yale University Press.

Brown, P. (1996) Gender, sport and the media: an investigation into coverage of women's sport in the *Newcastle Herald* and the *Sydney Morning Herald*. Unpublished PhD thesis, Newcastle, Australia: University of Newcastle.

Brown, P. and Rowe, D. (1998) The coming of the leisure society? Leisure time use in contemporary Australia, in D. Rowe and G. Lawrence (eds) *Tourism, Leisure, Sport: Critical Perspectives*. Sydney: Hodder Education.

Cardus, N. (1926) Kent v. Lancashire, 1, 2 and 3 July, in M. Engel (ed.) (1986) *The Guardian Book of Cricket*. Harmondsworth: Penguin.

Carlton and United Breweries Best Australian Sports Writing and Photography 1996. Melbourne: Heinemann.

Cashman, R. (1994) Cricket, in W. Vamplew and B. Stoddart (eds) *Sport in Australia: A Social History*. Melbourne: Cambridge University Press.

Cashman, R. and Hughes, A. (1998) Sydney 2000: cargo cult of Australian sport?, in D. Rowe and G. Lawrence (eds) *Tourism, Leisure, Sport: Critical Perspectives*. Sydney: Hodder Education.

Cashmore, E. (1990) *Making Sense of Sport*. London: Routledge.

Chandler, J.M. (1988) *Television and National Sport: The United States and Britain*. Urbana, IL: University of Illinois Press.

Chibnall, S. (1977) *Law and Order News*. London: Tavistock.

Chippindale, P. and Horrie, C. (1990) *Stick It Up Your Punter! The Rise and Fall of the Sun*. London: Heinemann.

Chomsky, N. (1989) *Necessary Illusions*. Boston, MA: South End Press.

Clarke, J. and Critcher, C. (1985) *The Devil Makes Work: Leisure in Capitalist Britain*. London: Macmillan.

Cockerill, M. (1997) The great sport hijack, *Sydney Morning Herald Sport*, 15 February.

Cohen, S. (1980 [1972]) *Folk Devils and Moral Panics: The Making of Mods and Rockers*. Oxford: Martin Robertson.

Cohen, S. and Taylor, L. (1976) *Escape Attempts: The Theory and Practice of Everyday Life*. London: Allen Lane.

Cohen, S. and Young, J. (1973) *The Manufacture of News: Deviance, Social Problems and the Mass Media*. London: Constable.

Coleman, N. and Hornby, N. (eds) (1996) *The Picador Book of Sportswriting*. London: Picador.

Collodi, C. (1911) *Pinocchio: The Story of a Puppet*. London: J.M. Dent.

Combe, C. (1997) Structural change in the UK broadcasting industry during the 1990's. Unpublished paper, University of Westminster.

Comisky, P., Bryant, J. and Zillman, D. (1977) Commentary as a substitute for action, *Journal of Communication*, 27: 150–3.

Connell, R.W. (1987) *Gender and Power*. Sydney: Allen and Unwin.

Correy, S. (1995) Who plays on pay? *Media Information Australia*, 75: 80–2.

Coulson, A. (1998) Our love, *Sun*, 26 January.

Cramer, J.A. (1994) Conversations with women sports journalists, in P.J. Creedon (ed.) *Women, Media and Sport: Challenging Gender Values*. Thousand Oaks, CA: Sage.

Creedon, P.J. (1994a) Women in toyland: a look at women in American newspaper sports journalism, in P.J. Creedon (ed.) *Women, Media and Sport: Challenging Gender Values*. Thousand Oaks, CA: Sage.

Creedon, P.J. (1994b) From whalebone to spandex: women and sports journalism in American magazines, photography and broadcasting, in P.J. Creedon (ed.) *Women, Media and Sport: Challenging Gender Values*. Thousand Oaks, CA: Sage.

Critcher, C. (1987) Media spectacles: sport and mass communication, in A. Cashdan and M. Jordin (eds) *Studies in Communication*. Oxford: Basil Blackwell.

Critcher, C. (1993) In praise of self abuse, in C. Brackenridge (ed.) *Body Matters: Leisure Images and Lifestyles*. Eastbourne: Leisure Studies Association.

Crook, S., Pakulski, J. and Waters, M. (1992) *Postmodernization: Change in Advanced Society*. London: Sage.

Crosswhite, J. (1996) Pay TV and its impact on women's sport, in R. Lynch, I. McDonnell, S. Thompson and K. Toohey (eds) *Sport and Pay TV: Strategies for Success*. Sydney: School of Leisure and Tourism Studies, University of Technology, Sydney.

Cunningham, S. (1992) *Framing Culture: Criticism and Policy in Australia*. Sydney: Allen and Unwin.

Cunningham, S. and Jacka, E. (1996) *Australian Television and International Mediascapes*. Cambridge: Cambridge University Press.

Cunningham, S. and Miller, T. (with Rowe, D.) (1994) *Contemporary Australian Television*. Sydney: University of New South Wales Press.

Curran, J. (1981a) The struggle for a free press, in J. Curran and J. Seaton (eds) *Power Without Responsibility: The Press and Broadcasting in Britain*, 4th edn. London: Fontana.

Curran, J. (1981b) The industrialisation of the press, in J. Curran and J. Seaton, *Power Without Responsibility: The Press and Broadcasting in Britain*, 4th edn. London: Fontana.

Curran, J. (1998) Newspapers: beyond political economy, in A. Briggs and P. Cobley (eds) *The Media: An Introduction*. Harlow: Longman.

Curran, J. and Seaton, J. (eds) *Power Without Responsibility: The Press and Broadcasting in Britain*, 5th edn. New York: Routledge.

Curry, J. (1998) Posada wants career to enter present tense, *New York Times Sports Wednesday*, 28 January.

Dahlgren, P. and Sparks, C. (eds) (1992) *Journalism and Popular Culture*. London: Sage.

Davis, T. (1995) The practice of gossip, in P. van Toorn and D. English (eds) *Speaking Positions: Aboriginality, Gender and Ethnicity in Australian Cultural Studies*. Melbourne: Victoria University of Technology.

DeLillo, D. (1997) *Underworld*. New York: Scribner.

Diamond, J. (1994) Match of the day, every day, *The Guardian*, 11 April.

Duncan, M.C. (1990) Sports photographs and sexual difference: images of women and men in the 1984 and 1988 Olympic Games, *Sociology of Sport Journal*, 7(1): 22–43.

Duncan, M.C. (1994) The politics of women's body images and practices: Foucault, the panopticon, and *Shape* magazine, *Journal of Sport and Social Issues*, 18(1): 48–65.

Duncan, M.C., Messner, M. and Williams, L. (1991) *Coverage of Women's Sport in Four Daily Newspapers*. Los Angeles: Amateur Athletic Foundation of Los Angeles.

Durkheim, E. (1960 [1893]) *The Division of Labour in Society*. Glencoe, IL: Free Press.

Dutton, K.R. (1995) *The Perfectible Body: The Western Ideal of Physical Development*. Sydney: Allen and Unwin.

Dyer, G. (1982) *Advertising as Communication*. London: Methuen.

Eagleton, T. (1989) *The Ideology of the Aesthetic*. Oxford: Basil Blackwell.

Eco, U. (1986) Sports chatter, in *Travels in Hyperreality*. New York: Harcourt Brace Jovanovich.

Elias, N. (1986a) The genesis of sport as a sociological problem, in N. Elias and E. Dunning, *Quest for Excitement: Sport and Leisure in the Civilising Process*. Oxford: Basil Blackwell.

Elias, N. (1986b) An essay on sport and violence, in N. Elias and E. Dunning, *Quest for Excitement: Sport and Leisure in the Civilising Process*. Oxford: Basil Blackwell.

Elias, N. (1986c) Introduction, in N. Elias and E. Dunning, *Quest for Excitement: Sport and Leisure in the Civilising Process*. Oxford: Basil Blackwell.

Elias, N. and Dunning, E. (1986a) *Quest for Excitement: Sport and Leisure in the Civilising Process*. Oxford: Basil Blackwell.

Elias, N. and Dunning, E. (1986b) Folk football in medieval and early modern Britain, in *Quest for Excitement: Sport and Leisure in the Civilising Process*. Oxford: Basil Blackwell.

Ellis, R. (1997) Albion want Royle, *Daily Star*, 18 December.

Engel, M. (1986) Introduction, in M. Engel (ed.) *The Guardian Book of Cricket*. Harmondsworth: Penguin.

Enzensberger, H.M. (1976) *Raids and Reconstructions*. London: Pluto.

Fiske, J. (1982) *Introduction to Communication Studies*. London: Methuen.

Fiske, J. (1983) Cricket/TV/culture, *Metro*, 62: 21–6.

Fiske, J. (1989a) *Understanding Popular Culture*. Boston, MA: Unwin Hyman.

Fiske, J. (1989b) *Reading the Popular*. Boston, MA: Unwin Hyman.

Foley, D. (1992) Making the familiar strange: writing critical sports narratives, *Sociology of Sport Journal*, 9(1): 36–47.

Fotheringham, R. (1992) *Sport in Australian Drama*. Melbourne: Cambridge University Press.

Foucault, M. (1979) *Discipline and Punish: The Birth of the Prison*. New York: Vintage.

Foucault, M. (1980) *Power/Knowledge: Selected Interviews and Other Writings, 1972–1977*, C. Gordon (ed.). New York: Pantheon.

Freeman, P. (1997) *Ian Roberts: Finding Out*. Sydney: Random House.

Galtung, J. and Ruge, M.H. (1970) The structure of foreign news, in J. Tunstall (ed.) *Media Sociology: A Reader*. London: Constable.

Galtung, J. and Ruge, M.H. (1973) Structuring and selecting news, in S. Cohen and J. Young (eds) *The Manufacture of News*. London: Constable.

Garrison, B. and Salwen, M. (1989) Newspaper sports journalists: a profile of the 'profession', *Journal of Sport and Social Issues*, 13(2): 57–68.

Garrison, B. and Salwen, M. (1994) Sports journalists assess their work: their place in the profession, *Newspaper Research Journal*, 15(2): 37–49.

Giddens, A. (1991) *Modernity and Self Identity*. Cambridge: Polity.

Gildea, W. (1992) For Ali, greatness takes another form, in T. McGuane (ed.) *The Best American Sports Writing 1992*. Boston, MA: Houghton Mifflin.

Given, J. (1995) Red, black, gold to Australia: Cathy Freeman and the flags, *Media Information Australia*, 75 (February): 46–56.

Golding, P. and Murdock, G. (1991) Culture, communications, and political economy, in J. Curran and M. Gurevitch (eds) *Mass Media and Society*. London: Edward Arnold.

Goldlust, J. (1987) *Playing for Keeps: Sport, the Media and Society*. Melbourne: Longman Cheshire.

Gordon, S. and Sibson, R. (1998) Global television: the Atlanta Olympics opening ceremony, in D. Rowe and G. Lawrence (eds) *Tourism, Leisure, Sport: Critical Perspectives*. Sydney: Hodder Education.

Grainger, G. (1996) The Broadcasting Services Act 1992: present and future implications, in R. Lynch, I. McDonnell, S. Thompson and K. Toohey (eds) *Sport and Pay TV: Strategies for Success*. Sydney: School of Leisure and Tourism Studies, University of Technology, Sydney.

Gruneau, R. and Whitson, D. (1993) *Hockey Night in Canada*. Toronto: Garamond.

Guttmann, A. (1978) *From Ritual to Record: The Nature of Modern Sports*. New York: Columbia University Press.

Guttmann, A. (1991) *Women's Sport: A History*. New York: Columbia University Press.

Guttmann, A. (1996) *The Erotic in Sports*. New York: Columbia University Press.

Habermas, J. (1989) *The Structural Transformation of the Public Sphere*. Cambridge: Polity.

Hall, M.A. (1997) Feminist activism in sport: a comparative study of women's sport advocacy organizations, in A. Tomlinson (ed.) *Gender, Sport and Leisure: Continuities and Challenges*. Aachen: Meyer & Meyer Verlag.

Hall, S. (1989) The meaning of new times, in S. Hall and M. Jacques (eds) *New Times: The Changing Face of Politics in the 1990s*. London: Lawrence and Wishart.

Hamilton, I. (ed.) (1992) *The Faber Book of Soccer*. London: Faber and Faber.

Hargreaves, Jennifer (1993a) Gender on the sports agenda, in A. Ingham and J. Loy (eds) *Sport in Social Development: Traditions, Transitions and Transformations*. Champaign, IL: Human Kinetics.

Hargreaves, Jennifer (1993b) Bodies matter! Images of sport and female sexualisation, in C. Brackenridge (ed.) *Body Matters: Leisure Images and Lifestyles*. Eastbourne: Leisure Studies Association.

Hargreaves, Jennifer (1994) *Sporting Females: Critical Issues in the History and Sociology of Women's Sports*. London: Routledge.

Hargreaves, John (1982) Sport, culture and ideology, in Jennifer Hargreaves (ed.) *Sport, Culture and Ideology*. London: Routledge and Kegan Paul.

Hargreaves, John (1986) *Sport, Power and Culture*. Cambridge: Polity.

Harris, H. (1997) Tel 'broke rules': official, *Mirror*, 27 March.

Harris, K. (1988) What do we see when we watch the cricket? *Social Alternatives*, 7(3): 65–70.

Harris, M. (1998) Sport in the newspapers before 1750: representations of cricket, class and commerce in the London press, *Media History*, 4(1): 19–28.

Harriss, I. (1990) Packer, cricket and postmodernism, in D. Rowe and G. Lawrence (eds) *Sport and Leisure: Trends in Australian Popular Culture*. Sydney: Harcourt Brace Jovanovich.

Hartley, J. (1982) *Understanding News*. London: Methuen.

Hartley, J. (1996) *Popular Reality: Journalism, Modernity, Popular Culture*. London: Arnold.

Harvey, D. (1989) *The Condition of Postmodernity: An Inquiry into the Conditions of Cultural Change*. Oxford: Basil Blackwell.

Haynes, R. (1995) *The Football Imagination: The Rise of Football Fanzine Culture*. Aldershot: Arena.

Heaven, P. and Rowe, D. (1990) Gender, sport and body image, in D. Rowe and G. Lawrence (eds) *Sport and Leisure: Trends in Australian Popular Culture*. Sydney: Harcourt Brace Jovanovich.

Hebdige, D. (1989) After the masses, in S. Hall and M. Jacques (eds) *New Times: The Changing Face of Politics in the 1990s*. London: Lawrence and Wishart.

Henningham, J. (1995) A profile of Australian sports journalists, *The ACHPER Healthy Lifestyles Journal*, 42(3): 13–17.

Herman, E.S. and Chomsky, N. (1988) *Manufacturing Consent: The Political Economy of the Mass Media*. New York: Pantheon.

Hill, C. (1992) *Olympic Politics*. Manchester: Manchester University Press.

Hilliard, D.C. (1994) Televised sport and the (anti) sociological imagination, *Journal of Sport and Social Issues*, 18(1): 88–99.

Hirsch, P. (1971) Processing fads and fashions: an organization-set analysis of cultural industry systems, *American Journal of Sociology*, 17(4): 641–57.

Hirst, P. and Zeitlin, J. (eds) (1989) *Reversing Industrial Decline?* Oxford: Berg.

Holland, P. (1998) 'The direct appeal to the eye?' Photography and the twentieth-century press, in A. Briggs and P. Cobley (eds) *The Media: An Introduction*. Harlow: Longman.

Hornby, N. (1992) *Fever Pitch*. London: Victor Gollancz.

Hughson, J. (1998) Is the carnival over? Soccer support and hooliganism in Australia, in D. Rowe and G. Lawrence (eds) *Tourism, Leisure, Sport: Critical Perspectives*. Sydney: Hodder Education.

Ingham, A. and Loy, J. (1993) Introduction: sport studies through the lens of Raymond Williams, in A. Ingham and J. Loy (eds) *Sport in Social Development: Traditions, Transitions and Transformations*. Champaign, IL: Human Kinetics.

Jameson, F. (1984) Postmodernism: or the cultural logic of late capitalism, *New Left Review*, 146: 53–92.

Janowitz, M. (1968) The study of mass communication, in D. Sills (ed.) *International Encyclopaedia of the Social Sciences Volume 2*. London: Macmillan.

Jellie, D. (1998) Talking torque, *Sydney Morning Herald – The Guide*, 2–8 March.

Jhally, S. (1989) Cultural studies and the sports/media complex, in L. Wenner (ed.) *Media, Sports and Society*. Newbury Park, CA: Sage.

Kane, M. and Disch, L. (1993) Sexual violence and the male reproduction of power in the locker room: a case study of the Lisa Olson 'incident'. *Sociology of Sport Journal*, 10(4): 331–52.

Kane, M. and Greendorfer, S. (1994) The media's role in accommodating and resisting stereotyped images of women in sport, in P.J. Creedon (ed.) *Women, Media and Sport: Challenging Gender Values*. Thousand Oaks, CA: Sage.

Kaufman, D. (1998) All angles covered, *Ralph*, June: 139.

Kerr, J. (1994) *Understanding Soccer Hooliganism*. Buckingham: Open University Press.

Kidd, B. (1982) Sport, dependency and the Canadian state, in H. Cantelon and R. Gruneau (eds) *Sport, Culture and the Modern State*. Toronto: University of Toronto Press.

Klatell, D. and Marcus, N. (1988) *Sports for Sale: Television, Money and the Fans*. New York: Oxford University Press.

Kuper, S. (1994) *Football Against the Enemy*. London: Orion.

Larson, J.F. and Park, H.S. (1993) *Global Television and the Politics of the Seoul Olympics*. Boulder, CO: Westview Press.

Lash, S. and Urry, J. (1994) *Economies of Signs and Space*. London: Sage.

Leiss, W., Kline, S. and Jhally, S. (1990) *Social Communication in Advertising*, 2nd edn. London: Routledge.

Lumpkin, A. and Williams, L.D. (1991) An analysis of *Sports Illustrated* feature articles, 1954–1987, *Sociology of Sport Journal*, 8: 1–15.

Lynch, R. (1993) The cultural repositioning of rugby league football and its men, in A.J. Veal and B. Weiler (eds) *First Steps: Leisure and Tourism Research in Australia and New Zealand*. Sydney: ANZALS Leisure Research Series 1.

Macdonald, K.M. (1995) *The Sociology of the Professions*. Thousand Oaks, CA: Sage.

McGuane, T. (1992) Introduction, in T. McGuane (ed.) *The Best American Sports Writing 1992*. Boston, MA: Houghton Mifflin.

McHoul, A. (1997) On doing 'we's': where sport leaks into everyday life, *Journal of Sport and Social Issues*, 21(3): 315–20.

McKay, J. (1990) Sport, leisure and social inequality in Australia, in D. Rowe and G. Lawrence (eds) *Sport and Leisure: Trends in Australian Popular Culture*. Sydney: Harcourt Brace Jovanovich.

McKay, J. (1991) *No Pain, No Gain? Sport and Australian Culture*. Sydney: Prentice Hall.

McKay, J. (1992) Sport and the social construction of gender, in G. Lupton, T. Short and R. Whip (eds) *Society and Gender: An Introduction to Sociology*. Sydney: Macmillan.

McKay, J. (1995) 'Just Do It': corporate sports slogans and the political economy of enlightened racism, *Discourse: Studies in the Cultural Politics of Education*, 16(2): 191–201.

McKay, J. and Miller, T. (1991) From old boys to men and women of the corporation: the Americanization and commodification of Australian sport, *Sociology of Sport Journal*, 8(1): 86–94.

McKay, J. and Rowe, D. (1997) Field of soaps: Rupert v. Kerry as masculine melodrama, *Social Text*, 50(1): 69–86.

McKay, J. and Smith, P. (1995) Exonerating the hero: frames and narratives in media coverage of the O J Simpson story, *Media Information Australia*, 75: 57–66.

McQuail, D. (1987) *Mass Communication Theory: An Introduction*, 2nd edn. Newbury Park, CA: Sage.

Maguire, J. (1990) More than a sporting touchdown: the making of American football in Britain 1982–1989, *Sociology of Sport Journal*, 7(3): 213–37.

Maguire, J. (1993) Globalization, sport development, and the media/sport production complex, *Sport Science Review*, 2(1): 29–47.

Maharaj, G. (1997) Talking trash: late capitalism, black (re)productivity, and professional basketball, *Social Text*, 50 (spring): 97–110.

Martin, R. and Miller, T. (eds) (1999) *SportCult*. Minneapolis, MN: University of Minnesota Press.

Marx, K. (1967 [1867]) *Capital: A Critique of Political Economy, Volume 1: A Critical Analysis of Capitalist Production*. New York: International Publishers.

May, N. (1984) *Gold! Gold! Gold! Norman May Looks at the Olympics*. Melbourne: Horwitz Grahame.

Mercer, K. (1992) Skin head sex thing: racial difference and the homoerotic imaginary, *New Formations*, 16 (spring): 1–23.

Messner, M.A. (1992) *Power at Play: Sports and the Problem of Masculinity*. Boston, MA: Beacon Press.

Miller, T. (1990) Sport, media and masculinity, in D. Rowe and G. Lawrence (eds) *Sport and Leisure: Trends in Australian Popular Culture*. Sydney: Harcourt Brace Jovanovich.

Miller, T. (1993) *The Well-Tempered Self: Citizenship, Culture, and the Postmodern Subject*. Baltimore, MD: Johns Hopkins University Press.

Miller, T. (1996) Film, in W. Vamplew, K. Moore, J. O'Hara, R. Cashman and I.F. Jobling (eds) *The Oxford Companion to Australian Sport*, 2nd edn. Melbourne: Oxford University Press.

Miller, T. (1997) '. . . the oblivion of the sociology of sport' (editorial), *Journal of Sport and Social Issues*, 21(2): 115–19.

Miller, T. (1998a) *Technologies of Truth: Cultural Citizenship and the Popular Media*. Minneapolis, MN: University of Minnesota Press.

Miller, T. (1998b) Hopeful signs? Arthur Ashe/working-class spectatorship (editorial), *Journal of Sport and Social Issues*, 22(1): 3–6.

Miller, T. (1998c) Scouting for boys: sport looks at men, in D. Rowe and G. Lawrence (eds) *Tourism, Leisure, Sport: Critical Perspectives*. Sydney: Hodder Education.

Miller, T., Lawrence, G., McKay, J. and Rowe, D. (in press) *Playing the World: Globalised Sport and the New International Division of Cultural Labour*. London: Sage.

Modleski, T. (1983) The rhythms of reception, in E.A. Kaplan (ed.) *Regarding Television*. Los Angeles: American Film Institute.

Montgomery, M. (1986) *An Introduction to Language and Society*. London: Methuen.

Moore, D. (1996) Pay TV: the Confederation of Australian Sport perspective, in R. Lynch, I. McDonnell, S. Thompson and K. Toohey (eds) *Sport and Pay TV: Strategies for Success*. Sydney: School of Leisure and Tourism Studies, University of Technology, Sydney.

Moore, M. (1997) Seven's 2000 advantage, *Sydney Morning Herald – The Guide*, 9–15 June.

Mowbray, M. (1993) Sporting opportunity: equity in urban infrastructure and planning, in A.J. Veal and B. Weiler (eds) *First Steps: Leisure and Tourism Research in Australia and New Zealand*. Sydney: ANZALS Leisure Research Series 1.

Murdock, G. (1992) Citizens, consumers, and public culture, in M. Skovmand and K.C. Schroder (eds) *Media Cultures: Reappraising Transnational Media*. London: Routledge.

Murdock, G. and Golding, P. (1989) Information poverty and political inequality: citizenship in the age of privatized communications, *Journal of Communication*, 39(3): 180–95.

Murphy, D. (1976) *The Silent Watchdog: The Press in Local Politics*. London: Constable.

Nack, W. (1992) O unlucky man, in T. McGuane (ed.) *The Best American Sports Writing 1992*. Boston, MA: Houghton Mifflin.

Ndalianis, A. (1995) Muscle, excess and rupture: female bodybuilding and gender construction, *Media Information Australia*, 75 (February): 13–23.

Nisbet, R. (1967) *The Sociological Tradition*. London: Heinemann.

Norris, C. (1993) Old themes for new times: postmodernism, theory and cultural politics, in J. Squires (ed.) *Principled Positions: Postmodernism and the Rediscovery of Value*. London: Lawrence and Wishart.

Novak, M. (1976) *The Joy of Sport*. New York: Basic Books.

Ono, K.A. (1997) 'America's' apple pie: baseball, Japan-bashing, and the sexual threat of economic miscegenation, in A. Baker and T. Boyd (eds) *Out of Bounds*. Bloomington, IN: Indiana University Press.

O'Regan, T. (1992) The international, the regional and the local: Hollywood's new and declining audiences, in E. Jacka (ed.) *Continental Shift: Globalisation and Culture*. Sydney: Local Consumption Publications.

Orwell, G. (1992 [1945]) The sporting spirit, in I. Hamilton (ed.) *The Faber Book of Soccer*. London: Faber and Faber.

Palmer, J. (1998) News values, in A. Briggs and P. Cobley (eds) *The Media: An Introduction*. Harlow: Longman.

Peterson, R. and Berger, D. (1975) Cycles in symbol production: the case of popular music, *American Sociological Review*, 40: 158–73.

Pilger, J. (1998) *Hidden Agendas*. London: Vintage.

Plimpton, G. (ed.) (1997) *The Best American Sports Writing 1997*. Boston, MA: Houghton Mifflin.

Pratchett, T. (1990) quoted in P. Cochrane, The end's nigh, but wait, *Sydney Morning Herald*, 17 August.

Pronger, B. (1990) *The Arena of Masculinity: Sport, Homosexuality, and the Meaning of Sex*. New York: St Martin's Press.

Rader, B. (1984) *In Its Own Image: How Television has Transformed Sports*. New York: Free Press.

Real, M. (1996) *Exploring Media Culture: A Guide*. Thousand Oaks, CA: Sage.

Real, M. (1998) MediaSport: technology and the commodification of postmodern sport, in L. Wenner (ed.) *MediaSport*. London: Routledge.

Redhead, S. (1991) *Football with Attitude*. Manchester: Wordsmith.

Richman, A. (1991) The death of sportswriting, *GQ*, September: 254–61, 334–7.

Rintala, J. and Birrell, S. (1984) Fair treatment for the active female: a content analysis of *Young Athlete* magazine, *Sociology of Sport Journal*, 1(3): 231–50.

Robbins, B. (1997) Head fake: mentorship and mobility in *Hoop Dreams*, *Social Text*, 50 (spring): 111–20.

Rodman, A. (with Scott, A.) (1997) *Worse than He Says He Is: White Girls Don't Bounce*. Los Angeles: Dove.

Rodman, D. (with Keown, T.) (1996) *Bad As I Wanna Be*. New York: Bantam.

Rodman, D. (with Silver, M.) (1997) *Walk on the Wild Side*. New York: Bantam.

Rogers, E. (1993) Foreword, in J. Larson and H. Park, *Global Television and the Politics of the Seoul Olympics*. Boulder, CO: Westview Press.

Rojek, C. (1985) *Capitalism and Leisure Theory*. London: Tavistock.

Rose, A. and Friedman, J. (1997) Television sports as mas(s)culine cult of distraction, in A. Baker and T. Boyd (eds) *Out of Bounds*. Bloomington, IN: Indiana University Press.

Rowe, D. (1992) Modes of sports writing, in P. Dahlgren and C. Sparks (eds) *Journalism and Popular Culture*. London: Sage.

Rowe, D. (1995) *Popular Cultures: Rock Music, Sport and the Politics of Pleasure*. London: Sage.

Rowe, D. (1996) The global love-match: sport and television, *Media, Culture and Society*, 18(4): 565–82.

Rowe, D. (1997a) Apollo undone: the sports scandal, in J. Lull and S. Hinerman (eds) *Media Scandals: Morality and Desire in the Popular Culture Marketplace*. New York: Columbia University Press.

Rowe, D. (1997b) Rugby League in Australia: the Super League saga, *Journal of Sport and Social Issues*, 21(2): 221–6.

Rowe, D. (1997c) Big defence: sport and hegemonic masculinity, in A. Tomlinson (ed.) *Gender, Sport and Leisure: Continuities and Challenges*. Aachen: Meyer & Meyer Verlag.

Rowe, D. (1998) Fessing up, moving on, *The UTS Review*, 4(1): 205–9.

Rowe, D. (1998) If you film it, will they come? Sports on film, *Journal of Sport and Social Issues*, 22(4): 350–9.

Rowe, D. and Lawrence, G. (1998) Framing a critical sports sociology in the age of globalisation, in D. Rowe and G. Lawrence (eds) *Tourism, Leisure, Sport: Critical Perspectives*. Sydney: Hodder Education.

Rowe, D. and Miller, T. (1999) Gays, in E. Cashmore (ed.) *Sports Culture: An A–Z*. London: Routledge (forthcoming).

Rowe, D. and Stevenson, D. (1995) Negotiations and mediations: journalism, professional status and the making of the sports text, *Media Information Australia*, 75: 67–79.

Rowe, D., Lawrence, G., Miller, T. and McKay, J. (1994) Global sport? Core concern and peripheral vision, *Media, Culture and Society*, 16(4): 661–75.

Rowe, D., McKay, J. and Miller, T. (1998) Come together: sport, nationalism and the media image, in L. Wenner (ed.) *MediaSport: Cultural Sensibilities and Sport in the Media Age*. New York: Routledge.

Sacks, H. (1992) in G. Jefferson (ed.) Volume 1, *Lectures on Conversation* (2 vols). Oxford: Basil Blackwell.

Salwen, M. and Garrison, B. (1998) Finding their place in journalism: newspaper sports journalists' 'professional problems', *Journal of Sport and Social Issues*, 22(1): 88–102.

Sargent, S.L., Zillmann, D. and Weaver III, J.B. (1998) The gender gap in the enjoyment of televised sports, *Journal of Sport and Social Issues*, 22(1): 46–64.

Sarris, A. (1980) Why sports movies don't work, *Film Comment*, 16(6): 49–53.

Schlesinger, P. (1991) *Media, State and Nation: Political Violence and Collective Identities*. London: Sage.

Schudson, M. (1991) The sociology of news production revisited, in J. Curran and M. Gurevitch (eds) *Mass Media and Society*. London: Edward Arnold.

Schultz, J. (ed.) (1994) *Not Just Another Business: Journalists, Citizens and the Media*. Sydney: Pluto.

Seidman, S. (ed.) (1996) *Queer Theory/Sociology*. Oxford: Basil Blackwell.

Sekula, A. (1984) *Photography Against the Grain*. Halifax, NS: The Press of the Nova Scotia College of Art and Design.

Shaw, P. (ed.) (1989) *Whose Game Is It Anyway? The Book of the Football Fanzines*. Hemel Hempstead: Argus.

Sheehan, P. (1998) Game, set and match: Murdoch, the champion of world sports, *Sydney Morning Herald – The Guide*, 23 February–1 March.

Simson, V. and Jennings, A. (1992) *The Lords of the Rings: Power, Money and Drugs in the Modern Olympics*. London: Simon and Schuster.

Singer, T. (1998) Not so-remote-control, *Sport*, March: 36.

Sloop, J.M. (1997) Mike Tyson and the perils of discursive constraints: boxing, race, and the assumption of guilt, in A. Baker and T. Boyd (eds) *Out of Bounds*. Bloomington, IN: Indiana University Press.

Smith, A. (1997) Back-page bylines: an interview with Liz Kahn, Mary Jollimore, and Wanda Jamrozik, *Social Text*, 50(1): 87–95.

Smith, P. (1996) Pay TV: perspective from a popular sport, in R. Lynch, I. McDonnell, S. Thompson and K. Toohey (eds) *Sport and Pay TV: Strategies for Success*. Sydney: School of Leisure and Tourism Studies, University of Technology, Sydney.

Smythe, D.W. (1977) Communications: blindspot of Western Marxism, *Canadian Journal of Political and Social Theory*, 1: 120–7.

Sobchack, V. (1997) Baseball in the post-American cinema, or life in the minor leagues, in A. Baker and T. Boyd (eds) *Out of Bounds*. Bloomington, IN: Indiana University Press.

Stevenson, N. (1995) *Understanding Media Cultures: Social Theory and Mass Communication*. London: Sage.

Stoddart, B. (1979) Cricket's imperial crisis: the 1932–33 MCC tour of Australia, in R. Cashman and M. McKernan (eds) *Sport in History*. St Lucia, QLD: University of Queensland Press.

Stoddart, B. (1986) *Saturday Afternoon Fever: Sport in the Australian Culture*. North Ryde, NSW: Angus and Robertson.

Stoddart, B. (1994a) *Invisible Games: A Report on the Media Coverage of Women's Sport*. Canberra: Sport and Recreation Ministers' Council.

Stoddart, B. (1994b) Sport, television, interpretation, and practice reconsidered: televised golf and analytical orthodoxies, *Journal of Sport and Social Issues*, 18(1): 76–88.

Stoddart, B. (1994c) Reflections past and present, in W. Vamplew and B. Stoddart (eds) *Sport in Australia: A Social History*. Melbourne: Cambridge University Press.

Stout, G. (1992) Foreword, in T. McGuane (ed.) *The Best American Sports Writing*. Boston, MA: Houghton Mifflin.

Sydney Morning Herald (1993) Sports computer is write on the ball, *Sydney Morning Herald*, 29 May.

Thompson, E.P. (1967) Time, work-discipline, and industrial capitalism, *Past and Present*, 38: 56–97.

Thompson, J.B. (1997) Scandal and social theory, in J. Lull and S. Hinerman (eds) *Media Scandals: Morality and Desire in the Popular Culture Marketplace*. New York: Columbia University Press.

Thwaites, T., Davis, L. and Mules, W. (1994) *Tools for Cultural Studies: An Introduction*. Melbourne: Macmillan Education.

Tomlinson, A. (1996) Olympic spectacle: opening ceremonies and some paradoxes of globalization, *Media, Culture and Society*, 18(4): 583–602.

Traub, J. (1991) Please don't mash the sportswriter, *Washington Journalism Review*, July/August: 34–7.

Trotsky, L. (1969) *The Permanent Revolution, and Results and Prospects*. New York: Merit.

Tudor, A. (1992) Them and us: story and stereotype in TV World Cup coverage, *European Journal of Communication*, 7: 391–413.

Turner, B.S. (1990) Australia: the debate about hegemonic culture, in N. Abercrombie, S. Hill and B.S. Turner (eds) *Dominant Ideologies*. London: Unwin Hyman.

Turner, B.S. (1992) *Regulating Bodies: Essays in Medical Sociology*. London: Routledge.

Urry, J. (1990) *The Tourist Gaze: Leisure and Travel in Contemporary Societies*. London: Sage.

Van Zoonen, L. (1991) Feminist perspectives on the media, in J. Curran and M. Gurevitch (eds) *Mass Media and Society*. London: Edward Arnold.

Van Zoonen, L. (1998) A professional, unreliable, heroic marionette (M/F):

structure, agency and subjectivity in contemporary journalisms, *European Journal of Cultural Studies*, 1(1): 123–45.

Weber, M. (1930 [1904/5]) *The Protestant Ethic and the Spirit of Capitalism*. London: Unwin University Books.

Weber, M. (1968 [1922]) *Economy and Society: An Outline of Interpretive Sociology*. New York: Bedminster Press.

Weber, S. (1996) Television: set and screen, in A. Cholodenko (ed.) *Mass Mediauras: Form, Technics, Media*. Sydney: Power Publications.

Wenner, L. (ed.) (1989) *Media, Sports, and Society*. Newbury Park, CA: Sage.

Wenner, L. (ed.) (1998) *MediaSport*. London: Routledge.

Whannel, G. (1992) *Fields in Vision: Television Sport and Cultural Transformation*. London: Routledge.

Wiechula, F. (1997) 'I play in the big league, Gazza Disney!' says Les Ferdinand, *Mirror*, 27 March.

Williams, C.L., Lawrence, G. and Rowe, D. (1986) Patriarchy, media and sport, in G. Lawrence and D. Rowe (eds) *Power Play: Essays in the Sociology of Australian Sport*. Sydney: Hale and Iremonger.

Williams, L. (1989) *Hard Core: Power, Pleasure and the 'Frenzy of the Visible'*. Berkeley, CA: University of California Press.

Williams, L.D. (1994) Sportswomen in black and white: sports history from an Afro-American perspective, in P.J. Creedon (ed.) *Women, Media and Sport: Challenging Gender Values*. Thousand Oaks, CA: Sage.

Williams, L.D. and Lumpkin, A. (1990) An examination of the sport, gender, race, and sporting role of individuals appearing on the covers of *Sports Illustrated*, 1954–1989. Unpublished paper.

Williams, R. (1974) *Television: Technology and Cultural Form*. London: Fontana/Collins.

Williams, R. (1989 [1970]) There's always the sport, in A. O'Connor (ed.) *Raymond Williams on Television: Selected Writings*. London: Routledge.

Wilson, H. (1998) Television's *tour de force*: the nation watches the Olympic Games, in D. Rowe and G. Lawrence (eds) *Tourism, Leisure, Sport: Critical Perspectives*. Sydney: Hodder Education.

Wilson, N. (1988) *The Sports Business: The Men and the Money*. London: Piatkus.

Windschuttle, K. (1984) *The Media: A New Analysis of the Press, Television, Radio and Advertising in Australia*. Ringwood, VIC: Penguin.

Windschuttle, K. (1998) The poverty of media theory, *Quadrant*, 42(3): 11–18.

Wolfe, T. and Johnson, E.W. (eds) (1975) *The New Journalism*. London: Pan.

INDEX